Effects of Stress on Human Health

Edited by Hülya Çakmur

Published in London, United Kingdom

IntechOpen

Supporting open minds since 2005

Effects of Stress on Human Health
http://dx.doi.org/10.5772/intechopen.79782
Edited by Hülya Çakmur

Contributors
Toyin Olowogbon, Aaron Yoder, Segun Fakayode, Abraham Falola, Heli Tissari, Surendra Shripati Wadikar, Haiyan Zhu, Guoxin Han, Shuoshuo Li, Kate Rygiel, Ertuğrul Allahverdi, José Jesús Vargas Delgado, Hülya Çakmur

First published in London, United Kingdom, 2020 by IntechOpen
IntechOpen is the global imprint of INTECHOPEN LIMITED, registered in England and Wales, registration number: 11086078, 7th floor, 10 Lower Thames Street, London, EC3R 6AF, United Kingdom
Printed in Croatia

British Library Cataloguing-in-Publication Data
A catalogue record for this book is available from the British Library

Additional hard and PDF copies can be obtained from orders@intechopen.com

Effects of Stress on Human Health
Edited by Hülya Çakmur
p. cm.
Print ISBN 978-1-78984-947-9
Online ISBN 978-1-78984-948-6
eBook (PDF) ISBN 978-1-83880-054-3

For EU product safety concerns:
IN TECH d.o.o., Prolaz Marije Krucifikse Kozulić 3, 51000 Rijeka, Croatia, info@intechopen.com or visit our website at intechopen.com.

Meet the editor

Hülya Çakmur graduated from medical school at the Atatürk University in Turkey. She completed her residency training in Family Medicine at the Trakya University. She has a PhD degree in Public Health from the Dokuz Eylül University. She has 25 years of practical experience as a specialist in family medicine, including 10 years of experience in public health as a PhD prepared professional. She studied sleep medicine at the UPMC in the USA, attended narrative medicine education at the STU in Canada, studied voluntarily in geriatrics, and published several studies in the field of elderly health. She is an active member of the Turkish Medical Association and European Academy of Teachers in General Practice/Family Medicine. She has eight years of teaching experience as an associate professor at the University of Kafkas and she is the Director of the Department of Family Medicine. She has published more than 30 papers in reputed journals.

Contents

Preface

Stress response is a biological need for homeostasis in the human body. Factors affecting a living organism's balance and the disruption of homeostasis may be called stressors. In this situation, organisms attempt to regain their own balance to maintain homeostasis. Hence, they consume too much biological, physiological, psychological, and chemical energy of the body. This process is defined as a stress reaction or response. The human body can handle small doses of acute stress. However, chronic or long-term stress adversely affects the organism and increases the risk of many disorders. The stress reaction of each organ in the human body is different. The harmful effects of stress depend on the intensity and duration of the stressful condition. The acute stress-activated endocrine system initiates a number of hormonal responses. As a result, the endocrine system releases adrenaline and cortisol during stress, which leads to several outcomes directly in the nervous system and indirectly in the whole body system. Persistent activation of the nervous system causes problems in visceral systems, e.g. metabolic, immune, gastrointestinal, respiratory, and cardiac. However, stress does not necessarily have negative effects on the human body. A tolerable dose of stress provides two coping outcomes for human beings: emotional coping, which is an increase in emotional resilience, and physiological coping, which is restorative for the immune system and homeostasis. Stress is not inevitable but it may be manageable. There are a number of effective ways to reduce stress response in the body. It has been established that relaxation techniques such as deep breathing, mindfulness, meditation, and other cognitive behavioral strategies could decrease stress-related health problems. The purpose of training programs for stress management is to mediate the harmful impact of stressors to emotional and physiological systems. The ultimate impact of these techniques is to reduce muscle tension and thus buffer the negative effects of stress on visceral systems. Also, it has been reported that having a purpose in life and the capability of environmental adaptation might decrease the stress response of the human body.

Dr. Hülya Çakmur
Kafkas University,
Turkey

Chapter 1

Introductory Chapter: How Does Stress Impact Human Body?

Hülya Çakmur

1. Introduction

Epidemiologic, clinical, and experimental studies show that the stress either acute or chronic affects deleteriously the functions of visceral system in some degree [1]. Stressors significantly impact physical and emotional well-being. Reported studies clearly show that there is a strong relationship between stress and several disorders from inflammation, metabolic, reproductive, autoimmune, and growth disorders to malignancy [1, 2]. It is well defined that all the biological systems of the human body, even skin and collagen tissue, were affected by stress [2]. In a stressful situation, the musculoskeletal system is also affected and muscles get tensed up. Actually, muscle tension is a reflex reaction to protect body against injury and pain. Clearly understand the molecular mechanisms and biochemical pathways of stress hormones provides better control of diseases arise from stress. The neuronal and endocrinal pathway of stress response is well understood [2, 3]. However, there is still necessity for further research to comprehend molecular mechanisms of the stress response. For this reason, researchers are exploring the exact mechanisms of stress-induced pathology which require molecular and biomedical research [3, 4]. Life always together with the stress and organism response to stressors varies individually. Also, the target organ of stress varies for each person. In this review it has been summarized the effects of stress in human body.

2. Nervous system

The nervous system is divided as the central (involving the brain and spinal cord—CNS) and the peripheral (consists of the autonomic and somatic nervous systems—ANSs). The central nervous systems directly regulate body's endocrine system. The CNS is particularly important in stress responses, but the ANS plays a key role in physical response to stressors. The ANS consists of sympathetic nervous system (SNS) and parasympathetic nervous system (PNS). The sympathetic nervous system activated adrenal gland to release hormones called stress hormones adrenalin (epinephrine) and cortisol [1, 3, 4]. These hormones are responsible for the activation of autonomic nerves that coordinate the cardiovascular, respiratory, gastrointestinal, and musculoskeletal systems. The SNS becomes active during stress reaction to regulate physiological functions of human body and provide adaptation to emergency situation. When emergency situation is over, the PNS activated several physiological functions to return organism to peaceful condition [1, 3, 4]. Namely, the PNS has opposite effects to the SNS. In summary, the SNS prepares organism for the "fight or flight" and the PNS for rest and digest. Continuous activation of the sympathetic nervous system causes several problems in visseral system. The response of the brain to stressors is complicated. It has been clearly shown that chronic stress decreases the brain mass and leads to atrophy in important parts of the human brain such as hypocampus, hypothalamus, and amygdala, thus disturbing main brain functions such as memory and cognition [6]. However, it has been reported that the effect of stress on memory was dependent on the time of exposure to the stressful stimulus. Researchers claim that exposure to stress before learning activity might be increased in the power of memory in their study [5].

3. Immune system

Both the SNS and the PNS interact with the immune system. Therefore, the immune system is affected by stressors, and it can also modulate stress reactions. It has been established that instant stressors do not change immune functions. Rather acute stressors cause to increase on natural immune factors such as natural killer cells, granulocytes, interleukin, and IgA [2]. However, it has been reported that chronic stressors activated hypothalamic-pituitary-adrenal (HPA) axis (one of the two main systems mediates a stress response) and HPA releasing glucocorticoids, hormones that suppress immune system in multiple levels. It has been proved that the long-term stress can impair the connection between the immune system and the HPA axis, and it is resulted as physical and mental health problems [1, 6]. It is clearly known that glucocorticoids decrease cytokines and other mediators of inflammation and cause cellular inflammation in the human body. Because of the sympathetic nervous system that innervates bone marrow and spleen, which are the main immunological structures, the long-term stress heavily influenced the function of these structures. Stressors depress immune functions of the organism and increase the susceptibility to host of several diseases. In a depressed immune system, the risk of several diseases such as collagen tissue, infection, inflammation, malignancy, connective tissue, and skin disorders increases [2].

4. Cardio-vascular system

Stressors may have profound inflammation especially in the coronary arteries and deleterious effect of cardiovascular system. Stressors activated the sympathetic nervous system and thus affect the function of the circulatory system. These activations initially lead to increase in the heart rate, venous narrowing, arterial vasodilation of skeletal muscles, and contraction of the splenic and kidneys' arteries and thus decrease sodium excretion. In course of time, it has led to increased coronary vasoconstriction, atherosclerosis, and increased blood pressure. Chronical stimulation of the sympathetic nervous system also increased the risk of myocardial ischemia, cardiac arrhythmias, platelet aggregation, endothelial dysfunction and, finally, sudden death [1, 3].

5. Gastrointestinal system

The brain-gut axis is a bidirectional connection between the brain (parasympathetic-sympathetic pathways) and the enteric nervous system. Stress strongly influences the brain-gut pathway. The corticotropin-releasing hormone (CRH) manages this process. It has been reported that stress can have several negative effects on gastrointestinal functions. The various gastrointestinal problems were defined related to stress from gastroesophageal reflux and peptic ulcer to inflammatory bowel disease. Either acute or chronic stress affects gastrointestinal motility patterns. Stress increases the intestinal permeability and colonic inflammation [1, 7]. Stress also changes microbiata. While acute stress decreased gastric motility and increased colonic motility, the chronic stress decreased colonic motility. Acute stress leads to delayed gastric emptying, and the long-term exposure to gastric acid results to gastric ulcer. Acute and chronic stress affects brain-gut communication and thus influences emotions [1, 7].

6. Endocrine system

Actually, the stress response is an adaptive reaction of the organism. The purpose of the stress response is to sustain homeostasis. Hypothalamic-pituitary-adrenal axis is primarily responsible for endocrine stress response. HPA axis activated the production of glucocorticoids. During stress, the hypothalamus activated the pituitary gland, and pituitary gland activates adrenal glands to produce cortisol. Cortisol directly affects human biological systems. Cortisol has an important role for the circadian rhythm, glucose and lipid metabolism, and regulation of blood pressure. Cortisol production is necessary throughout the day to maintain daily cycle of energy. But the production of cortisol needs to be slowly declining according to biological rhythm. During a long-term stress, an increased level of cortisol leads to prolonged or extreme challenge for biological system [1–3].

7. Respiratory system

Many emotional and physical stressors increase the ventilation in humans such as excitement, fear, exposure to sudden and long-term cold, heat, hypoxia, and severe pain. Several clinical studies show that there is a strong relationship between lung disease and chronic anger. Acute stress causes many of distresses in respiratory system from rapid breathing and hyperventilation to shortness of breath. Acute stress could trigger asthma attacks but it has been reported that chronic stress aggravate asthma and chronic obstructive pulmonary disease, chronic bronchitis, and emphysema [8–11].

8. Reproductive system

Acute stress and chronic stress cause several problems in female reproductive system, from menstruation, premenstrual syndrome, sexual desire, pregnancy to menopause. It has been shown that high levels of stress could be associated with absent or irregular menstrual cycles, more painful periods, and changes in the length of cycles. Also, the male sexual desire, reproduction, and diseases of the reproductive system are affected by the nervous system. Long-term and excessive cortisol releasing might affect the normal biochemical functioning of the male reproductive system. While the parasympathetic nervous system causes relaxation, the sympathetic nervous system activates sexual desire in males [12, 13].

9. How to cope with the stress

It has been reported that some people are more vulnerable than others to stress-related health problems [4]. Because of the stress that is not inevitable in life, it is important to learn how one can manage it. There are myriad of effective ways to reduce stressors in life. Living accordingly with the circadian rhythm is one of the most important stress-reduced factors. Regular physical activity, especially the long distance walking, healthy nutrition, adequate sleep, living in healthy environment, solve economic problems, life satisfaction, and healthy social network and support are known as stress-relieving lifestyles. It has been clearly shown that applying relaxation techniques and adapting stress-relieving lifestyles improve the emotional function and reduce stress-influenced disorders, such as chronic pain, headache, obesity, diabetes, heart disease, hyperthyroidism, gastric ulcer, hair loss, and sexual dysfunction. Physical activity is the most effective way to manage endocrine system and mediate stress. It has been reported that diaphragmatic breathing practice improves the cognitive performance and reduces the adverse effect of stress in healthy adults [6, 14–17]. It has been provided that effective stress management strategies such as meditation, yoga, deep breathing, which is defined as a mindfulness activity efficient for integrative body-mind training and reduces stress-related disorders, contribute to healthy lifespan, increase the quality of life, and prevent sudden death [18].

Author details

Hülya Çakmur
Kafkas University, Turkey

*Address all correspondence to: hulyacakmur@gmail.com

References

[1] Yaribeygi H, Panahi Y, Sahraei H, Johnston TP, Sahebkar A. The impact of stress on body function: A review. EXCLI Journal. 2017;**16**:1057-1072. DOI: 10.17179/excli2017-480 eCollection 2017

[2] Khanam S. Impact of stress on physiology of endocrine system and on immune system: A review. International Journal of Diabetes and Endocrinology. 2017;**2**(3):40-42. DOI: 10.11648/j.ijde.20170203.12

[3] Kiss A, Goldstein DS, editors. Catecolamines and stress. In: Endocrine Regulations. Vol. 37. Slovak Republic: AEPress; 2003. pp. 69-80. ISSN: 1210-0668

[4] Pulopulos MM, Kozusznik MW. The moderating role of meaning in life in the relationship between perceived stress and diurnal cortisol. Stress. 2018;**21**(3):203-210. DOI: 10.1080/10253890.2018.1429397

[5] Schwabe L, Bohringer A, Chatterjee M, Schachinger H. Effects of pre-learning stress on memory for neutral, positive and negative words: Different roles of cortisol and autonomic arousal. Neurobiology of Learning and Memory. 2008;**90**:44-53. DOI: 10.1016/j.nlm.2008.02.002

[6] Hölzel BK, Carmody J, Evans KC, Hoge EA, Dusek JA, Morgan L, et al. Stress reduction correlates with structural changes in the amygdala. Social Cognitive and Affective Neuroscience. 2010;**5**(1):11-17. DOI: 10.1093/scan/nsp034

[7] Bhatia V, Tandon RK. Stress and the gastrointestinal tract. Journal of Gastroenterology and Hepatology. 2005;**20**(3):332-339. DOI: 10.1111/j.1440-1746.2004.03508

[8] Lehrer P. Anger, stress, dysregulation produces wear and tear on the lung. Thorax. 2006;**61**(10):833-834. DOI: 10.1136/thx.2006.057182

[9] Lehrer P, Feldman J, Giardino N, et al. Psychological aspects of asthma. Journal of Consulting and Clinical Psychology. 2002;**70**(3):691-711. DOI: 10.1037//0022-006x.70.3.691

[10] Tipton MJ, Harper A, Julian FR, Paton JFR, Costello JT. The human ventilatory response to stress: Rate or depth? Journal of Physiology. 2017;**595**(17):5729-5752. DOI: 10.1113/JP274596

[11] Ma X, Yue ZQ, Gong ZQ, Zhang H, Duan NY, Shi YT, et al. The effect of diaphragmatic breathing on attention, negative affect and stress in healthy adults. Frontiers in Psychology. 2017;**6**(8):874. DOI: 10.3389/fpsyg.2017.00874

[12] Mousavi MS, Riazi G, Imani A, Meknatkhah S, Fakhraei N, Pooyan S, et al. Comparative evaluation of adolescent repeated psychological or physical stress effects on adult cognitive performance, oxidative stress, and heart rate in female rats. Stress. 2019;**22**(1):123-132. DOI: 10.1080/10253890.2018.1507021

[13] Li G, Jiang Z, Han X, Shang X, Tian W, Kang X, et al. A moderated mediation model of perceived stress, negative emotions and mindfulness on fertility quality of life in women with recurrent pregnancy loss. Quality of Life Research. 2020;**28**. DOI: 10.1007/s11136-020-02460-2

[14] Snippe E, Dziak JJ, Lanza ST, Nyklíček I, Wichers M. The shape of change in perceived stress, negative affect, and stress sensitivity during mindfulness-based stress reduction. Mindfulness (NY). 2017;**8**(3):728-736. DOI: 10.1007/s12671-016-0650-5

[15] Agathokleous E, Calabrese EJ. A global environmental health perspective and optimisation of stress. Science of the Total Environment. 2019;**18**:135263. DOI: 10.1016/j.scitotenv.2019.135263

[16] Christopher M, Bowen S, Witkiewitz K. Mindfulness-based resilience training for aggression, stress and health in law enforcement officers: Study protocol for a multisite, randomized, single-blind clinical feasibility trial. Trials. 2020;**21**(1):236. DOI: 10.1186/s13063-020-4165-y

[17] Köpsen S, Sjöström R. Patients' experiences of a stress-management programme in primary care. Journal of Multidisciplinary Healthcare. 2020;**21**(13):207-216. DOI: 10.2147/JMDH.S235930

[18] Barnhill JL, Gerkin JS, Moura VL, Weil AB. Mindful opportunity to reflect on experience: Interdisciplinary mind-body medicine skills training for health-care professionals. Global Advances in Health and Medicine. 2020;**9**:2164956120907876. DOI: 10.1177/2164956120907876

Chapter 2

Chronic Fatigue Stress and Sudden Death

Haiyan Zhu, Guoxin Han and Shuoshuo Li

Abstract

Stress refers to a series of neuroendocrine reactions, such as sympathetic nerve excitation and pituitary-adrenal cortex secretion increase, which occur when the body is stimulated by various stressors, and the changes of various functions and metabolism caused by these reactions. Chronic fatigue stress is a fatigue state caused by long-term physical and psychological stress. When the stress reaches a certain intensity or the individual is not well-tolerated, the body stability is impaired, resulting in various pathophysiological reactions leading to various diseases, such as stress hyperglycemia, stress cardiomyopathy, stress arrhythmia, stress ulcer hemorrhagic shock, or even stress ulcer hemorrhagic shock. Eventually lead to sudden death and other adverse events.

Keywords: chronic fatigue stress, epidemiology, sudden death, acute coronary syndrome, arrhythmia

1. Introduction

With the development of today's society, people's pace of work and life is accelerating, resulting in increasing physical and mental stress on people, the main productive forces of society. Long-term physical fatigue and excessive mental load, as well as consequent adverse emotions such as depression and irritability, constitute the unfavorable stress state that is currently common among people. The sudden death of young people caused by chronic fatigue stress is not uncommon, especially in the first-tier cities of developed countries. The early death of these lives not only brought huge disasters to their families, but also caused serious negative impacts on social production. It has created a huge medical and social burden. Chronic fatigue stress and sudden cardiac death in people will be introduced in this passage.

2. Epidemiology

According to the latest research survey, 80% of white-collar workers in China are in the state of overfatigue at present. About 95.7% of young people have died of fatigue-related fatal diseases [1]. According to statistics, the annual incidence of sudden death in Western European and American countries is 0.1–0.2%. According to the epidemiological survey in China, the annual incidence of sudden death in China is 4184 cases per 100,000 people, which is about 0.04% of the general population. Although it is lower than that in European and American countries, because of the large population base in our country, according to the national population of

1.3 billion, nearly 544,000 people die suddenly every year, with an average of about 1500 people per day [2]. Due to the immature pre-hospital first aid transfer system in the past, the success rate of rescue for sudden death outside hospital is <1%. Therefore, the mechanism of sudden death induced by chronic fatigue stress needs to be studied urgently.

3. Acute coronary syndrome and sudden death

The causes of cardiopulmonary arrest are mainly divided into two aspects: primary cardiopulmonary arrest and secondary cardiopulmonary arrest. Eighty percentage of the primary causes are sudden cardiac death, and the leading cause is acute coronary syndrome. Other causes were dilated cardiomyopathy, genetic disorders of rhythm and various types of cardiomyopathy (such as stress cardiomyopathy). The main causes of secondary cardiopulmonary arrest are accidental casualties such as electric shock, drowning, severe trauma, poisoning, etc. Acute coronary syndrome (ACS) is a common and serious cardiovascular disease. It is common in postmenopausal women, men and the elderly. High risk factors include smoking, hypertension, diabetes, hyperlipidemia, obesity and family history of coronary heart disease. Acute coronary syndrome (ACS) patients are usually characterized by paroxysmal anterior pain, chest tightness, suffocation and other symptoms, which can lead to arrhythmia, even heart failure, and ultimately cardiopulmonary arrest. The main mechanism is that after the occurrence of ACS, myocardial activity is more unstable than before, and myocardial autonomy will increase, which will lead to arrhythmia in patients. Abnormal phenomenon, after myocardial ischemia and reperfusion, myocardium will appear abnormal sympathetic nerve regeneration problems, myocardial damage, myocardial hypoxia and ischemia problems, make electrolyte ions imbalance, lead to acidosis, affect ECG activity, arrhythmia, and eventually lead to sudden death [3].

3.1 Establishment of predictive and early warning model for acute coronary syndrome

Now that medical care has entered the era of big data, turning big data into scientific facts and knowledge is the future direction of medicine. The goal of big data analysis is to use data to generate predictions and make more reasonable plans and operational decisions. In this information age, research on big data support for acute coronary syndromes is still rare at home and abroad. Since there is no classification method to predict acute coronary syndrome, the two-category method is used to construct the predictive and early warning model of acute coronary syndrome. The aortic dissection is most easily misdiagnosed as acute chest syndrome with chest pain, so aortic dissection is chosen as a control group. This study systematically summarized the etiology, risk factors, risk stratification, treatment methods and prognosis of acute coronary syndrome in young people, and established a standardized early warning model to gain time for patients' rescue. A total of 58 variables were selected, 14 variables were deleted, and the missing values were >25%. The remaining variables are used to analyze the correlation between variables and ACS and AD, and the variables are filtered by feature selection before the model is built using machine learning algorithms. While maintaining the performance of the machine learning model, some of the most effective features were selected from the original data set to reduce the dimensions. Firstly, the indicators are normalized, and the recursive feature elimination method is adopted. The machine learning model method is used to select random

	Average error rate	Sensitivity	Specificity	Accuracy	AUC
Logistic	0.131	0.868(5.31e-04)	0.869(2.55e-03)	0.869(6.42e-04)	0.915(1.50e-04)
SVM	0.133	0.835(6.86e-03)	0.895(2.88e-03)	0.867(1.06e-03)	0.935(1.61e-04)
RF	0.093	0.913(3.60e-03)	0.902(7.66e-04)	0.907(1.36e-03)	0.964(5.94e-06)

Table 1.
Model evaluation indicators.

forests for feature selection. The results show that when the characteristic variable is 33, the prediction accuracy of the model is the highest. Among them, 13 variables are most closely related to AD and ACS, including plasma D-dimer, troponin T, creatine kinase, creatine kinase isoenzyme, aspartate aminotransferase, urea, platelet count, glucose, creatinine, serum albumin, total protein, direct bilirubin and sodium. The selection of these eigenvalues is based on their specific expression of different pathological processes for ACS and AD. The risk prediction model of young patients with acute chest pain was constructed by logistic regression, SVM method and random forest method. The model evaluation index was obtained by five-fold cross-validation. The prediction accuracy of the three classifiers was >85%. The risk prediction model constructed by the random forest algorithm is the most effective. Sensitivity, specificity and accuracy are all >90%. These results indicate that the random forest risk prediction model can distinguish between acute coronary syndrome and aortic dissection, and has a high recognition ability. According to the average accuracy rate and the average kappa value of the model evaluation index, the prediction model established by the random forest method has the best effect, and the accuracy rate reaches 90.17%. Therefore, the results of this study can achieve early, non-invasive, accurate and safe diagnosis and early warning of acute coronary syndrome. As a result of the updated criteria for assessing coronary stenosis, such as the non-invasive coronary angiography-based blood flow reserve fraction (FFRCT) assessment method, it is becoming a new non-invasive standard to evaluate the functional significance of coronary artery disease and determine whether the lesion leads to myocardial ischemia. We will introduce this method in the next study, comprehensively evaluate the correlation between stress indicators and non-invasive detection, and further evaluate the clinical value of GDF-15, catecholamine and HSP-70 (**Table 1**).

4. Stress and sudden death

Acute coronary syndrome (ACS) is a process of ischemic events caused by the formation of unstable plaques in the coronary artery. After the formation of atherosclerotic plaques, acute stress, such as fatigue, emotional excitement and infection, excites the sympathetic nervous system, promotes the release of inflammatory factors such as norepinephrine, adrenaline and dopamine, and acts on B receptor and a receptor in the body. The body, dopamine receptor, causes a series of reactions such as systolic peripheral blood vessels and visceral blood vessels of the body, leading to increased blood pressure, which causes unstable atherosclerotic plaques to become more vulnerable to rupture, forming coronary artery thrombosis, leading to severe reduction of distal blood supply to myocardial tissue, thus causing a series of clinical manifestations, including ventricular arrhythmia, cardiac insufficiency, shock, etc. Clinical manifestation. At the same time, a large amount of catecholamine release, resulting in increased blood pressure, accelerated heart rate, increased cardiac contractility, increased oxygen demand, excitation of sympathetic nerve receptors, increased coronary artery tension, on the contrary, oxygen supply seriously reduced, affecting blood flow shear stress, accelerating the formation of plaque, leading to plaque rupture, which can trigger the occurrence of arrhythmia and arrhythmia. Platelet aggregation [4]. Inflammatory factors play an important role in the process of stimulation and promotion. In addition, stress can aggravate the severity of acute coronary syndrome, because stress hyperglycemia can lead to glycosylation of low density lipoprotein in blood and transform into foam cells, accelerate coronary atherosclerosis [5–8]. It can also affect the occurrence and development of acute coronary syndrome from the aspects of endothelial dysfunction, insufficient collateral filling, abnormal coagulation mechanism, vasculitis, oxidative stress and increased myocardial oxygen consumption. At the same time, when acute coronary syndrome occurs, the more extensive the myocardial injury is, the more severe the stress is.

Protective inflammatory factors play an important role in the formation of unstable atherosclerotic plaque in coronary artery, besides the involvement of endothelial cells and lipids. A large number of experimental and clinical studies have confirmed the role of inflammatory factors in it. A meta-study found that Bootcov et al. first published a literature report on the structure and function of GDF-15 protein in Proceedings of the National Academy of Sciences of the United States of America in 1997 [9]. Later studies found that GDF-15 is a stress response protein, which is highly expressed in the prostate and placenta under physiological conditions, and weakly expressed in most other tissues, including heart tissue, but under pathological and environmental stresses such as ischemia-reperfusion injury. GDF-15 is abundantly expressed in cardiac myocytes under conditions of injury, cardiac hypertension, heart failure and atherosclerosis, and plays a regulatory role in the structure and apoptotic process of cardiac myocytes [10, 11]. At the same time, GDF-15 is closely related to inflammation. It is an endogenous anti-inflammatory factor, which promotes the repair and survival of infarcted myocardium, inhibits leukocyte infiltration, and inhibits the activation of macrophages and the occurrence of inflammation [12]. In addition, some studies have found that GDF-15 may be related to the basic pathology of cardiovascular diseases. Long-term physical and mental stress can lead to the exhilaration of neuroendocrine system, the increase of corticotropin secretion, and the hyperfunction of sympathetic-adrenal medullary system and pituitary-adrenal cortex system, resulting in the excessive release of adrenaline and noradrenaline, which has an impact on hemodynamics, hemorheology, lipid metabolism and peripheral blood vessels. Increased resistance, increased blood viscosity, increased cardiac load, increased myocardial oxygen consumption and myocardial ischemia are a series of factors that together lead to the occurrence of ACS [13]. Heat shock protein 70 (HSP-70) is a kind of stress protein widely existing in bacteria and mammals. It is a group of proteins that increase rapidly in cells when stimulated by heat, ischemia, hypoxia or metabolic toxicants. According to its molecular weight, it can be divided into HSP30, HSP60, HSP70, HSP90 and so on. Heat shock protein-70 was expressed in normal cells and maintained normal physiological activity, but was low in normal tissues. HSP70 is highly induced during stress. It can mediate the occurrence of vascular inflammation through inflammatory reaction and immune response, destroy vascular endothelium and promote the formation and development of atherosclerosis. At the same time, it can stimulate the expression level of inflammatory factors such as IL-6 to increase the immune response and increase the instability of atherosclerotic plaque. Its serum expression level is correlated with ACS [14]. In recent years, more attention has been paid to its pathophysiological significance.

4.1 Analysis of relationship between stress and ACS

Forty patients with ACS were included in the case group, aged 29–85 years, including 28 males and 12 females. There were 17 cases of unstable angina and 23 cases of myocardial infarction. Forty healthy volunteers were selected from the physical examination center, aged 35–74 (52.53 ± 8.397), including 30 males and 10 females. The acute coronary syndrome was used as the catecholamine in the plasma of the case group and the healthy control group (46592.15 ± 30931.27, $p < 0.001$), GDF-15 (21.94 ± 14.23, $p = 0.007$), HSP-70 (369.56 ± 300.44, $p < 0.001$). Statistical analysis showed that the case group compared catecholamine in the control group (46592.15 ± 30931.27, $p < 0.001$), GDF-15 (21.94 ± 14.23, $p = 0.007$), HSP-70 (369.56 ± 300.44, $p < 0.001$). The level was significantly elevated ($p < 0.05$), which was statistically significant (**Table 2**).

4.2 The relationship between stress and the degree of coronary artery stenosis

Lesion vascular stenosis in the case group ACS patients was divided into <20 group, 20–39 group, <40 group according to Gensini score. Statistical analysis was performed on risk factors such as age, BMI, smoking history, history of hypertension, and stress and severity of diseased vessels. The results showed that serum stenosis >40 group GDF-15 serum levels were significantly higher than <20 group (324.27 ± 198.81 vs. 77.43 ± 699.22, $p = 0.03$), vascular stenosis >40 group serum catecholamines (adrenalin, norepinephrine, dopamine). The level was significantly higher than the <20 group (18.71 ± 7.32 vs. 18.6 ± 46.1, $p = 0.017$), the difference was statistically significant, and the other results were not statistically significant (**Table 3**).

With reference to domestic and foreign literature, the degree of coronary stenosis is evaluated by coronary artery lesion count and Gensini score in this study. It is found that the serum levels of GDF-15, HSP-70, catecholamine (adrenalin, norepinephrine, dopamine) in the ACS case group were higher than those in the control group, and it is speculated that the chronic fatigue stress indicators GDF-15, HSP-70, catecholamine (adrenalin, norepinephrine, dopamine) is associated with ACS. The research team further studied the relationship between these stress indicators and the severity of ACS. The study found that the elevated serum levels of GDF-15 were linearly related to the Gensini score. The correlation coefficient was 0.131 ($p > 0.05$), but the difference was not of statistical significance, which indicates that GDF-15 has a correlation with ACS, but there is no linear regression relationship. GDF-15 and vascular stenosis studies showed that serum levels of GDF-15 in the multivessel disease group were significantly higher than those in the single vessel disease group ($p = 0.035$, $p < 0.05$), and stenosis <40 group GDF-15 serum levels. Compared with the <20 group ($p = 0.033$, $p < 0.05$), serum GDF-15 levels increased with the

Group	GDF-15	HSP-70	Catecholamine
Case group	21.94 ± 14.23	369.56 ± 300.44	46592.15 ± 30931.27
Control group	7.059 ± 5.53	107.76 ± 54.23	5507.14 ± 2083.28
F	1.922	19.024	43.841
P	0.007※	<0.001※	<0.001※

※*P < 0.05 means statistically significant.*

Table 2.
Comparative analysis of stress indexes between case group and control group.

Parameter	<20分(n = 3)	20–39分(n = 5)	>40分(n = 15)	P1	P2	P3
Age	46 ± 12.17	66.6 ± 9.40	63.93 ± 14.33	0.035	0.704	0.061
BMI	25.90 ± 1.46	25.95 ± 6.27	27.07 ± 5.83	0.990	0.720	0.742
Smoke	0.33	0.8	0.533	0.244	0.317	0.555
Hypertension	0.33	0.8	0.8	0.244	1.000	0.111
GDF-15	77.43 ± 699.22	400.98 ± 294.1	324.27 ± 198.81	0.318	0.515	0.035※
HSP-70	74453.4 ± 69224.2	45655.2 ± 45185.1	43978.25 ± 17068.4	0.496	0.902	0.119
Catecholamine	18.6 ± 46.1	19.94 ± 6.15	18.71 ± 7.32	0.317	0.741	0.017※

P1 stands for comparison between Gensini <20 and Gensini 20–39, P2 stands for comparison between Gensini 20–39 and Gensini <40, P3 stands for comparison between Gensini <20 and Gensini <40.
※$P < 0.05$ means statistically significant.

Table 3.
Stress and known risk factors and severity of stenosis.

increase of coronary artery disease count and stenosis, GDF-15 level and coronary artery disease. There is a significant positive correlation between the number and the degree of stenosis Gensini score, which is consistent with the current research results related to GDF-15 and ACS. The meta-study found that GDF-15 is a stress-responsive protein, which represents the level of stress in the body. Through this study, it is found that the state of chronic fatigue stress is related to the severity of ACS. GDF-15 can be used as a potential indicator of risk classification and treatment prognosis. At the same time, the level of serum catecholamine (epinephrine, norepinephrine, dopamine) in the stenosis <40 group was significantly higher than that in the <20 group ($p = 0.017$, $p < 0.05$), indicating that the degree of vascular stenosis was correlated with the expression level of catecholamine. The more severe the vascular stenosis is, the higher the serum catecholamine level will be, which is closely related to the long-term chronic fatigue stress. Long-term stress leads to hyperactivity of the sympathetic-adrenal-pituitary neuroendocrine axis, which secretes a large number of catecholamine antibodies, resulting in their high expression in the body.

5. The pathogenesis of arrhythmia induced by chronic fatigue stress

Stress can cause a variety of arrhythmias, including tachyarrhythmias and bradyarrhythmias, including sinus arrhythmias, atrial arrhythmias and ventricular arrhythmias. It is closely related to stress intensity and basic heart disease. The mechanism of stress-induced cardiorespiratory arrest has been proved by some studies from the aspects of myocardial ischemia and the increase of ECG instability caused by autonomic nervous system. In the process of research, people have found important indicators and pathophysiological processes involved in stress-induced cardiopulmonary arrest, such as intracellular calcium homeostasis, central nervous system and so on. The arrhythmia caused by intracellular calcium homeostasis is still the focus of current research. When the human body is under fatigue stress for a long time, excessive production of highly active molecules such as reactive oxygen species (ROS) in mitochondria leads to a series of changes in myocardial ion channels leading to ventricular arrhythmia. The mutation of calmodulin gene induced by chronic fatigue stress may affect the structural changes of calmodulin, such as the increase of sulfhydryl group content. Both of them may increase the incidence of arrhythmia by influencing the function of calcium channel. In the pathological injury of myocardial ischemia or pressure overload, various signaling molecules and ionic mechanisms induce the increase of intracellular calcium level, while elevated calcium ion promotes the production of ROS. Too much ROS further increases the levels of calcium ion and ROS by triggering mitochondrial calcium signal and regulating calcium regulatory proteins, eventually forming positive feedback of calcium ion and ROS, causing myocardial fineness. Persistent cell damage and electrophysiological disorders [15]. At the same time, ROS can change the membrane lipid environment or activate signal transduction molecules such as protein kinase C and calmodulin-dependent protein kinase II. Thus, it can affect the phosphorylation of sodium channels, reduce the peak sodium current, and lead to arrhythmia. Activation of calmodulin-dependent protein kinase II can also phosphorylate subunits of Ca channel, opening L-type calcium channel. With the increase of calcium influx, delayed post depolarization and cardiac systolic dysfunction will eventually lead to arrhythmia. Young people under high intensity and high pressure under fatigue stress belong to the group at high risk of sudden death. Preventive measures should be taken in advance to provide an insurance for the people who are the backbone of society and make some contributions to the health of the main construction forces of the family and society.

Author details

Haiyan Zhu[1,2*], Guoxin Han[3] and Shuoshuo Li[1]

1 Emergency Department, The First Medical Center of Chinese PLA General Hospital, Beijing, China

2 Emergency Department, Hainan Hospital of Chinese PLA General Hospital, Sanya City, Hainan Province, China

3 Emergency Department of Strategic Support Force Special Medical Center, Beijing, China

*Address all correspondence to: zhuhy301@aliyun.com

References

[1] Meng X, Wang RL, Gao S, et al. Effect of ulinastatin on paraquat-induced-oxidative stress in human type II alveolar epithelial cells. World Journal of Emergency Medicine. 2013;**4**(2):133-137

[2] Luft R, Ikos D, Palmieri G, et al. A case of severe hypermetabolism of non-thyroid origin with a defect in the maintenance of mitochondrial respiratory control: A correlated clinical, biochemical, and morphological study. The Journal of Clinical Investigation. 1962;**41**:1776-1804

[3] Jie Wang, Gailu, Guangdong, Duluoshan, et al. Multivariate analysis of left ventricular dysfunction in elderly patients after acute myocardial infarction. Chinese Journal of Cardiovascular Diseases for the Aged. 2000;**2**(4):233-236

[4] Bazhen Y, Xuecheng L, Jiong T, et al. Stress and myocardial infarction. Advances in Cardiovascular Disease. 2004;**25**(5):404

[5] Bellodi G, Manicardi V, Malavasi V, et al. Hyperglycemia and prognosis of acute myocardial infarction in patients without diabetes mellitus. The American Journal of Cardiology. 1989;**64**:885-888

[6] Andersen GO, Eritsland J, Aasheim A, et al. Impaired glucose tolerance in patients with acute myocardial infarction. Tidsskrift for den Norske lægeforening: tidsskrift for praktisk medicin, ny række. 2006;**126**:2264-2267

[7] Bhadriraju S, Ray KK, De Franco AC, et al. Association between blood glucose and long-term mortality in patients with acute coronary syndromes in the OPUS-TIMI 16 trial. The American Journal of Cardiology. 2006;**97**(11):1573-1577

[8] Scott AR, Cheng A, Greenacre M, et al. Implications of hyperglycaemia and ethnicity and apos; in patients with acute coronary syndromes in New Zealand. Diabetes, Obesity & Metabolism. 2007;**9**:121-126

[9] Bootcov MR, Bauskin AR, et al. MIC-1, a novel macrophage inhibitory cytokine, is a divergent member of the TGF-b superfamily. Proceedings of the National Academy of Sciences of the United States of America. 1997;**94**:11514-11519

[10] Xu J, Kimball TR, Lorenz JN, et al. GDF15/MIC-1 functions as a protective and antihypertrophic factor released from the myocardium in association with SMAD protein activation. Circulation Research. 2006;**98**(3):342-350

[11] Yuying G, Yintao Z, Yian Y, Ming Z, Liying F, Daifu Z. Analysis of correlation between serum GDF-15 level and severity of coronary artery disease. Shandong Medicine. 2010;**50**(24):84-85

[12] Barma M, Khan F, Rosemary J. Association between GDF-15 levels and changes in vascular and physical functions in older patients with hypertension. Aging Clinical and Experimental Research. 2017;**29**:1055-1059

[13] Chuping G. Clinical significance of plasma catecholamine and serotonin detection in patients with type A behavioral coronary heart disease. Contemporary Chinese Medicine. 2016;**23**(23):126-128

[14] Qiu FY, Tian RL, Qiang Y, et al. Association of occupational chronic psychological stress with heat shock protein 70 in serum and tumor necrosis factor-alpha expression levels. Zhonghua Yu Fang Yi Xue Za Zhi. 2016;**50**(5):423-428

[15] Akar FG, O'Rourke B. Mitochondria are sources of metabolic sink and arrhythmias. Pharmacology & Therapeutics. 2011;**131**:287-294

Chapter 3

Taming Occupational Stress among Farmers in Developing Nations

Toyin Samuel Olowogbon, Aaron M. Yoder, Segun B. Fakayode and Abraham O. Falola

Abstract

Agriculture is a major sector in most developing nations of the world. The world food poverty is on the rise, with almost one in seven people around the world who are chronically hungry and lacking enough food to be healthy and lead active lives. The race is on to explore agriculture to produce enough food to feed the rapidly growing population. Consequently, there has been a change in the dimensions of agricultural health risks among farm workers in most developing countries. Occupational health-related studies are very important, yet research outputs in these regions of the world are yet to target this area extensively to stimulate appropriate policy formulations. Farm workers therefore have low adaptive capacity to workplace stress-related issues. These peculiar constraints have exposed farmers to work-related stressors affecting their well-being. In this context, farm stress occurs as a result of adverse reaction farmers' faced including excessive pressure, seasonality, rural lifestyle, job demands or reactions to some uncertainty in their farming businesses. This chapter X-rayed the concept of farm stress in a developing nation context, providing empirical basis for the formulation of appropriate interventions to reduce farm stressors with particular focus on stress in the crop and poultry ventures.

Keywords: farmers, developing nations, occupational stress, stressors, well-being

1. Introduction

Agriculture is tipped to be the largest provider of jobs globally, as the sector's share of the global workforce stood at 32% in 2013 [1–3]. Asia and the Pacific (59%) are ranked first followed by Africa, which is ranked second (52%) as regards workforce share in agriculture. Globally, agricultural occupation has been described as one of the most hazard-prone occupations. This industry has one of the worst records for high incidence of occupational ill health, injuries and work-related fatalities after construction industry [4].

Agriculture plays a major role in Nigeria's economy. This sector has been described to be the primary rescue of the nation from economic recession. It has been documented that about 121 million of the 175 million Nigerian population are farmers out which about 80% of this figure are smallholder farmers [5, 6]. These smallholder crop farmers are poor, typically not literate, have limited infrastructure, solely depend on rainfed agriculture and have limited adaptive and coping capacity [7, 8]. On the other hand, poultry subsector is the most commercialised (capitalised) of all the subsectors of the Nigeria's agriculture [9]. This subsector contributes about 15% of the total annual protein intake with approximately 1.3 kg of poultry products consumed per head per annum in Nigeria [10].

Despite the role played by the agricultural industry in reducing poverty, agriculture has been described as a hazardous occupation exposing farm workers to several work-related risks including agricultural stressors [4, 11–16].

In spite of the documented hazards in agriculture, the agricultural sector in Nigeria has a culture of unwise risk-taking and is yet to appreciate the role a good health and safety management can play in attaining safe and sustainable agriculture. In Nigeria, agriculture is largely practiced as a way of life and usually not regulated as such, and the safety and health of the workers are yet to be prioritised [4, 17]. Incidence of injuries and illness in agriculture is high and may be directly linked to workplace stress [18]. Workplace stress may not be observed at the early stages in most cases. However, as it progresses, ill health makes an individual grasp that he/she is under stress.

Recent development in agriculture in most developing countries has increased the exposure of agricultural workers to agricultural risks and hazards in their workplaces. This high exposure may be due to increased need to meet food and monetary demands of farming households. Agricultural productivity has been very low in developing countries. This has been attributed in part to climate change effects and erratic rainfall pattern in recent times. These issues have further exposed farmers to work-related stressors. This in turn affects farmers' total well-being.

On the one hand, stress is described as the response, while stressor is the stimulus eliciting a need for adaption on the other. A publication by European Commission on the Guidance on Work-Related Stress defined work-related stress as a pattern of emotional, cognitive, behavioural and physiological reactions to adverse and harmful aspects of work. This includes work contents, the organisation and the workplace environment as the major sources of stress [19]. The United States National Institute for Occupational Health and Safety [NIOSH] defined work-related stress as the damaging physical and emotional responses that occur when the necessities of a job do not mat competence, resources and needs of a worker [20] and expresses the view that working conditions are a key factor while personal factors are also influential to stress.

The UK Health and Safety Executives (HSE) further classified work-related stress as a key occupational health crisis among workers [21].Work-related stress is a major source of psychosocial hazards that has not been prioritised in the agricultural sector of most developing nations. The origin of stressors could be of physical, psychological or social. This is probably due to the intricate way agriculture is carried out in these developing nations [17].

Generally, agriculture includes many other associated activities, such as cropping, crop processing and packaging, irrigation, pest management, grain storage, animal husbandry and farm construction. Agriculture is usually demanding and time-consuming. There is no shortage of farm tasks to complete under constrained seasonal conditions. This can be stressful for most farm workers especially those who like to feel a sense of completion [22].

Stress in farm workplaces occurs when an individual response to unfavourable reaction from excessive pressure or other types of demand placed on them relates to their farming activities. This is often due to exposure of farm workers to workplace stressors that cause frustration or anxiety exerting pressure on the farmer. In addition, agricultural operations are mostly seasonal, mostly self-owned, and peasant in nature coupled with rural lifestyle, exposing farmers to numerous stressors.

The University of California report has revealed that younger farmers, especially those younger than 50 years, are more stressed compared to farmers of older age group. Farmers who practiced mixed farming (e.g. crop and livestock farming) self-reported higher stress intensity than those in crop farming only. Farmers who also engaged off-farm jobs apart from farming report more stress than full-time farm operators [22]. It was also reported that women working on farms experience additional stressors compared with those not engaged in farm works. It was also documented that working as a full partner in the farm business leads to many women taking sole responsibility for the home and family matters. A woman with an off-farm job faces more difficult demands in addition to being the traditional nurturer for the rest of the family [23].

The agricultural-based stressors affect farm workers' total well-being including physical and mental well-being [18]. Exposure to workplace stress causes ill health, affecting mental health and human body physiology leading to low labour productivity. The way an individual reacts to stress differs; some of the documented reactions to stress include gastrointestinal disorders, behavioural changes, exhaustion and sleep disorders. It also increases the danger of other diseases such as cardiovascular diseases and other psychological disorders [24].

Empirical evidences have provided information on agricultural workplace health issues such as farm chemical poisoning, ocular injuries, hearing loss and ergonomic injuries, but little is known about the psychosocial hazards such as stress in agricultural workplaces (see [25–37]). General workplace stressors have been identified from sources such as the National Institute for Occupational Safety and Health (USA) (NIOSH), the Health Safety Executive and the International Labour Organisation (ILO). The HSE identified workplace stressors including demand, relationship, role change, control and lack of support [20]. The NIOSH reported workplace stressors to include management style, design of tasks, interpersonal relationships, career concerns, work roles and environmental conditions [37].

The ILO reported job control, social support, out-of-a-job demands, physical environment, working time, work-life balance, recognition at work, job security, information and communication as workplace stressors [38]. Agriculture in most developing countries is practiced as a means of livelihood, social security and way of life. This underscores the importance of the sector in sustainable development effort. Investigating work-related stress in agriculture in Nigeria is important in understanding the mechanism underlying agricultural stressors in cropping and poultry operations. This will help in developing adequate coping (adapting to stress situations) strategies and making efforts at removing some of the identified stressors. This may in the long run enhance farmers' total health, agricultural productivity and food security. No doubt, studying agricultural stressors as it linked to agricultural sector productivity is important. However, little is known about stressors in crop and poultry production in developing countries like Nigeria. Studies in Nigeria on agricultural-related stressors especially crop production and poultry industry is rare. This present study intends to bridge this information gap and offers a pragmatic solution to these pertinent health risks and occupational stress in agriculture.

2. Materials and methods

2.1 Study area for the crop farmers

In addressing the stressors associated with crop farming, 70 crop farmers were sampled from Ekiti State, Nigeria. The state has 16 local government areas with coordinates 7° 40°N, 5°15°E. The total land area is 6353 km2 and has a population of

2,237,186 people, with agriculture providing income and employment for more than 75% of the population [39, 40]. Ekiti State is also categorized by the Ekiti State Agricultural Development Project (EKADP) into Zones A, B and C based on agronomic and ecological considerations. These zone headquarters are situated at Aramoko, Ikere and Isan, respectively [40].

2.2 Study area for poultry farmers

For the poultry venture, a structured questionnaire was administered to 80 randomly selected poultry farmers in Ilorin Metropolis. Ilorin, is the state capital of Kwara State, North Central, Nigeria. The state lies between latitudes 7°45′N and 9°30′N and longitudes 2°30′E and 6035′E and has an estimated population of about 2.37 million people [40]. The state has an annual rainfall range of 1000–1500 mm. The months of December and January coincide with the cold and dry harmattan period, while the annual rainfall pattern across the state extends between the months of April and October with minimum temperature ranging from 21.1 to 25°C and average maximum temperature varying between 30°C and 35°C.

2.3 Study type and instruments

The study engaged a descriptive survey to collect information on agricultural stressors among crop farmers in Ekiti State, Nigeria. Farmers who had farming as their major occupation across the farming communities in the state were approached for the study. About 85 farmers were informed about the purpose of the study, and 74 gave their consent via information letters. However, after data collection and cleaning, 70 of the questionnaires were found useful (N = 70). Similar approach was engaged in eliciting information from 80 poultry farmers in Kwara State, Nigeria. Information were elicited with the aid of a structured questionnaire and semi-structured interview. The questionnaires were designed to elicit information on socio-economics, agricultural stressors and their causes and perceived effects among the farming population as experienced by crop and poultry farmers. The instrument for crop farmers was taken through a test and retest method of 3-week interval to ensure the internal reliability of the instrument. The reliability index was found to be 0.73, while that of the poultry farmers was found to be 0.71. The instruments were augmented with a semi-structured interview to elicit qualitative information on the stressors associated with their occupation. The research instrument was developed based on the available information empirically (see [19, 20, 41, 42]). Various components of the instrument include the following: Section A, the socio-economic characteristics of the respondents; Section B, stressor identification and causes of farm stress on a four-point Likert scale [4 = strongly agree (SA), 3 = agree (A), 2 = disagree (D), 1 = strongly disagree (SD)]; and Section C, the ascribed effects of farm stressors and intensity of effects on a three-point Likert type [2 = mostly affected (MA), 1 = occasionally affected (OC) and 0 = not affected (NA)]. Authors sought the consent of the respondents via a consent form in which participants were informed of the purpose of the study and the confidentiality of the information provided. Respondents signed/thumb printed to show approval. The farmers were provided brief education on the concept of farm stress. This education included farm stress, sources and effects of farm stress using oral presentation. This was followed with a semi-structured interview using probing and prompting to elicit more information of farm stress-related issues from farmers. Authors are aware of the limitation of this method to include biassed results leading to overestimation of stressor prevalence and effects. However, this was corrected by cross-checking responses from the structured questionnaire and interview with the use of probing and prompting responses to check for internal validity and consistency.

2.4 Data analysis

Collected data were analysed using descriptive statistics such as frequency and percentage, means, standard deviation and range. Stressors were ranked from the Likert scale mean as reflected in Eq. 1:

$$\mathrm{X} = \sum_{n}^{1} \frac{Fx}{N} \tag{1}$$

where X is the mean response to an item, Σ is the summation, F is the number of respondents choosing a particular scale point, x is the numerical value of a scale point and N is the total number of respondents to an item.

The mean response to a particular item was interpreted using the concept of real limit of numbers. The numerical values of the scale points and their respective real limits are as follows:

- SA = points with real limits of 3.50–4.0
- A = points with real limits of 2.50–3.49
- D = points with real limits of 1.50–2.49
- SD = points with real limits of 0.50–1.49

Mean values were calculated from the responses interpreted accordingly, e.g. a mean of range 0.5–1.49 is interpreted as SD. The intensity of effects was also computed using the above model real limits as follows: mostly affected = 1.5–2.0; occasionally affected = 0.6–1.50; and not affected = 0.00–0.50 accordingly.

We collected data from poultry farmers for this study which were analysed using descriptive statistics. In analysing the effects of stressors on poultry business, the following rating is used for the mean remark:

- Not affected (NF) = points with real limits of 0.50–1.49
- Fairly affected(FA) = points with real limits of 1.50–2.49
- Affected (AF) = points with real limits of 2.50–3.49
- Highly affected (HF) = points with real limits of 3.50–4.0

3. Results and discussion

Our findings showed that about 80% of the sampled farmers planted maize and cassava, while 10% of the farmers planted cassava and watermelon and solely cassava, respectively. We found that most (86%) of the sampled farmers had previous agriculture-related trainings, while about 14% had no previous agricultural training.

Further results from the study revealed that the mean age was 34 years, with about 38% of the respondents in the age class of 31–35 years and the age ranging between 20 and 50 years. The average schooling years was found to be 14 years, with about 43 and 33% having technical and degree qualifications accordingly. The average years of farming stood at 14 years, with about 43% in the class of 11–15 years. The average farm size among respondents was 9.3 hectare with household size median of five persons (see **Table 1**).

Our study revealed that about 98% of the respondents identified stressors that are related to their occupations. These stressors included unfavourable government policies, long hours of farm labour, labour scarcity, poor harvest anxiety, poor transport infrastructure, poor access to credit facilities, untimely access to farm inputs, poor market proximity and poor access to market information, among others (see **Table 2**). The study shows that about 80% perceived that farm stressors had affected them in a number of ways including extreme tiredness, intense headache, forgetfulness, back pain, insomnia (sleep disorder), loss of temper, relaxation problem and worry (see **Table 3**).

Our study further revealed in **Table 4** that most of the farmers were mostly affected by the identified farm stressors and they were able to perceive their effects accordingly. Ninety-eighth percent of the farmers were yet to develop structured coping strategies in dealing with the stressors (see **Table 5**).

The age distribution from our study showed that most of the respondents were under 40 years of age. This shows agility, activeness, vigour and the likelihood to take risks and adopt innovation. Education has been described as a tool for change. This implies that the level of education is related to the level of innovativeness of an individual. This study reported that the average educational years of respondents

S/N	Characteristics	Value
1	Age (years)	
	Mean	33.57
	Standard deviation	2.34
	Coefficient of variation	6.97%
2	Years spent in school	
	Mean	13.97
	Standard deviation	1.17
	Coefficient of variation	8.38%
3	Farming experience (years)	
	Mean	13.57
	Standard deviation	4.430
	Coefficient of variation	32.65%
4	Household size (persons)	
	Mean	3.62
	Standard deviation	1.17
	Coefficient of variation	32.32%
5	Farm size (ha)	
	Mean	9.30
	Standard deviation	4.94
	Coefficient of variation	53.12%
Field Survey, 2015.		

Table 1.
Socio-demographic characteristics of crop farmers (N = 70).

S/N	Stress items (stressors)	Frequency SA	A	D	SD	Mean	Remark
1	I am usually on farm for long hours, and I work myself out	25 (35.7)	25 (35.7)	18 (25.7)	2 (2.9)	3.04	A
2	I am usually disturbed about how to secure seeds, fertilisers and chemicals for my farm	30 (42.9)	20 (28.6)	10 (14.3)	10 (14.3)	3.00	A
3	I am usually frustrated on how to secure financial support for my farm	42 (60)	25 (35.7)	3 (4.3)	0 (0)	3.55	SA
4	I always get worried on where I am going to sell my farm produce	32 (45.7)	20 (28.6)	11 (15.7)	7 (10)	3.10	A
5	I am always disturbed on how to transport my produce to the market	41 (58.6)	23 (35.7)	6 (8.6)	0 (0)	3.50	SA
6	I get worried because I do not have access to market information on my produce	28 (40)	24 (34.3)	8 (11.4)	10 (14.3)	3.00	A
7	I get disturbed about the poor prices in market for my farm produce	51 (72.9)	19 (27.1)	0 (0)	0 (0)	3.72	SA
8	I get disturbed about weather-related issues as regards my crops: rains, floods,	30 (42.9)	27 (38.6)	10 (14.3)	3 (4.3)	3.20	A
9	I get worried about my crops; I am not going to have good harvest	40 (57.1)	20 (28.6)	7 (10)	3 (4.3)	3.38	A
10	I get disturbed because I do not see extension agents regularly to help me	28 (40)	20 (28.6)	11 15.7)	11 (15.7)	2.92	A
11	I get worried because I do not have labour regularly for my farming activities	30 (42.9)	25 (35.7)	10 (14.3)	5 (7.1)	3.14	A
12	I am usually worried about my farm because this land does not belong to me	25 (35.7)	22 (31.4)	17 (24.3)	6 (8.6)	2.94	A
13	Usually, I am not happy being a farmer	25 (35.7)	22 (31.4)	13 (18.6)	10 (14.3)	2.88	A
14	Usually, I get worried that government policies do not favour farmers	35 (50)	15 (21.4)	17 (24.3)	3 (4.3)	3.17	A
15	Usually, I get worried about the future of my farming business	25 (35.7)	25 (35.7)	10 (14.3)	12 (17.1)	2.96	A
16	Usually, I get worried about the costs of inputs such as fertiliser, labour and chemicals	49 (70)	18 (25.7)	3 (4.3)	0 (0)	3.66	SA
17	Usually, I get worried about Fulani herdsmen intruding my farm	38 (54.3)	22 (31.4)	10 (14.3)	0(0)	3.40	A

Source: Field Survey, 2015. (Figures in brackets are the percentages of responses).

Table 2.
Identified agricultural stressors by crop farmers.

For the identified stressors, in what ways have you been affected by these stressors?		
Perceived stressor effects	**Frequency**	**Percentage**
Headache	66	94.0
Extreme tiredness	56	80.0
Forgetfulness	54	77.1
Sleeping difficulty	50	71.4
Back pain	48	68.6
Loss of temper	47	67.1
Relaxation problem	45	64.3
Excessive worry	43	61.3
Field Survey, 2015.		

Table 3.
Perceived effects of stressors on crop farmers.

Perceived stressor effects	Intensity of effects				
	Mostly affected (MA)	**Occasionally affected (OA)**	**Not affected (NA)**	**Mean**	**Remark**
Headache	45	21	4	1.68	MA
Extreme tiredness	50	6	14	1.89	MA
Forgetfulness	42	12	16	1.78	MA
Sleeping difficulty	40	10	10	1.80	MA
Back pain	47	1	22	1.93	MA
Loss of temper	20	27	23	1.43	OA
Relaxation problem	30	15	25	1.67	MA
Excessive worry	37	6	27	1.86	MA
Field Survey, 2015.					

Table 4.
Intensity of the perceived effects of stressors among crop farmers.

Have you developed any planned coping strategies against the identified stressors?		
Item	**Frequency**	**Percentage**
Yes	1	1.4
No	68	97.1
Do not know	1	1.4
Total	70	100
Field Survey, 2015.		

Table 5.
Coping strategies adopted by crop farmers.

was 14 years. The 14 years average of schooling years reported in this study is an indication that most of the respondents had tertiary education. The educational status of respondents shows they are literate and could easily engage technology to improve their work and source for relevant information. Years of farming were expected to influence skill acquisition and ability to adopt innovation in the production in agribusiness. The study showed that the average years of farming stood at 14 years, with a range of 4–20 years. The study showed that the average household size is four persons per household. The mean farm size among respondents was 9.3 hectares. This farm size is an indication that most of the farmers are smallholders.

The findings from the study as shown in **Table 2** showed about 98% identified occupational-related stressors such as labour scarcity, poor transport infrastructure, poor harvest anxiety, unfavourable government policies, uncertain future for Nigerian agriculture, poor access to credit facilities, poor market proximity, insufficient funds and poor access to market information, among others. The study also shows that most of the stressors are linked to insufficiency of resources.

Our research identified long hours of labour in farm workplace as a stressor. This finding corroborated an earlier study in England and Wales by Simkin et al.. The authors reported that about 70% of farmers worked more than 10 hours a day, a practice that is unhealthy and hazardous [43]. The research conducted in Europe by Katalin identified physical exhaustion leading to extreme tiredness as stressor. The respondents admitted that this had affected their health negatively [44]. From our own study, it could be implied that long hours of working on the farm will lead to physical exhaustion leading to excessive tiredness which was identified by farmers as one of the perceived effects of exposure to occupational stress. The study by Phelps in North Yorkshire showed that farmers' major stressors were government policies and legislation, financial problems and time pressures [45]. Our study corroborated these findings that poor credit access and unfavourable government policies as regards financial concerns were identified as stressors. Other studies had also suggested that financial concerns are a key source of stress to farmers. It was also reported that hazardous working conditions and geographical isolation are also significant concerns [46, 47].

A study in London by Hawton et al. reported that the majority of respondents worried about money. The researchers further noted that the unclear boundaries between farmers' home and working lives made it difficult to escape from occupational-related problems [48]. A study in North Yorkshire by Raine reported that farmers perceived their occupation as becoming even more stressful and that key factors in this were paperwork and finances [49]. The stressors for farmers identified in a study by Booth and Lloyd were new legislation, paperwork and media criticism of agricultural communities [50]. The results from a study in the UK by Deary et al. found that stress was linked to government legislation and increased bureaucracy [51]. Another study from the UK by the Health and Safety Executives (HSE) showed that workload intensity, the non-controllability of certain aspects of farming (such as disease and seasonality) and insecure futures and finances were farm stress factors [18]. The findings from our own study corroborated these findings by identifying poor harvest anxiety, unfavourable government policies and unpredictable weather conditions as stressors to crop farmers. Unpredictable weather conditions are attributed to climate change impact, to which Nigeria has been identified as being vulnerable since its economy is largely based on weather-sensitive agricultural production systems [52]. Evidence has earlier shown that climate change is already affecting crop yields in many countries [49, 53–55]. This climate change effect will affect farmers' holistic well-being.

Other farm workplace stressors identified in this study that may be common to developing nations due to their developmental stage include labour scarcity, uncertain future for the agricultural sector, poor agricultural extension services/contact, poor land availability, poor road infrastructure, unfavourable market prices, poor access to credit facilities, poor access to market information, high cost of farm inputs, poor market for farm produce (in this case farmers produced but do not have buyers leading to postharvest losses) and poor public perception for the agricultural occupation (farmers are perceived to be poor and uneducated in the Nigeria since most farmers are peasants).

We found poor labour availability as a stressor to Nigerian crop farmers. This has been attributed to "push factors" such as poverty and unemployment, lack of farmland, poor infrastructures, crop failures, famine, insurgence and long work hours of farm work with lower wage than other employment opportunities such as motorcycle riding business, all leading to rural–urban migration labourers from rural areas.

Crop farmers identified uncertain future for their business as a stressor. This could be due to the neglect that the agricultural sector had suffered in recent times as a result of the nation's overdependence on crude oil.

Inadequate access to agricultural extension services was identified as a source of stress. Earlier studies in Nigeria have revealed that non-provision of relevant agricultural information to farmers is a key factor limiting farmers' productivity [6]. This has been attributed to insufficient number of extension agents. As revealed from the agricultural development programmes (ADP) in 27 states of Nigeria, an extension agent and farm family ratio of 1:826 was reported in Gombe State; this was reputed to be the highest in Nigeria, while Niger, Lagos and Ebonyi States' extension agent to farm family ratio is in the neighbourhood of 1:5000 [56]. With this statistics, there will be poor agricultural extension contact leading to inefficient information dissemination to farmers.

Poor access to land for agricultural activities by farmers in Nigeria could be a stressor due to land grabbing challenges, the land use act of the nation and the land tenure-related challenges that farmers encounter in their farm operations. Poor road infrastructure is a major stressor for farmers as the road networks are bad and this has led to high transport cost. The poor road network has led to postharvest losses for farmers as such products attract unfavourable market prices. Crop farmers also identified poor market for agricultural produce as stressor. Due to their size of farms and financial capacity, these farmers are unable to add values to this product and as such are sceptical on where and how to sell their farm produce.

In Nigeria, an average farmer depicts neglect and poverty, even though these small-scale farmers produce the bulk of the food consumed in the country. Farmers are not respected, and as such poor public perception for the agricultural occupation was identified as a stressor to Nigerian crop farmers.

In recent time in Nigeria, Fulani herdsman intrusion to farmlands is a threat to the existence of crop farming especially peasants. These farmers lack the capacity to protect and secure their farmlands from herdsmen. This has recently contributed to farm stressor among Nigerian crop farmers. Empirical evidence has revealed that herdsman intrusion to farmland has contributed to crop yield reduction, poverty due to farmers' income decline and farmers' displacement from their farms [8, 57].

Farm stress affects farmers' physical, social and mental well-being. Further findings from this study show that about 80% of respondents perceived that agricultural stressors had affected them in a number of ways including back problem, irregular sleep, relaxation problem, extreme tiredness, temper loss, excessive worry and headache. The UK HSE found that the common effects of farm stressors on farmers were back problems, lack of sleep, worrying about work, irritability and feeling down [18]. Smith et al. [18] found that 20% of the respondents were suffering from high levels of occupational stress, the effects of which were manifest in terms of health complaints, disrupted family life and elevated levels of sick leave and workplace accidents. Corroborating this, a study in Canada by Walker and

Walker found that farmers scored higher than nonfarmers on a range of stress-related symptoms, including chronic tiredness, forgetfulness, difficulty relaxing, loss of temper, poor concentration, sleep disruption and back pain [58].

Evidence from this study further documented effects of farm stress on well-being. Most of the respondents (about 98%) are yet to develop structured coping strategies to deal with the stressors. This finding could be due to poor access to stress management information among crop farmers in Nigeria.

Further findings from the study are shown in **Table 6**; the mean age was 49 years, with the age ranging between 25 and 65 years. This finding showed most of the poultry farmers are about 50 years. Education has been noted as a tool for change, and the level of education has been correlated to innovativeness of an individual. The Nigerian educational system is 9 years of education in the basic class, 3 years in the senior secondary and 4 years in tertiary totalling 16 years. The average years spent in school was 15 years, with about 34 and 55% having secondary education and degree qualifications accordingly. The 15 years average of schooling years reported in this study shows that most of the respondents possessed tertiary education. The educational status of respondents shows they are literate and could easily give accurate information on stress-related issues in their businesses and engage information technology in improving themselves on stress-related issues. Years of experience in poultry were expected to influence the acquisition of skills and capability to adopt technological innovation in poultry business. The average years of poultry experience was 6 years, with about 50% in the class of 1–5 years. The average of 6 years in poultry business is sufficient for farmers to give accurate information on stressors in poultry business. Households had a median of four persons, and the average farm size in terms of number of birds among respondents was 151 birds/farmer. This farm size is an indicator that most of the farmers have smallholdings for their birds. The average poultry income per cycle of production was N80,450 ($224).

S/N	Characteristics	Value
1	Age (years)	
	Mean	49.20
	Standard deviation	3.20
2	Years spent in school	
	Mean	14.5
	Standard deviation	2.34
3	Poultry experience (years)	
	Mean	6.0
	Standard deviation	1.12
4	Household size (persons)	
	Mean	4.0
	Standard deviation	1.3
5	Farm size (no. of birds)	
	Mean	151 birds
	Standard deviation	4.34
6	Income per cycle	
	Mean	80,450 naira ($224)
	Standard deviation	1200

Field Survey, 2015.

Table 6.
Socio-economic characteristics of poultry farmers (N = 80).

The findings revealed the classification of stress items. These items include climate change effects. Notable effects includes reduction in egg size, reduction in egg quality, reduction in egg shell thickness, continuous outbreak of diseases in poultry and high death rate among birds were found to fairly affect (FA) poultry farmers. The results of this study is similar to those obtained by [9] who submitted that climate change (such as low rainfall, high temperature and other climatic factors) affects the cost of poultry production and also the spread of poultry disease. This view was also shared by [10], who stated that variance in climatic variables can lead to variance in poultry egg production, feed intake and outbreak of poultry diseases.

Farmers were found to be affected (AF) by stressors that are financial based including poor credit access and high collateral demand. Farmers also reported that

Stress items	Highly affected (HF)		Affected (AF)		Fairly affected (FA)		Not affected (NF)			Mean rating
	Freq	%	Freq	%	Freq	%	Freq	%	Total	
Climate change										
a. Reduction in egg size	09	11.2	21	26.2	32	40.0	18	22.5	182	2.28 (FA)
a. Reduction in egg quality	06	7.5	18	22.5	31	38.7	25	31.3	165	2.06 (FA)
a. Reduction in eggshell thickness	04	5.0	12	15.0	51	63.7	13	16.3	167	2.09 (FA)
a. Continuous outbreak of diseases in poultry	06	7.5	11	13.7	38	47.5	25	31.3	158	1.97 (FA)
a. High death rate among birds	04	5.0	15	18.8	27	33.7	34	42.5	149	1.86 (FA)
Financials										
a. Poor credit access	28	35.0	36	45.0	16	20.0	0	0	252	3.15 (AF)
a. High collateral demand	21	26.3	32	40.0	27	33.7	0	0	234	2.92 (AF)
Health										
a. Highly demanding and time-consuming	41	51.3	21	26.3	18	22.5	0	0	263	3.28 (AF)
a. Highly stressful	31	38.8	30	37.5	19	23.7	0	0	252	3.15 (AF)
Institutional										
a. Poor government support	54	67.5	36	45.0	0	0	0	0	324	4.0 (HF)
a. Poor policies	63	78.7	17	21.3	0	0	0	0	303	3.79 (HF)
a. Poor market for product	30	37.5	32	40.0	18	22.5	0	0	252	3.15 (AF)
a. Poor market prize	32	40.0	33	41.2	15	18.8	0	0	194	2.42 (FA)
Business management										
a. Inadequate access to relevant trainings	14	17.5	27	33.7	11	13.8	18	22.5	177	2.21 (FA)
a. Inadequate access to inputs	32	40.0	18	22.5	17	21.3	13	16.3	229	2.86(AF)
a. Inadequate access to farm labour	08	10.0	08	10.0	28	35.0	36	45.0	148	1.85 (FA)

Stress items	Highly affected (HF)		Affected (AF)		Fairly affected (FA)		Not affected (NF)			Mean rating
	Freq	%	Freq	%	Freq	%	Freq	%	Total	
a. Inadequate access to clean water	06	7.5	21	26.3	30	37.5	23	28.7	170	2.12 (FA)
a. Poultry waste disposal issues	06	7.5	24	30.0	40	50.0	10	12.5	186	2.32 (FA)
a. Poor light and energy access	18	22.5	34	42.5	15	18.8	13	16.2	217	2.71 (AF)

Field Survey, 2015.

Table 7.
Poultry-related stressors and perceived effects (N = 80).

S/N	Disease	Frequency	%	Remark
1	Malaria	21	26.3	3rd
2	Diarrhoea	9	11.3	7th
3	Headache	20	25	4th
4	Vomiting	1	1.3	12th
5	Catarrh	13	16.3	5th
6	Joint pain	22	27.5	2nd
7	Abdominal pain	1	1.3	12th
8	Respiratory difficulty	2	2.6	11th
9	Skin irritation	5	6.3	8th
10	Dizziness	10	12.5	6th
11	Muscular weakness	27	33.8	1st
12	Heart problem	1	1.3	12th
13	Eye irritation	4	5.0	10th
14	Loss of appetite	5	6.3	8th

Field Survey, 2015.

Table 8.
Self-reported health issues among poultry farmers (N = 80).

they are affected by health stressors including highly demanding, time-consuming and highly stressful. Farmers reported that their businesses were highly affected (HF) by poor government support and policies. Business management stressors were identified and affected by farmers including inadequate access to inputs and poor energy access/stability (see **Table 7**).

As shown in **Table 8**, the prominent health issues reported among poultry farmers in Nigeria include muscular weakness, joint pain, malaria, headache and catarrh accordingly. As seen in **Table 9**, about 63% were yet to come up with planned coping strategies to the stressors. However, 20% reported they have adopted coping strategies, and these include intensive and semi-intensive systems of poultry keeping where the birds are kept within a cage or in a poultry and the required warmth needed particularly in cold weather is generated artificially

Have you developed any planned coping strategies against these stressors?		
Response	**Frequency**	**Percentage**
Yes	20	25
No	50	63
Do not know	10	12
Total	80	100
Field Survey, 2015.		

Table 9.
Response to stressor coping strategies (N = 80).

through the use of electricity. In coping with financial challenges, some of the poultry farmers resolved to self-financing, borrowing from family members and taking loans from cooperatives as well as banks. Some farmers cope with health challenges by observing adequate rest, while others maintain good hygiene and good housekeeping in the poultry to reduce the risk of infections, among others. Due to poor access energy supply, poultry farmers resolve to the use of generators, solar panels and inverters in providing energy particularly for the storage of poultry products.

4. Conclusion and recommendations

We concluded that exposure to work-related stress is common in the Nigerian crop and poultry workplaces in Nigeria. This finding could be linked to the composite nature of agricultural work and the way agriculture is practiced in Nigeria. Agricultural stressors affect farmers' total well-being. The elimination of stressors removes stress. Identifying stress factors (stressors) is the first stage in designing efficient stress management plan. The identified stressors by farmers are developmental, economic, environmental, institutional, governmental, sociocultural and educational/information and business management based, among others. Most of the identified stressors are due to failure on the part of stakeholders of the industry in carrying out their responsibilities. These farmers were able to identify these stressors, engaging a stress management-oriented attitude which is the most excellent agricultural health practice that can improve agricultural stress management. Our recommendations include:

i. Researchers should engage in field experiments using randomised control trials in the design of appropriate interventions to reduce stress among poultry and crop farmers.

ii. Targeted agricultural enterprise insurance package should be developed with collaboration with farmers to help reduce stress among farmers.

iii. The government, foreign development partners and the private sector have been the major stakeholders supporting agricultural productive activities in Nigeria. These stakeholders should embark on stress management campaign and surveillance among farmers to improve mental health.

iv. These stakeholders should help farmers in their challenged areas including infrastructure provision, favourable agri-policies, credit facilities, input access, stock grazing reserves for herders and prompt extension services.

v. Based on our findings from the intensity of the perceived effects of stress, there should be integration of mental health focused on agricultural health in primary health care by the Nigerian government.

vi. Farmers should engage in the good use and management of their time as good time management practices and planning can reduce workplace stress.

Acknowledgements

This book chapter is derived in part from an article published in *Journal of Agromedicine*, November, 2018 24(1) Copyright Taylor & Francis. Available online: http://www.tandfonline.com/loi/wagr20//; https://doi.org/10.1080/1059924X.2018.1538915.

Conflict of interest

We have no conflict of interest to declare.

Author details

Toyin Samuel Olowogbon[1*], Aaron M. Yoder[2], Segun B. Fakayode[3] and Abraham O. Falola[1]

1 Department of Agricultural Economics, PMB 1515, University of Ilorin, Ilorin, Nigeria

2 Department of Environmental, Agricultural and Occupational Health, University of Nebraska Medical Center, Omaha, USA

3 Department of Agricultural Economics and Extension, Federal University, Oye-Ekiti, Ekiti, State, Nigeria

*Address all correspondence to: olowogbonsamuel@gmail.com

References

[1] International Labour Organization and World Bank. Labour Force Total International Labour Organization, using World Bank Population Estimates [Internet]. 2014 [Cited: 07 July 2016]. Available from: http://data.worldbank.org/indicator/SL.TLF.TOTL.IN?end=2014&start=1990&view=chart

[2] International Labour Organization. Safety and Health in Agriculture. Geneva: International Labour Organization Office; 2011

[3] International Labour Organization (2014) Global Employment Trend Report. Risk of a Jobless Recovery. Available from: https://www.ilo.org/global/research/global-reports/global-employment-trends/2014/lang–en/index.htm

[4] Chris I. Pastoral Care. Safety Health Practitioner Magazine. Borehamwood, London: United Media; 2008

[5] National Bureau of Statistics (NBS) Annual Report. 2014

[6] Omotesho OA. Let the Small-Scale Farmer be in Good Standing. The 158th Inaugural Lecture Series. Ilorin Nigeria: University of Ilorin; 2015

[7] Nigerian Environmental Study Team (NEST). Building Nigeria's Response to Climate Change (BNRCC):Annual Workshop of Nigerian Environmental Study Team (NEST): The Recent Global and Local Action on Climate Change, held at Hotel Millennium, Abuja, Nigeria; 8-9th October, 2008

[8] Ifeanyi-obi CC, Etuk UR, Jike-wai O. Climate change, effects and adaptation strategies: Implication for agricultural extension system in Nigeria. Greener Journal of Agricultural Sciences. 2012; **2**(2):053-060

[9] Adene DF, Oguntade AF. The Structure and Importance of the Commercial and Village Based Poultry Industry in Nigeria FAO (Rome) Study October 2006; 2006

[10] Ologbon AC, Ambali I. Poultry enterprise combination among small-scale farmers in Ogun state, Nigeria: A technical efficiency approach. Journal of Agriculture and Veterinary Sciences. 2012;**12**:8-13

[11] World Health Organization (WHO). Building Healthy and Equitable Workplaces for Women and Men: A Resource for Employers and Worker Representatives. [Internet]. 2011 [Cited 2014 August 2011] Protecting Workers' Health Series, 11. Available from: www.who.int

[12] Asenso-Okyere K, Chiang C, Thangata P, Andam K. Interactions Between Health and Farm Labor Productivity. Food Policy Report of International Food Policy Research Institute Washington, DC; 2011

[13] Grovermann C, Schreinemachers P, Berger T. Quantifying pesticide overuse from farmer and societal points of view: An application to Thailand. Elsevier. Crop Protection. 2013;**53**:161-168

[14] Suwanna P, Pepijn S, Piyatat P, Prasnee T. Pesticides, external costs and policy options for Thai agriculture. Environmental Science & Policy. 2013; **27**:103-113

[15] Helitzer DL, Hathorn G, Benally J, Ortega C. Culturally relevant model program to prevent and reduce agricultural injuries. Journal of Agricultural Safety and Health. 2014;**20**: 175-198

[16] Occupational Safety & Health Administration (OSHA). Agricultural Operations [Internet]. 2014 [Cited: 10 November 2014]. Available from:

https://www.osha.gov/dsg/topics/agriculturaloperations/

[17] Olowogbon TS. Stress management: An abandoned work-ethic in agriculture. African Newsletter on Occupational Health and Safety. 2014; **24**:9-11. ISSN 1239-4386

[18] Health and Safety Executives. Farmers, Farm Workers and Work-Related Stress. Research report 362. 2005: ISBN 0 7176 6135 0

[19] OSH in Figures: Stress at Work-Facts and Figures [Internet]. 2005 European Agency for Safety and Health at Work.[Cited: 25 February 2014] Available from www.osha.europa.eu/en/publications/ reports/TE-81-08-478-EN-C_OSH_in_figures_stress_at_work

[20] Health and Safety Executive-UK. Managing the Causes of Work-Related Stress: A Step-by-Step Approach Using the Management Standards (2n edn.), 2007:HMSO

[21] United States National Safety Council. International Accident Facts: Illinois. United States; 1995

[22] Kristin R. Stress Management for Women Farmers & Ranchers. Oakland, CA: University of California (UC) Small Farm Program Publication, Agriculture and Natural Resources, 1111 Franklin Street, 6th Floor; nd 94607, (510) 987-0096

[23] Molgaard V, Miller L. Manage Stress to Increase Farm Safety. SAFE FARM-Promoting Agricultural Health & Safety Project. Ames: Iowa State University Extension; 2002. Available from: www.cdc.gov/nasd/

[24] Lajini P. Why stress should be managed in the workplace. African Newsletter on Occupational Health and Safety. 2014;**24**(1) Healthy workplaces - managing stress. ISSN 1239-4386

[25] Erondu ES, Anyanwu PE. Potential hazards and risks associated with the aquaculture industry. African Journal of Biotechnology. 2005;**4**:1622-1627

[26] Ajayi M, Solomon O, Ajayi I. Farmers' perception and knowledge of health problems affecting their agricultural productivity in Edo State Nigeria. Journal of Agriculture and Social Research. 2007;7(2):38-45

[27] Ajani OIY, Ugwu PC. Impact of adverse health on agricultural productivity of farmers in Kainji Basin north-Central Nigeria using a stochastic production frontier approach. Trends in Agriculture Economics. 2008;**1**:1-7

[28] Fathallah FA, Miller BJ, Miles JA. Low back disorders in agriculture and the role of stooped work: Scope, potential interventions, and research needs. Journal of Agricultural Safety and Health. 2008;**14**:221-245

[29] Onasanya AS. Perceived effects of farming related health problems on farmers productivity in Yewa north area of Ogun state, Nigeria. Medwell Journal of Social Sciences. 2009;**4**:42-48

[30] Tekwa IJ, Ambali OY, Gabdo BH. Economic analysis of farm hazards associated with the use of agrochemicals on agricultural farms. Australian Journal of Agricultural Engineering. 2010;**1**:7-13

[31] Myers ML. Review of occupational hazards associated with aquaculture. Journal of Agromedicine. 2010;**15**:412-426

[32] Verma A. Visual Impairment and Eye Health and Safety among Latino Farmworkers [Internet]. 2010 [Cited: 23 November 2012]. Available from: http://libres.uncg.edu/ir/uncg/f/Verma_uncg_0154D_10479.pdf

[33] Durborow RM, Myers ML, Cole HP, Ogunsanya TO, Thompson SL. Health

and Environment in Aquaculture. Presented at the National Symposium on Agriculture, Forestry, & Fishing Health and Safety in Boise, Idaho, June 28, 2011

[34] Quandt AS, Schulz RMW, Talton WJ, Verma A, Arcury TA. Occupational eye injuries experienced by migrant farmworkers. Journal of Agromedicine. 2012;**17**:63-69

[35] Earle-Richardson G, Jenkins P, Fulmerc S, Mason C, Burdick P, May P. An ergonomic intervention to reduce back strain among apple harvest workers in New York state. Applied Ergonomics. 2005;**36**:327-334

[36] Vanderwal L, Rautiainen R, Kuye R, Peek-Asa C, Cook T, Ramirez M, et al. Evaluation of long- and short-handled hand hoes for land preparation, developed in a participatory manner among women vegetable farmers in the Gambia. Applied Ergonomics. 2011;**42**:749-756

[37] National Institute for Safety and Health Stress at Work [Internet]. 2014: [Cited: 25 February 2014]. Available from: www.cdc.gov/niosh/docs/99-101/

[38] International Labour Organization. Stress Prevention at Work Checkpoints [Internet]. 2014 [Cited: 24 February 2014]. Available from: www.ilo.org/wcmsp5/groups/public/@dgreports/@dcomm/@publ/documents/publication/wcms_168053.pdf

[39] Ekiti State Government. Ekiti State Government Diary. Ado-Ekiti, Nigeria: Ekiti State Government; 2008

[40] Nigerian Population Census (NPC). National Population Commission. Sample Survey, Nigeria. 2007

[41] Travers C, Cooper C. Increasing costs of occupational stress for teachers. In: Dunham J, Varma V, editors. Stress in Teachers: Past, Present and Future. London: Whurr; 1998

[42] Wainwright D, Calnan M. Work Stress – The Making of a Modern Epidemic. Buckingham: Open University Press; 2002, 2002

[43] Simkin S, Hawton K, Fagg J, Malmberg A. Stress in farmers: A survey of farmers in England and Wales. Occupational and Environmental Medicine. 1998;**55**:729-773

[44] Katalin B. High Levels of Work Rrelated Stress in Aagricultural Sector. [Internet]. 2009 [Cited: 10 October 2015]. Available from: www.eurofound.europa.eu/observatories/eurowork/articles-high-levels-of-work related-stress-in-agricultural-sector

[45] Phelps C. Stress in Farming in North Yorkshire. WPS/01/06. Phase 1 Report. Sheffield: Health and Safety Laboratory; 2001

[46] Eberhardt BJ, Pooyan A. Development of the farm stress survey: Factorial structure, reliability and validity. Educational and Psychological Measurement. 1990;**50**:393-402

[47] McGregor M, Willock J, Deary I. Farmer stress. Farm Management. 1995; **9**:57-65

[48] Hawton K, Simkin S, Malmberg A, Fagg J, Harris L. Suicide and Stress in Farmers: Department of Health Funded Research. London: The Stationary Office; 1998

[49] Sulaiman A, Ja, afar-Furo MF. Economic effects of farmer-grazier conflicts in Nigeria: A case study of Bauchi state. Trends in Agricultural Economics. 2010;**3**:147-157

[50] Booth NJ, Lloyd K. Stress in farmers. International Journal of Social Psychiatry. 1999;**46**:67-73

[51] Deary IJ, Willock J, McGregor M. Stress in farming. Stress Medicine. 1997; **13**:131-136

[52] Walker LS, Walker J. Stressors and symptoms predictive of distress in farmers. Family Relations. 1987;**36**: 374-378

[53] Deressa T, Hassen R, Alemu T, Yesuf M, Ringler C. Analyzing the Determinants of Farmers' Choice of Adaptation Measures and Perceptions of Climate Change in the Nile Basin of Ethiopia. International Food Policy Research Institute (IFPRI) Discussion Paper No. 00798. Washington, DC: IFPRI; 2008

[54] Intergovernmental Panel on Climate Change (IPCC). Climate change: Impacts, adaptation, and vulnerability. In: Parry ML, Canziani OF, Palutikof JP, van der Linden PJ, Hanson CE, editors. Contribution of Working Group II to the Third Assessment Report of the Intergovernmental Panel on Climate Change. Cambridge, United Kingdom: Cambridge University Press; 2007, 1000 p

[55] Raine G. Causes and effects of stress on farmers: A qualitative study. Health Education Journal. 1999;**58**:259-270

[56] Oladipupo AM, Egbenyabuwa OF, Sede C. Effect of T&V innovation on income and farmers' performance in Edo state, Nigeria. American Journal of Agriculture and Forestry. 2014;**2**: 159-167

[57] Olobatoke R, Amusain O. Effects of Fulani herder's intrusion on economic livelihood of crop farmers in Yagba east local government of Kogi state, Nigeria. Inter Journal of Agricultural Policy and Research. 2017;**5**(3):80-85

[58] Dinar A, Hassan R, Kurukulasuriya P, Benhin J, Mendelsohn R. The Policy Nexus between Agriculture and Climate Change in Africa. A Synthesis of the Investigation under the GEF/WB Project: Regional Climate, Water and Agriculture: Impacts on and Adaptation of Agro-Ecological Systems in Africa. CEEPA Discussion Paper No. 39. Pretoria: Centre for Environmental Economics and Policy in Africa, University of Pretoria; 2006

Chapter 4

Psychosomatic Pain

Ertuğrul Allahverdi

Abstract

Disorders that are not clearly attributable to an organic disease are called somatoform disorders. Their symptoms are called psychosomatic symptoms and include insomnia, fatigue, and weakness. These disorders can also be associated with heartburn, depression, irregular heartbeat, dizziness, pain, cardiovascular problems, gastrointestinal discomfort, erectile dysfunction, a sensation of pressure in the throat, chest problems, hallucinations, and double vision. Somatoform disorders can be an expression of untreated mental pain and life experiences, resulting from serious loss, profound personal injury, or disrespect. Such symptoms occur in almost all humans, but these disorders can have a serious effect in 4–20% of the population.

Keywords: psychosomatic, pain, chronic pain, stress

1. Introduction

Psychosomatic pain: "A combination of symptoms of physical pain in various body areas that occur during any life period, where treatment is sought for the pain by going to many health clinics, and resulting in disruption of social and/or occupational activities" [1–3].

"Soma" means the body. "Psychosomatic" diseases in psychiatry are mainly due to psychological causes that are not based on an organic etiology or physical disorders.

It is currently believed that conscious or unconscious emotions, thoughts, and behaviors are also effective in psychosomatic disease in biological organisms and should be evaluated together with the dual thoughts related to the body and mind status. The patient may use more atypical and exaggerated expressive words from time to time when defining psychogenic pain. The localization and periodicity of the patient's pain can also be persistently atypical. The pain of the patient usually begins after some important life events and stresses. The emotional burden of the factors stimulating and triggering pain is reflected in the patient's voluntary posture and the relevant muscle groups. A psychological dimension, depression and anxiety are usually noted among the accompanying symptoms. It is noteworthy that the characteristics of the pain do not conform to anatomical facts and physiological functioning. Besides, the response to analgesics is also often atypical. Accompanying symptoms such as anger, impatience, helplessness, boredom, and restlessness must be considered in patients with psychological pain.

Both psychosocial and biological factors always play a role in the development and pathophysiological mechanism of psychogenic pain [1–4].

The *Diagnostic and Statistical Manual of Mental Disorders* (DSM-IV) reference book of diagnostic criteria in psychiatry explains psychosomatic diseases as follows [1–3]:

> *"A combination of multiple physical symptoms that occur within a period of time, with continuing search for treatment, and resulting in deterioration of social or professional life."*

The following criteria must be present to make a diagnosis of a psychosomatic disorder according to the DSM-IV:

- *Having at least four separate pains* (headache, abdominal pain, pain in the arms and legs, back pain, etc.)
- *Two gastrointestinal tract symptoms* (nausea, bloating, vomiting without pregnancy, diarrhea, gastric irritation)
- *One sexual function or genital system symptom* (menstrual irregularity, impotence in men, sexual aversion to women and men, etc.)
- *One neurological symptom* (impaired balance, regional paralysis or decreased strength, difficulty swallowing, double vision, deafness, loss of consciousness, etc.)
- *Lack of an organic disorder to explain these symptoms as a result of medical examination, laboratory investigations, and imaging methods*
- *No addiction to alcohol, drugs, or other substances*
- *Insecure and skeptical approach to psychiatric examination*
- Stress is one of the major causes of psychosomatic diseases. Stress causes many bodily functions to deteriorate or not work properly.
- The most common trigger of psychosomatic diseases is loss and separation.

The American Board of Medical Specialties and the American Psychiatry and Neurology Board have approved specialization in psychosomatic medicine in 2003. This decision has emphasized the importance of this field and also reintroduced the widespread use of the "psychosomatic" term [1–3].

The Diagnostic Criteria for Psychosomatic Research (DCPR) are considered to be more explanatory than the DSM-IV [1–3].

2. DCPR definition criteria

Persistent somatization subjects with a psychosomatic disorder are believed to have a higher incidence of other nonfunctional system (chronic fatigue) syndromes in the future with this approach, and these are called "multisomatoform disorder," "pure somatization," or "chronic somatization." The functional somatic symptoms secondary to a psychiatric disorder are as follows:

a. **Conversion symptoms**

b. **Anniversary reaction:** the anniversary reaction defines the somatic, emotional, and behavioral responses at the anniversary of the period where a loss has been suffered.

2.1 Abnormal behavior

a. **Health anxiety:** the health anxiety concept includes many different types of beliefs and fears related to illness and pain.

b. **Fear of illness:** fear of illness is the unsupported and persistent fear that a specific illness (such as AIDS or cancer) is present despite examination results and assurances to be contrary, as defined in the DCPR.

c. **Denial of illness:** the denial concept as specified in psychoanalytic theory is an ego defense mechanism against unpleasant thoughts. Denial has later been included in the emotion-focused coping strategies when faced with stressful conditions.

d. **Fear of death (thanatophobia):** this is a sudden feeling or belief that the subject is about to die despite the lack of a medical reason. It must not be confused with the fear of unavoidable death.

3. The psychological aspect of disease: psychological factors influencing medical conditions

Demoralization (lack of resistance): hopelessness is the most important aspect. There is a loss of the feeling of usefulness/effectiveness. Mood reactivity is usually preserved.

Alexithymia: alexithymia is a personality type that is characterized by difficulty in recognizing emotions, difficulty communicating, and a cognitive structure and operative thought that focuses on external focus and external center adaptation.

Type A behavior: Type A behavior leads to taking care of more work in continually shorter times. Coronary disorders are more common in these subjects. They have irritable mood and are impatient and agitated.

Irritable mood: irritable mood is characterized by decreased anger control and usually results in verbal or behavioral bursts of anger.

It is important to have knowledge about the pain and its variety before psychosomatic pain, because pain can cause psychosomatic problems as well as result.

Pain is thought to be an important clinical and socioeconomic problem all around the world. We investigated the incidence, prevalence, and economic burden of pain conditions in children, adolescents, and adults based on the electronic scanning of databases for articles published between 2000 and 2014 in this review. Differences in methodology and the epidemiological studies make it difficult to give precise predictions of prevalence and incidence; however, the economic burden of psychosomatic pain is clearly high. There is a need to develop concepts and methods to examine pain from a population perspective and to advance the development of pain prevention and management strategies. Family physicians and clinicians have great responsibilities in the diagnosis and treatment of pain and especially psychosomatic pain within this context. The participation of physicians in multidisciplinary training and studies is also a fundamental principle [3, 5].

It is appropriate to explain psychosomatic pain primarily in accordance with general principles. Pain is a defining characteristic in the diagnosis of many diseases. It can serve as an index of the symptoms and activity of the disease or diseases and as a prognostic indicator and a predictor of the use of health care for the underlying etiology [1, 2]. The International Association for the Study of Pain (IASP) and the World Health Organization (WHO) describe pain as "an unpleasant sensory and emotional experience associated with or described in relation to real or potential tissue damage or associated with such damage," "an unpleasant sensory and emotional experience associated with existing or possible tissue damage or associated with such damage," and "a protection mechanism" [2].

An overview of the epidemiology and economic burden of pain conditions in children, adolescents, and adults is summarized below under the relevant headings. The incidence and prevalence of pain conditions as well as the risk factors and the effect of pain on individuals have also been described. The wide range of pain conditions in clinical and research areas include pain in children and adolescents, spinal pain, neuropathic pain, musculoskeletal pain, and fibromyalgia/chronic diffuse pain. In addition to the factors associated with the prevalence of pain, the individual, economic, and social burden of pain conditions should also be considered.

4. Classification of pain

1. According to neurophysiological mechanisms
   a. Nociceptive
   b. Somatic
   c. Visceral
   d. Neuropathic (non-nociceptive) central or peripheral
   e. Psychogenic
2. According to the duration
   a. Acute
   b. Chronic
3. According to the etiologic factors
   a. Cancer pain
   b. Postherpetic neuralgia
   c. Pain due to sickle cell anemia
   d. Arthritis pain
4. According to the pain region
   a. Headache
   b. Facial pain
   c. Low back pain
   d. Pelvic pain

Before making a diagnosis of **psychogenic pain**, somatic pathology must be definitely eliminated. A diagnostic nerve block can be used for the diagnosis, and psychological or psychiatric conditions should be evaluated as a factor in pain etiology using the criteria in the DSM-IV and DCPR classifications. One must know the general pain definitions, classifications, and criteria well to be able act objectively when dealing with the diagnosis and criteria of psychosomatic pain. Psychosomatic pain is often found in the etiology together with the definitions provided below [1–3, 5].

5. Pain incidence and definition

Describing the epidemiology of pain is difficult because of the subjective nature of symptoms and the lack of consensus on the definitions of specific diagnoses and conditions. It is problematic to identify pain areas, especially with musculoskeletal pain. Many pain conditions are episodic, and the majority of patients express recurrent symptoms at varying intervals and durations during periods with and without pain. The actual incidence of most pain conditions may therefore remain unknown.

Similarly, study results vary due to differences in the identification of diffuse pain cases and the specific diagnosis. While case definitions may also vary depending on the duration, intensity, or psychological burden of pain in the patient, the diagnoses are based on subjective patient experience, clinical tests, or results of imaging and pathological studies. It may be difficult to compare studies reporting different periods of prevalence (e.g., timepoint, weekly, monthly, lifetime) [5].

6. The incidence and distribution of pain

6.1 Pain in children and adolescents

Pain conditions in children and adolescents have gradually become the focus of the scientific literature in recent years. The occurrence of pain in children evidence as indicates childhood or adolescence pain can predict adulthood pain. Children with pain discontinue their education or become withdrawn. Physical inactivity is a possible result. Low back pain, headache, and abdominal pain are the most common types of childhood and adolescence pain.

The reported 1-year incidence of low back pain in children and adolescents varies from 11.8 to 33.0% (median, 22.4%), while the 1-month prevalence varies from 9.8 to 36.0% (median, 22.9%). Since there are a lower number of studies on the prevalence of neck pain (49.0%) and upper back pain (30.0%), some doubt remains about the accuracy of these predictions. A systematic review of chronic pain epidemiology in children and adolescents (pain continuing for more than 3 months) has reported that the 1-month prevalence of chronic back pain was between 18.0 and 24.0% (median, 21.0%) [6–9]. In addition to these predictions obtained from systematic reviews, the 1-month prevalence of low back pain was reported to be 37.0% in more than 400,000 children and adolescents aged 11–15 years [10–14].

The predicted 1-month headache prevalence in children and adolescents is 26.0–69.0% (median, 47.5%) in systematic investigations. Swain et al. have reported this figure to be 54.1% in a survey based on 312 schools [15]. Recurrent abdominal pain (at least three episodes that limit the child's functions for at least 3 months) is the focus of most childhood and adolescence pain studies [16]. Recurrent abdominal pain prevalence has been reported as 0.3–19.0% (median, 8.4%) [17] and 3.8–41.2%

(median, 12.0%) [7]. Childhood and adolescence monthly multiple pain prevalence was 12.1–35.7% (median, 23.9%).

Further studies on pain epidemiology in children and adolescents are still required to evaluate the effect of age on the pain prevalence. The effects of the increased pain rates in childhood and adolescence and of the transition to adolescence on the incidence and prevalence of pain conditions are not clear at present [17].

6.2 Spinal pain

Spinal pain, and especially low back pain, is a common problem that most people experience at a certain point in their lives. The lifetime prevalence of low back pain is reported to be between 51.0 and 84.0%. There are many studies on the epidemiology of low back pain compared to other pain conditions.

Predictions for the 1-year first low back pain events varied between 6.3 and 15.4% (median, 10.9%) in one review [18] and between 13.5 and 26.2% (median, 19.9%) in others [11, 16, 18–22]. Predictions of the 1-year incidence of low back pain events (including patients with previous episodes) vary between 1.5 and 38.9% (median, 20.2%). Many people who experience activity-limiting low back pain recover quickly [23], but some have recurrent pains [24]. Predictions for the 1-year recurrence vary between 24.0 and 80.0% (median, 52.0%) [18].

Important information is present on the prevalence of low back pain. The 1-month prevalence is predicted to be between 24.0 and 49.5% (median, 36.8%) [25]. The prevalence of thoracic spine pain varies between 1.4 and 34.8% (median, 18.1%) [26], while the 1-month prevalence of neck pain varies between 15.4 and 45.3% (median, 30.4%) [27].

Chronic low back pain (CLBP) is usually defined as low back pain continuing for more than 12 weeks [28]. The prevalence of CLBP in the general European population has been predicted as 5.9–18.1% (median, 12%).

6.3 Neuropathic pain and sciatica

Neuropathic pain has been defined by the International Association for the Study of Pain as "pain caused by a lesion or disease of the somatosensory nervous system" [29]. It is differentiated from other inflammatory conditions by characteristic signs and symptoms such as "burning" or "freezing," numbness, tingling, or "pins and needles" sensations [29]. There are only a few studies on the incidence and prevalence of neuropathic pain in the population.

Chronic pain with neuropathic features has a prevalence of 0.9–17.9% (median, 9.4%) [13]. Prevalence in cancer is 19.0–39.1% (median, 29.1%) [14]. The incidence is 3.9–42.0 per postherpetic neuralgia, 12.6–28.9 for trigeminal neuralgia, 0.2–0.4 for glossopharyngeal neuralgia, and 15.3–72.3 for painful diabetic peripheral neuropathy, respectively, all per 100.000 person years [13].

Sciatica is also called radiculopathy, nerve root compression-irritation, nerve root pain, or lumbosacral radicular syndrome [30]. The pain is believed to arise in the lumbar spine but is felt in the leg pain by the patline. The 1-year sciatica incidence is reported as 9.3% [30]. The 1-month sciatica prevalence varies between 0.4 and 16.4% (median, 8.4%) [31].

6.4 Musculoskeletal pain

Musculoskeletal system disorders are among the most common causes of disability and incapacity, especially in the elderly [32]. Upper extremity pain is also common; monthly shoulder pain symptoms are present in 18.6–31.0% (median, 24.8%) of adults [33]. Monthly knee pain prevalence in adults is 13.0–28.0% (median, 20.5%) [34]. The prevalence was 28.0, 15.0, and 14.0% for foot ankle and toe pain in a review combining the reported figures [35].

6.5 Fibromyalgia and chronic diffuse pain

Chronic diffuse pain is defined as the presence of chronic pain with diffuse localization [36]. The American College of Rheumatology defines chronic diffuse pain as bilateral axial skeleton pain continuing for 3 months or more in its 1990 guidelines [37]. Fibromyalgia diagnostic criteria have been defined using the same definition [38]. Some fibromyalgia prevalence figures are 2.0–5.0% in the USA, 0.7% in Denmark, and 10.5% in Norwegian women. Fibromyalgia is a clinical diagnosis similar to other chronic pain conditions, and the lack of a clear definition therefore limits the comparison of prevalence predictions. The diagnostic criteria for fibromyalgia in the American College of Rheumatology's 2010 Criteria include the evaluation of diffuse pain together with the other symptoms (such as fatigue and cognitive symptoms) to develop a more specific case definition [38]. Future studies on the epidemiology of fibromyalgia are likely to increase the accuracy of current prevalence predictions by using this definition [39].

7. Prevalence tendencies over time

Only a few studies have evaluated the prevalence of pain conditions, and most have focused on the prevalence of low back pain. Palmer et al. [40] reported that the 1-year prevalence of low back pain increased by 12.7% over a 10-year period from 1987 to 1997, and this increase was associated with gender, age group, social class, and residence area. A contrasting decrease in the 1-month prevalence from 26.1 to 22.6% has been reported over a 7-year period in another study [41]. The chronic low back pain frequency In the USA has increased from 3.9 in 1992 to 10.2% in 2006 [42].

8. The effects of pain on health

Pain, and especially chronic pain, creates a significant burden for patients and their families. It adversely affects the general health perception, significantly inhibits daily activities, is associated with depressive symptoms, and significantly and negatively affects the relationships and interactions with others. The World Health Organization Global Burden of Disease uses the term "disability" to assess the potential for non-mortality-related disease. They define disability as any short- or long-term loss of health [43]. Disability-adjusted life years (DALYs) and years lived with disability (YLDs) are needed to measure and compare the limitations of a wide range of disorders associated with pain. Pain-related disorders that are characterized or defined by the presence of pain (low back pain, neck pain, other musculoskeletal disorders, migraine, and falls) constitute 5 of the top 10 conditions responsible for YLDs in the world. Acute low back pain has caused 83 million DALYs, and according to the effects of the chronic types of back pain, this constitutes 10.7% of all YLDs [43]. Neck pain and migraine/headache each account for about 24 million DALYs. Other musculoskeletal disorders are responsible for 28 million DALYs and traumas due to falls for 19 million DALYs. Other important contributions include osteoarthritis (17 million DALYs) and accident-related injuries

(13 million DALYs) [44]. These results for 1990 and 2010 supersede all previously published Global Burden of Disease results.

9. Risk factors for pain

It is difficult to determine the factors initiating pain episodes in the population as studies only specify an estimate due to the differences in the methodology and reporting. It is necessary to focus on the main risk categories such as age, gender, social group, and individual factors. Generally, there is no evidence for the risk factors of pain. Future studies that evaluate all aspects of the pain experience from both the individual and the population point of view are needed. These studies must employ multidimensional methods in the case of psychosomatic pain.

10. Age and gender

Studies on pain in children and adolescents have shown that females generally suffer more pain than males. The relationship between pain and gender is clear in adults. Females report more severe pain, more frequent pain, and longer-lasting pain than males in most studies. However, it is not known whether this gender difference is due to underlying biological pain mechanisms or the effects of psychological and social factors.

As regards age, the prevalence of some pain disorders such as back pain increases from childhood to adolescence. The effect of age is not relevant on the pain prevalence in the elderly as some studies report that it increases, while others report it decreases with age. The effect also varies by gender and the pain location [41]. It is believed that musculoskeletal pain is most common in adults in the employment age and the prevalence therefore decreases from the middle of the sixth decade [41]. However, recent studies have shown that pain continues to be a widespread and serious problem in the elderly. The prevalence of chronic pain in the active elderly (>65 years) varies between 25.0 and 76.0%, while it is much higher in the sedentary elderly at between 83.0 and 93.0% [41].

11. Social factors

The role of social factors continuously increases throughout life [45]. The socioeconomic status is usually measured by the complex created by education, income, and occupation. Many studies in children and adolescents have evaluated the relationship between pain and socioeconomic status, but there is some evidence of a conflict between these studies [7]. An inverse relationship is present between the socioeconomic status and pain prevalence in adults. The data show that lower educational status, low income, and being unemployed are related to increased pain prevalence [5].

More recently, pain prevalence studies have been conducted in populations of various cultural, ethnic, and socioeconomic statuses. Native Americans, Alaska Natives, and Aboriginal Canadians have been found to have a higher prevalence of pain than the general population of the United States [45]. Studies in Africa have found the 1-year prevalence of pain to be 33.0% in adolescents and 50.0% in adults [46]. This value is higher than reported in studies conducted in most Western countries (mean prevalence of 38.1%) [25]. However, it is difficult to make a definite comparison due to the differences in methodology. Another study based on the World Bank Human Development Index has reported the prevalence of chronic pain to be 24.8% in less developed countries and 28.1% in more developed countries [47].

12. Individual factors

Various individual risk factors have been associated with the development of pain disorders. The demands of employment, lack of job security, an immobile job position, dissatisfaction with work, low levels of social support at work, and vibrating bodily work conditions have been associated with various occupational factors that lead to musculoskeletal pain. Individual lifestyle factors that create health problems such as smoking and obesity can also play a role in the development of pain disorders [34]. The psychosocial variables believed to influence the pain prevalence include stress, anxiety, lack of sleep, depression, low self-confidence, and the presence of chronic health problems (irregular heartbeat, dizziness, pain, cardiovascular problems, gastrointestinal discomfort, erectile dysfunction, feeling of lump or pressure in the throat, chest problems, hallucinations, and double vision).

Pain and disorders that are not clearly attributable to an organic disease are called somatoform disorders. These disorders can be an expression of untreated mental pain and life experiences resulting from serious loss, profound personal injury, and disrespect. These symptoms occur in almost all humans, but they can become a serious problem in 4–20% of the population [1–3, 5–9, 48].

Genetic research on pain is increasing, and chronic pain is being seen as a classic example of the gene–environment interaction [49]. It is generally believed that the first trigger of chronic pain syndromes are inflammatory processes or nerve trauma. Once chronic pain develops, the pain intensity and response to analgesics are also quite variable. However, evidence is lacking regarding the influence of genetic effects and the interaction with psychosocial environmental factors as regards the development of chronic pain. Patients with chronic pain feel that the cause is life challenges, but the disease also makes life more difficult. This contradictory approach is related to the importance attributed to the pain. A person with intrapsychic conflict may not have to express the problem verbally and may have to use the organs to do so (alexithymia).

The presence of enhancers in the environment: one example is caring for one's wife when she has pain but not caring when she does not. Other examples are as follows: finding comfort by suffering pain for a bad action; excessive interest in pain and then relaxing when the test results are normal (somatization); and feeling sure an illness is present and changing physicians frequently (hypochondriasis).

Type A persons (hasty, impatient, hyperactive) perceive pain more easily than type B persons (calm, cool), probably due to autonomic hyperactivity. The risk of hypertension and coronary heart disease is 3–5 times higher in type A persons [50, 51].

13. The financial effects of pain

13.1 Total cost

The cumulative cost of chronic pain to the patient, the health-care system, and the economy is huge. In Australia, with a population of 22.7 million, the total annual cost of chronic pain was estimated as 34.3 billion dollars in 2007 or 10.847 dollars per person [52]. The total cost in Europe is estimated as 1.5–3.0% of the European GDP [53]. In the USA, approximately 100 million adults have been affected by chronic pain in 2008, including joint pain and arthritis [54]. The total cost in 2010 was 560–635 billion dollars. The annual cost of pain is higher than that of heart disease (309 billion dollars), cancer (243 billion dollars), and diabetes (188 billion dollars) [53, 55–60].

The term psychosomatic means the person. It combines two basic components, including the mind and the body. The reason is that physical complaints are at the forefront. However the research will investigate if there are any physical symptoms to explain such bodily complaints.

There is no medical illness, and this is a definable psychiatric disorder.

14. Examples of psychological problems seen with psychosomatic pain disorders

1. **Somatoform disorders:** (a) somatization disorder, (b) conversion disorder, (c) pain disorder, (d) hypochondriasis, and (e) body dysmorphic disorder

2. **Mood disorders:** (a) generalized anxiety disorder (objective anxiety, neurotic anxiety, or traumatic anxiety and moral anxiety), b) panic disorder, (c) agoraphobia, (d) dysthymic disorder, and (e) major depressive disorder

Pain experts still do not know whether pain is one of the senses or an experience. The fact that pain can be learned and that it can be affected by beliefs, expectations, and emotional states is quite important in its diagnosis and treatment. It is known that psychological disorders increase pain, while extreme fear, stress, and shock decrease pain. Many studies have reported that cultural norms and expectations play a major role in feeling pain and the related behavior.

The gate control system that monitors pain is especially influenced by neurotransmitter modulation that is associated with cortical stimulants in anxious subjects. The lack of an adequate 5-hydroxyl tryptamine (5HT) level in the synapse disturbs pain perception and decreases the pain threshold and pain tolerance [50, 51].

The physical and psychological problems of the person described under the following titles also play a role in psychosomatic pain.

Emotional crises. Emotional crises and chronic distress can lead to various psychosomatic complaints. The whole organism can be affected and the effects are therefore not listed here.

Somatoform pain disorder. Somatoform pain disorder is characterized by intense and agonizing pain that is subjectively felt in a part of the body for at least 6 months and that cannot be reasonably explained by a physical disorder or physiological event. The onset of the pain is related to a significant problem that has created serious emotional and/or psychosocial stress, conflict, or trauma. The increased interest in the person and the medical care received are the possible gains from the disorder. When compared with somatization disorders, these pains are long-lasting, and the patient focuses on them. The differential diagnosis of pain syndromes requires differentiation of organic physical pain from histrionic processing.

Dissociative disorder. The absence or modification of physical functions without a physical cause is usually the result of an intrapsychic conflict and can lead to psychogenic paralysis, coordination disorders, tremors, and myoclonus (muscle twitching).

Major depression. Major depression affects the entire body including the metabolism and the musculoskeletal system. Inactivity or pain syndromes may be present. The pain, lack of exercise, social withdrawal, smoking habits, and malnutrition lead to significant difficulties in the patient's life.

The patient comes to the doctor because of the somatic complaints as he/she has usually not noticed the depression: it is therefore not an independent disease. It is possible to determine the real psychic etiology during the examination if retrospective evaluations are also performed. Neurobiological studies have demonstrated that somatic symptoms are associated with brain dysfunction that is also responsible for depression. Psychological pain and emotional pain have been shown to cause activation of the same sites as physical pain stimuli on MR investigations.

Evaluation of the stress axis. The documentation of neuroendocrine abnormalities in cases of depression and pain have revealed the parallel course of the functional changes in depression and pain and the hypothalamus-hypophysis-adrenal axis with excess production of corticotropin-releasing hormone (CRH). It is also known that a deficiency in the serotonin and norepinephrine monoamines can play an important role in the decreased inhibition of pain pathways and the development of somatic symptoms in depression [50, 51].

Comorbid symptoms. Masked depression can have various symptoms. Urogenital system symptoms include dysuria, painful urination and defecation, signs of urinary and fecal incontinence, functional prostate problems (prostatitis), and bladder dysfunction in women without additional genital muscle weakness. There may also be upper abdominal discomfort, bloating, colic-like abdominal discomfort, stomach pain, and constipation [51].

Weakened immune system. Negative emotions such as fear and anger permanently weaken our immune system and defense. The risk of catching infections such as influenza increases many times, and wounds heal slower and in a worse manner.

Sleep disorders. Sleep problems are common when pain is present. Lack of sleep affects both the social life and performance of the patient. Fatigue can lead to depression and accidents. Sleep disorders have various signs such as difficulty falling asleep, waking up frequently and quickly, long period of staying awake during the night, being irritable, superficial sleep, loud and irregular snoring, leg restlessness, waking up early in the morning, and disturbing thoughts. Anger and hopelessness can also have a strong effect on sleep disorders.

It has recently been found that our brain is active in a very special manner during sleep. The brain sends impulses, produces active substances, and is involved in coding and storing data 24 h a day with its 100 billion nerve cells, and it is the organ that benefits most from a good night's sleep. This has been demonstrated with decreased brain capacity when we get little sleep. The first sign of cerebral fatigue is difficulty with concentrating and performing coordinated tasks such as driving or tasks that require a great deal of attention. We then become irritated and feel pain because of the related fatigue.

Sleep apnea. Snoring during sleep is present in 10–30% of adults and it is usually not dangerous. However, pauses in respiration during sleep are an indicator of sleep apnea syndrome, which affects approximately 3 million people in Germany alone. The most common type of the disorder is "obstructive sleep apnea." The pharyngeal muscles relax excessively and do not let air pass, leading to a pause in the respiration during sleep. This breathing problem goes on for about 2 min, usually with explosive snoring, and the subject then starts to breath normally again. In severe cases, these periods of paused respiration can recur hundreds of times every night. These patients are usually prone to falling asleep during the day, and the muscles can be weak and painful.

The most important diagnostic step in the diagnosis of sleep apnea syndrome is talking to the patient and family. In case of increased sleep apnea suspicion, the next step is a sleep laboratory investigation. Electrodes record the ECG, blood pressure, and brain waves; observe movements of the eyes and legs; measure the oxygen content of the blood; and record each snoring and breathing sound during this test.

Lungs: shortness of breath. Our breathing becomes quite shallow in case of stress, depression, or sadness. The lungs receive less oxygen and can provide less oxygen to the blood, increasing the risk of infection. Pneumonia is five times more common in the elderly than in healthy subjects.

Coronary heart disease and somatization disorder. Somatization disorder and pain syndromes develop after a heart attack in approximately 30% of all patients. A heart attack is experienced as a "spontaneous infarction." Physician appointments are frequently avoided and the recommended medication is not used. This increases the risk of new infarction development two to four times when added to the biological changes in the metabolism.

The infarction risk is increased several times (deaths due to a heart attack are four to five times more common in depression patients). The more severe the somatization disorders, the worse the prognosis of a heart disorder. Factors such as emotional stress, dissatisfaction with work and the partner, anxiety, and long-term stress increase the heart attack risk more than classical risk factors such as smoking and high blood pressure.

Hair problems. The reason for white hair is mineral deficiency in the hair and scalp, and there can be several causes: decreased nutrition due to age, acidity or nutritional disorder, and psychological reasons. Mineral intake is decreased with fear or stress, resulting in hair loss or white hair.

Skin disorders and skin structure problems. The metabolism slows down and the body functions deteriorate during stress. Free radicals that attack the skin cells and slow down the regeneration of the natural protective layer are created. The skin ages faster and spots develop. The face appears stressed.

Gastric disorders. Gastric absorption becomes difficult in patients with repressed emotions, anger, or anxiety. The stomach becomes tense with stress and anger, leading to increased gastric acid secretion. This in turn causes heartburn and can result in gastric ulcer, bloating, nausea, and cramps. Many subjects suffer from irritable stomach or irritable colon. Psychological components also play a role. Excitement and anxiety increase irritable stomach or irritable colon symptoms.

15. Examples of psychosomatic comorbidity in orthopedics

It is very important to investigate the relationship of psychosomatic pain in many patients admitted between orthopedics and traumatology clinics. In this context;

Osteoarthritis (arthrosis). Depression leads to a long period of internal stress and increased muscle tension, causing a predisposition to motility disorders, immobility, and arthritis. The patient usually sees an orthopedist before going to a neurologist.

Fractures and depression. Patients suffering from depression for a long time can be exposed to fractures more commonly as the mineral content of bone is decreased. Heavy psychological burdens can significantly decrease the blood oxygen content in the elderly as the breathing becomes superficial. The cells cannot receive adequate nutrition and renewal deteriorates. Inflammation and arthritis can develop in the joints.

Orthopedic pain syndromes. Orthopedic surgeons believe that back pain is the result of emotional problems, not organic ones, in most cases. If job dissatisfaction is high, the person feels overwhelmed and does not seek solutions to change the circumstances, leading to a high risk of pain as the spinal system reacts very strongly to mental stress.

Neuropathic pain. Approximately 6% of Germans are affected by neuropathic pain. At least 20% of the patients at pain centers suffer from neuropathic pain syndromes. Peripheral neuropathies can commonly develop after postherpetic neuralgia or trauma. Generalized neuropathies include those due to chemotherapy and diabetic neuropathies.

Nociceptor pain. Nociception is the perception of pain. The responsible receptors are called nociceptors. Nociceptors are present in all the pain-sensitive tissues of the body as the free nerve ends of sensitive neurons of the spinal cord. Nociceptors trigger various types of pain according to their localizations:

- **Surface pain** is perceived superficially by the skin nociceptors. The pain can be clearly localized to the damaged region.

- **Severe pain** can be **muscle pain** or **bone pain** (localized in the periosteum) according to the localization of the nociceptors. It is poorly localized as deep pain due to the different fiber characteristics and the various projection areas of pain fibers.

- **Internal organ pain** develops following stimulation of nociceptive receptors in the internal organs. Classic examples are renal or biliary colic due to smooth muscle stretching.

Myofascial pain. Myofascial pain has local causes. Individual muscles are affected more intensely by chronic pain than muscle groups. Individual muscles contain trigger points that signify very sensitive areas. Overloading of the muscle can prevent excess calcium intake and the related muscle relaxation and therefore create localized oxygen deprivation.

Long-term contraction treatment becomes difficult in the case of myofascial pain. The sensitivity leads to the corresponding areas creating a perception of pain even with mild contact, and these areas are therefore called trigger points.

Excessive stress on such muscles can be the result of muscle damage, inadequate nutrition, hormonal imbalances, immobility, muscle weakness, hypothermia, contractions, and neurological damage.

Myofascial pain mainly develops in the **facial muscles, the neck muscles, the shoulder, and the pelvis region**. The trigger points can be activated spontaneously or with light pressure to make the diagnosis [61].

Psychotherapy in the treatment of pain can be explained as follows:

Patients with psychosomatic pain may have had a very disturbing experience in the past. This event can create links with the memory and senses, and the traumatic disorder may occur at any time when the present experience is once again dominant. Psychological stress may also cause physical illnesses. Within the soul-soma-soul sequence, an ever-growing chain of causes can be present. Life-threatening diseases such as cancer or myocardial infarction and the relevant medical interventions can also lead to mental trauma.

Traumas, undesirable social experiences, accidents, or stressful experiences have been scientifically proven to be the most common triggers and the causes of many physical disorders, pain, and other illnesses without a physical cause.

Changes related to psychological trauma in the brain can now be scientifically demonstrated by imaging (such as fMRI, a magnetic resonance method) and other diagnostic methods. Brain structure and brain metabolism are altered by the corresponding changes in the autonomic nervous system during the stress process. The entire spectrum of mental trauma should be considered. Psychotherapy for psychosomatic pain due to trauma is performed in three stages and with multiple sessions.

There are some fundamental differences between type I and type II trauma.

Type I trauma is a one-time event such as a traffic accident. The result is a short-term mental balance disorder such as adaptation disorder or posttraumatic stress disorder (PTSD). The patient will not forget the accident and will, for example, be afraid of driving. However, the disorder is also accompanied by physical symptoms (sweating, palpitation, sleep disorders, etc.).

Recurrent trauma (type II trauma) can lead to complicated disorders from all types of neurosis to emotional disorders, anxiety disorders, and phobias, in addition to personality disorders and changes or dependence on psychotropic drugs. Type II trauma can develop after life-threatening disorders such as cancer or myocardial infarction or as a result of chronic diseases. Intensive or long-term medical treatment can lead to helplessness in patients with psychosomatic pain.

The results of type II trauma include the consequences of childhood and long-term adult violence. This violence can also be mental as seen with coldness, extreme violence and indifference, emotional wounds, and frequently repeated trauma, especially in childhood. Type II traumas can lead to complex symptoms as in borderline disorder with comorbidities.

A three-stage model is used for the treatment of disorders that are psychosomatic or accompanied by pain. These stages consist of **stabilization**, **confrontation**, and **integration**.

It is not mandatory to include each stage in every treatment process. Stabilization is the foundation of all treatment steps. It can be integrated into other therapeutic methods such as specific interventions for trauma, behavioral therapy, systemic treatment, or deep psychology-associated therapies.

Stabilization stage. Sufficient time is allocated to get to know the patient and to create the basis of trauma therapy while building a mutually trusting relationship.

The stabilization stage creates a foundation for a common understanding of the clinical picture. An objective viewpoint is obtained about the emotions as much as possible. Anxiety and depression are responses to psychologically disturbing experiences and the emotional dissociations within the patient or those around him/her. An emergency state plan is developed together with the patient at this stage. Relaxation techniques such as meditation or Jacobson's progressive muscle relaxation are then used as guides for self-passivation techniques, and the patient thus learns the relevant methods to use the powers of healing within.

Confrontation stage. Behavioral therapy for the confrontation state has been specifically designed to treat phobias and anxiety. Cognitive behavioral therapy and especially systematic desensitization techniques are used. The aim is to re-evaluate the traumatizing event.

Special therapeutic procedures for trauma are also used such as eye movement desensitization and reprocessing (EMDR), imagery rescripting and reprocessing therapy (IRRT), and psychodynamic imaginative trauma therapy (PITT).

Eye movement desensitization and reprocessing has been developed by the American psychologist Francine Shapiro (* 1948). The literary translation indicates "eye movement, desensitization and reprocessing." This method is not hypnosis. When the patient focuses on an especially stressful stage of the emotionally traumatic experience, the therapist slowly asks the patient to perform rhythmic eye movements by slowly moving his fingers and gives the patient confidence. This stimulates cerebral processes. The aim is to decrease and even eliminate the fears produced by the memories. More than 20 controlled studies have shown the long-term effect of EMDR. EMDR is also included in guidelines as a preferred procedure.

Imagery rescripting and reprocessing therapy has been developed by the American clinical psychologist Mervin Smucker (* 1949). A traumatizing experience is created together with the therapies as though it had happened today. The patient imagines how he dealt with it in the past and how he is dealing with it now. The patients no longer view themselves as helpless victims and feel they are the designers of the condition who can act and maintain control even in the most difficult situations. We can think about it as deleting an old text and then writing over it.

Psychodynamic imaginative trauma therapy has been developed by psychoanalyst Luise Reddemann (* 1943). PITT is based on the idea that people have self-regulating powers to cope with disturbing events even after terrible experiences. Establishing a supportive therapeutic relationship is very important for such self-understanding, and it is also important for helping oneself. At the heart of PITT's therapeutic approach is the "internal phase" that the person is currently acting on.

In this mental "imaginary" game, the patient confronts the previous ego states with the therapist's support. Understanding the multiple egos in the consciousness comes from a scientific and philosophical tradition that has been present in all cultures for a thousand years, and the treatment relies on a systemic approach to therapy. With PITT, you can experience the injustice you have experienced and the area where you feel helpless from a safe distance. The patient learns to accept this part of his personality and to relax and make others relax at the same time. The patient also learns to heal his/her emotional wounds and therefore regains his/her confidence.

Symbol work: the study of symbols has been developed by psychotherapist Maria-Elisabeth Wollschläger and theologian Gerhard Wollschläger in the 1970s. If you associate a certain feeling with an object such as a chair, a doll, or something else, that item becomes the symbol of your senses. Symbol work is used in places where the traumatizing event can leave you speechless and where you cannot find the words to describe your mental wounds, what happened to you, and your anger, grief, or helplessness. By transferring your emotions to objects or using the object to present them, you can activate the brain areas responsible for mental processing. Conditions of loss, for example, can increase a person's confidence in his/her abilities. You regain your ability to move and to understand that what you are doing has a meaning, enabling further progress (self-efficacy).

Integration stage. This is the moment the joy of living and the relevant control are regained and understood.

The aim of this stage is to gradually integrate the traumatic experiences of the patient into his/her consciousness. These events are parts of the person's life, and control over life and social integration can be achieved once again by confronting these events [4, 61–64].

16. Conclusion

Our understanding of the epidemiology of psychosomatic pain is limited to a small number of studies that provide estimates of the prevalence in the general population. These studies are usually difficult and costly to conduct and require very large samples. The way data is collected and reported may also have an impact on the estimates with various results obtained from studies that depend on surveys, interviews, or clinical investigations. Large-scale population-based studies can provide richer data related to the age and gender distribution of pain, and assessments over extended periods of time can provide comprehensive information about the incidence and risk factors. Epidemiological studies in various cultural, social, and ethnic groups can clarify the effects and also the interactions between the individual and population-based risk factors. Physicians should be able to understand the information related to psychosomatic pain, search the relevant information available, and perform research on the subject themselves.

> *"The biggest misconception of today is the separation of the mind and body by physicians." - Socrates*

> *"What influences us is not the events themselves but the meanings we assign to them." - Epictetus*

Author details

Ertuğrul Allahverdi
Department of Orthopedics and Traumatology, School of Medicine, Kafkas University, Kars, Turkey

*Address all correspondence to: ertugrulallahverdi@hotmail.com

References

[1] Güleç MY. Temperament and character in psychosomatic disorders. Current Approaches in Psychiatry. 2009;**1**:201-214

[2] Porcelli P, Rafanelli C. Criteria for psychosomatic research (*DCPR*) in the medical setting. Current Psychiatry Reports. 2010;**12**(3):246-254

[3] Aral G, Arslan FC. A new operational guide against to traditional classification systems in Consultation-Liaison psychiatry: Diagnostic criteria for psychosomatic research (DCPR). Klinik Psikiyatri Dergisi. 2019;**22**(2):228-242

[4] Lazarus RS. From psychological stress to the emotions: A history of changing books. Annual Review of Psychology. 1993;**44**:1-22

[5] Henschke N, Kamper SJ, Maher CG. The epidemiology and economic consequences of pain. Mayo Clinic Proceedings. 2015;**90**(1):139-147. DOI: 10.1016/j.mayocp.2014.09.010

[6] McBeth J, Jones K. Epidemiology of chronic musculoskeletal pain. Best Practice & Research. Clinical Rheumatology. 2007;**21**:403-425

[7] King S, Chambers CT, Huguet A, et al. The epidemiology of chronic pain in children and adolescents revisited: A systematic review. Pain. 2011;**152**:2729-2738

[8] Jeffries LJ, Milanese SF, Grimmer-Somers KA. Epidemiology of adolescent spinal pain: A systematic overview of the research literature. Spine (Phila Pa 1976). 2007;**32**:2630-2637

[9] Palermo TM. Impact of recurrent and chronic pain on child and family daily functioning: A critical review of the literature. Journal of Developmental and Behavioral Pediatrics. 2000;**21**:58-69

[10] Hestbaek L, Leboeuf-Yde C, Kyvik KO, Manniche C. The course of low back pain from adolescence to adulthood: Eight-year follow-up of 9600 twins. Spine (Phila Pa 1976). 2006;**31**:468-472

[11] Juniper M, Le TK, Mladsi D. The epidemiology, economic burden, and pharmacological treatment of chronic low back pain in France, Germany, Italy, Spain and the UK: A literature-based review. Expert Opinion on Pharmacotherapy. 2009;**10**:2581-2592

[12] Reid KJ, Harker J, Bala MM, et al. Epidemiology of chronic non-cancer pain in Europe: Narrative review of prevalence, pain treatments and pain impact. Current Medical Research and Opinion. 2011;**27**:449-462

[13] van Hecke O, Austin SK, Khan RA, Smith BH, Torrance N. Neuropathic pain in the general population: A systematic review of epidemiological studies. Pain. 2014;**155**:654-662

[14] Bennett MI, Rayment C, Hjermstad M, Aass N, Caraceni A, Kaasa S. Prevalence and aetiology of neuropathic pain in cancer patients: A systematic review. Pain. 2012;**153**:359-365

[15] Swain MS, Henschke N, Kamper SJ, Gobina I, Ottová-Jordan V, Maher CG. An international survey of pain in adolescents. BMC Public Health. 2014;**14**:447

[16] Apley J, Naish N. Recurrent abdominal pains: A field survey of 1,000 school children. Archives of Disease in Childhood. 1958;**33**:165-170

[17] Fearon P, Hotopf M. Relation between headache in childhood and physical and psychiatric symptoms in adulthood: National birth cohort study. BMJ. 2001;**322**:1145

[18] Carragee EJ, Alamin TF, Miller JL, Carragee JM. Discographic, MRI and psychosocial determinants of low back pain disability and remission: A prospective study in subjects with benign persistent back pain. The Spine Journal. 2005 Jan-Feb;**5**(1):24-35

[19] Calvo-Muñoz I, Gómez-Conesa A, Sánchez-Meca J. Prevalence of low back pain in children and adolescents: A meta-analysis. BMC Pediatrics. 2013;**13**:14

[20] Taylor JB, Goode AP, George SZ, Cook CE. Incidence and risk factors for first-time incident low back pain: A systematic review and meta-analysis. The Spine Journal. 2014;**14**:2299-2319

[21] Briggs AM, Smith AJ, Straker LM, Bragge P. Thoracic spine pain in the general population: Prevalence, incidence and associated factors in children, adolescents and adults; a systematic review. BMC Musculoskeletal Disorders. 2009;**10**:77

[22] Hogg-Johnson S, van der Velde G, Carroll LJ, et al. The burden and determinants of neck pain in the general population. Spine Journal. 2008;**17**:39-51

[23] Henschke N, Maher CG, Refshauge KM, et al. Prognosis in patients with recent onset low back pain in Australian primary care: Inception cohort study. BMJ. 2008;**337**:a171

[24] Pengel LH, Herbert RD, Maher CG, Refshauge KM. Acute low back pain: Systematic review of its prognosis. BMJ. 2003;**327**:32

[25] Hoy D, Brooks P, Blyth F, Buchbinder R. The epidemiology of low back pain. Best Practice & Research. Clinical Rheumatology. 2010;**24**:769-781

[26] Briggs AM, Smith AJ, Straker LM, Bragge P. Thoracic spine pain in the general population: Prevalence, incidence and associated factors in children, adolescents and adults; a systematic review. BMC Musculoskeletal Disorders. 2009;**10**:77

[27] Hogg-Johnson S, van der Velde G, Carroll LJ, et al. The burden and determinants of neck pain in the general population. European Spine Journal. 2008;**17**:39-51

[28] Furlan AD, Pennick V, Bombardier C, van Tulder M, Editorial Board, Cochrane Back Review Group. Updated method guidelines for systematic reviews in the Cochrane Back Review Group. Spine (Phila Pa 1976). 2009;**34**:1929-1941

[29] Berk HÖS. Kronik Ağrı Yaşantısı Ve Ağrı İnançları: Ağrı İnançları Ölçeğinin Türkçe Geçerlik Ve Güvenirlik Çalişması [PhD thesis]. Turkey: Istanbul University; 2006

[30] Cook CE, Taylor J, Wright A, Milosavljevic S, Goode A, Whitford M. Risk factors for first time incidence sciatica: A systematic review. Physiotherapy Research International. 2014;**19**(2):65-78. DOI: 10.1002/pri.1572. Epub 2013 Dec 11

[31] Konstantinou K, Dunn KM. Sciatica: Review of epidemiological studies and prevalence estimates. Spine (Phila Pa 1976). 2008;**33**(22):2464-2472. DOI: 10.1097/BRS.0b013e318183a4a2

[32] Coggon D, Ntani G, Palmer KT, et al. Disabling musculoskeletal pain in working populations: Is it the job, the person, or the culture? Pain. 2013;**154**:856-863

[33] Luime JJ, Koes BW, Hendriksen IJ, et al. Prevalence and incidence of shoulder pain in the general population: A systematic review. Scandinavian Journal of Rheumatology. 2004;**33**:73-81

[34] Peat G, McCarney R, Croft P. Knee pain and osteoarthritis in older adults:

A review of community burden and current use of primary health care. Annals of the Rheumatic Diseases. 2001;**60**:91-97

[35] Thomas MJ, Roddy E, Zhang W, Menz HB, Hannan MT, Peat GM. The population prevalence of foot and ankle pain in middle and old age: A systematic review. Pain. 2011;**152**:2870-2880

[36] Cimmino MA, Ferrone C, Cutolo M. Epidemiology of chronic musculoskeletal pain. Best Practice & Research: Clinical Rheumatology. 2011;**25**:173-183

[37] Arnold LM, Clauw DJ, McCarberg BH, Fibro Collaborative. Improving the recognition and diagnosis of fibromyalgia. Mayo Clinic Proceedings. 2011;**86**:457-464

[38] Freburger JK, Holmes GM, Agans RP, et al. The rising prevalence of chronic low back pain. Archives of Internal Medicine. 2009;**169**:251-258

[39] Froud R, Patterson S, Eldridge S, et al. A systematic review and meta-synthesis of the impact of low back pain on people's lives. BMC Musculoskeletal Disorders. 2014;**15**:50

[40] Palmer KT, Walsh K, Bendall H, Cooper C, Coggon D. Back pain in Britain: Comparison of two prevalence surveys at an interval of 10 years. BMJ. 2000;**320**:1577-1578

[41] Macfarlane GJ, McBeth J, Garrow A, Silman AJ. Life is as much a pain as it ever was. BMJ. 2000;**321**:897

[42] Froud R, Patterson S, Eldridge S, et al. A systematic review and meta-synthesis of the impact of low back pain on people's lives. BMC Musculoskeletal Disorders. 2014;**15**:50

[43] Murray CJ, Vos T, Lozano R, et al. Disability-adjusted life years (DALYs) for 291 diseases and injuries in 21 regions, 1990-2010: A systematic analysis for the Global Burden of Disease Study 2010. Lancet. 2012;**380**:2197-2223

[44] Macfarlane TV, Glenny AM, Worthington HV. Systematic review of population-based epidemiological studies of oro-facial pain. Journal of Dentistry. 2001;**29**:451-467

[45] Jimenez N, Garroutte E, Kundu A, Morales L, Buchwald D. A review of the experience, epidemiology, and management of pain among American Indian, Alaska Native, and Aboriginal Canadian peoples. The Journal of Pain. 2011;**12**:511-522

[46] Louw QA, Morris LD, Grimmer-Somers K. The prevalence of low back pain in Africa: A systematic review. BMC Musculoskeletal Disorders. 2007;**8**:105

[47] Elzahaf RA, Tashani OA, Unsworth BA, Johnson MI. The prevalence of chronic pain with an analysis of countries with a Human Development Index less than 0.9: A systematic review without meta-analysis. Current Medical Research and Opinion. 2012;**28**:1221-1229

[48] Hush JM, Nicholas M, Catherine M. Embedding the IASP pain curriculum into a 3-year pre-licensure physical therapy program: Redesigning pain education for future clinicians. Pain Reports. 2018;**3**(2):e645

[49] Côté P, van der Velde G, Cassidy JD, Carroll LJ, Hogg-Johnson S, Holm LW, et al. The burden and determinants of neck pain in workers: Results of the bone and joint decade 2000-2010 task force on neck pain and its associated disorders. Spine (Phila Pa 1976). 2008;**33**(4 Suppl):S60-S74

[50] Morris CG. Psikolojiyi Anlamak/Understanding Psychology. Third Edition. Türk Psikologlar Derneği Yay. No: 23 2002-Ankara

[51] Lopez-lber JJ. Masked depression. British Journal of Psychiatry. 1972;**120**:254-257

[52] Limited AEP. The High Price of Pain: The Economic Impact of Persistent Pain in Australia. Sydney, Australia: Access Economics Pty Limited; 2007

[53] Phillips CJ. Economic burden of chronic pain. Expert Review of Pharmacoeconomics & Outcomes Research. 2006;**6**:591-601

[54] Gaskin DJ, Richard P. The economic costs of pain in the United States. The Journal of Pain. 2012;**13**:715-724

[55] Reid KJ, Harker J, Bala MM, et al. Epidemiology of chronic non-cancer pain in Europe: Narrative review of prevalence, pain treatments and pain impact. Current Medical Research and Opinion. 2011;**27**:449-462

[56] Mogil JS. Pain genetics: Past, present and future. Trends in Genetics. 2012;**28**:258-266

[57] EngbersLH,Vollenbroek-HuttenMM, van Harten WH. A comparison of patient characteristics and rehabilitation treatment content of chronic low back pain (CLBP) and stroke patients across six European countries. Health Policy. 2005;**71**:359-373

[58] Dagenais S, Caro J, Haldeman S. A systematic review of low back pain cost of illness studies in the United States and internationally. The Spine Journal. 2008;**8**:8-20

[59] Schofield DJ, Shrestha RN, Passey ME, Earnest A, Fletcher SL. Chronic disease and labour force participation among older Australians. The Medical Journal of Australia. 2008;**189**:447-450

[60] Vet HC, Heymans MW, Dunn KM, et al. Episodes of low back pain: A proposal for uniform definitions to be used in research. Spine (Phila Pa 1976). 2002;**27**:2409-2416

[61] Emre M, Mathies H, Radvila A. Psychogenic aspects of muscle spasms and pain. Muscle spasms and pain. The Parthenon Publishing Group, New Jersey. 1988;**5**:43-46

[62] Ettlin T, Kischka U. Psychosomatic Rehabilitation: An Overview. Therapeutische Umschau. German. 2019;**76**(8):460-464. DOI: 10.1024/0040-5930/a001115

[63] Gomez J. "Pain" Liaison Psychiatry, Mental Health Problems in the General Hospital. London: The Free Press; 1987. p. 53-61/180-189

[64] Schmidt AJM. Cognitive factors in the performance level of chronic low back pain patients. Journal of Psychosomatic Research. 1985;**29**:183-189

Chapter 5

Deep Diaphragmatic Breathing: A "Portable Intervention" for Stress Reduction among University Students

Katarzyna (Kate) Rygiel

Abstract

Students are at risk for daily stress, often caused by an increasing load of the material to study, limited time and resources necessary to fulfill assignments, personal or family demands, high expectations, pressures, and frustrations. All these factors can create distress, decreased learning abilities, and psychosomatic disorders or diseases. To mitigate such negative biopsychosocial effects of stress, different types of relaxation techniques can be used. Addressing these issues early (e.g., among the 1st and 2nd year university students) seems particularly important, due to possible prevention of the long-term adverse health consequences of stress (compared to no intervention). To fulfill this important need, a "portable intervention," such as stress management brief training (SMBT), focused on the reduction of the perceived stress levels among students will be briefly outlined. The SMBT consists of a short review of stress and coping approaches, followed by the instruction of a simple stress management relaxation/technique [e.g., deep diaphragmatic breathing (DDB)]. Practical considerations regarding the DDB will be highlighted. The feasibility and usefulness of the DDB training for stress management among the 1st and 2nd year university students should encourage implementation of this innovative, safe, inexpensive, and friendly technique.

Keywords: distress, stress reduction, coping, relaxation techniques, deep diaphragmatic breathing (DDB), university students

1. Introduction

Students are at risk for daily stress, often caused by the increasing load of the material to study, limited time and resources necessary to fulfill assignments, personal demands, high expectations, as well as socioeconomic pressures, and frustrations. In some cases, the above problems can be aggravated by difficulties in adjusting to the new environment and lack of support from family and friends. All these factors can create distress and subsequently may contribute to decreased ability to learn, impaired academic performance, psychosomatic disorders or diseases, and decreased quality of life among many students. There is no doubt about the fact that dealing with multiple negative biopsychosocial consequences of daily stress is very difficult and expensive. Therefore, addressing these issues early, among 1st and 2nd year university students seems particularly important. A review of the literature on reducing stress, and preventing its damaging consequences in student population, indicates that person-focused interventions, such as different types of relaxation techniques, can be effective in reducing anxiety, irritability, sadness, depressed mood, insomnia, and many other general symptoms of distress, compared to no intervention. The beneficial results of various stress reduction programs may last from 6 months to 2 years, after their formal ending [1]. For instance, beneficial effects of one specific relaxation technique, mindfulness-based stress reduction (MBSR), developed by Kabat-Zinn, have been documented in various populations (both among healthy individuals, exposed at high level of a daily stress, and among patients, suffering from different psychosomatic diseases) in diversified medical and psychological contexts [2–7]. In particular, some studies related to students and professionals in the medical field have revealed positive effects of mindfulness on stress reduction, health condition, quality of life, empathy, and quality of patient care [8, 9]. Furthermore, a small recent study, conducted among university students, provided data, which support the possibility that a deep breathing technique is able to induce some improvements in mood and control of stress (e.g., illustrated in the form of self-reports and objective parameters, like heart rate and cortisol levels, measured in saliva) [10]. Although MBSR has been successfully used for the last 40 years in the USA, Canada, and Western Europe in many psychosomatic disorders related to stress [11–13], it is still little known as a relaxation technique in Eastern or Central Europe. Due to some logistic obstacles, the entire MBSR program may be too difficult to implement at the universities in this location. However, an important component of the MBSR, the deep diaphragmatic breathing (DDB) technique, has also been separately studied as a stress reduction modality, and convincing evidence exists that DDB is useful in stress management [14]. For instance, a recent study has demonstrated a beneficial influence of DDB on mental functions and normalization of stress-induced cortisol levels. This indicates that such a simple and easily available technique has enormous implications for the promotion of mental hygiene and prevention of adverse health consequences of stress [14]. However, the specific advantages of DDB on stress reduction, cognitive abilities, and mood among students still remain largely unknown. To explore this topic in mere details and fulfill the unmet needs, a "portable intervention," such as stress management brief training (SMBT), focused on the reduction of the perceived stress levels among students will be outlined. The SMBT consists of a short review of stress mechanisms and coping approaches, followed by the instruction of a simple stress management relaxation/technique [e.g., deep diaphragmatic breathing (DDB)]. Practical considerations regarding the DDB will be emphasized.

2. Review of the literature on stress and coping: a focus on the student population

A review of the literature was conducted using PubMed. The following keywords: stress, stress management, perceived stress, coping, relaxation, and students were utilized. The review was limited to full-text articles, in English language, which were published within the last 15 years. After this search, the following study-specific areas were determined: the hypothalamic-pituitary-adrenal (HPA) axis; the HPA axis dysregulation from stress; impact of chronic stress on memory and cognition; stress perception; stress-related maladaptive behaviors; appraisal of the stressors; coping with stress among students; relations between stress, coping strategies, academic performance, and quality of life; managing stress in the students; relaxation techniques; deep diaphragmatic breathing; and the effects of stress management programs.

2.1 Stress and the hypothalamic-pituitary-adrenal (HPA) axis

Human stress is the psychophysiological reaction of a person, who confronts a situation, in which there is an imbalance between the demands (e.g., real or imagined) and the ability to fulfill them [15]. When a person confronts a stressor (e.g., an internal or external, physical, or psychological factor, which creates disequilibrium), the body activates a series of reactions to enhance coping with the stressful situation. In particular, when an individual experiences different stressors, the hypothalamus (the main hormone-regulating brain "station") releases corticotrophin-releasing hormone (CRH), which stimulates the release of adrenocorticotropic hormone (ACTH) from the pituitary gland [16]. ACTH stimulates the production of glucocorticoids (e.g., cortisol) by the adrenal glands. In this manner, the hypothalamic-pituitary-adrenal (HPA) axis is "in charge" of the systemic adaptive changes that are induced by stressors [17]. Simultaneously, catecholamines are being secreted from the adrenal glands.

2.2 The HPA axis dysregulation from stress: negative consequences for health

In the case of the prolonged HPA axis activation (e.g., due to some undesirable, cumulated stressors, such as difficult tasks and personal, family, or financial problems), the chronically increased stress hormone levels can cause negative psychosomatic consequences [18]. An adaptation to stress initially includes the physiological mobilization of resources, such as an increased catecholamine's release [19]. This is often followed by the resistance stage, which represents a prolonged adaptation to stressful challenges (e.g., increased cortisol levels) [19]. Finally, decompensation of the HPA axis, which is often characterized by decreased cortisol and catecholamine production, can cause serious disorders and diseases in each organ or system of the human body [19]. In particular, chronic stress elevates the risk for central obesity, metabolic syndrome, type 2 diabetes mellitus (T2DM), cardiovascular disease (CVD) [e.g., arterial hypertension, coronary artery disease (CAD), myocardial infarction (MI), heart failure (HF), and stroke], neoplastic, degenerative, or inflammatory diseases, allergies, asthma, gastroesophageal reflux disease, peptic ulcer disease, osteoporosis, and mental disorders (e.g., major depression and insomnia) [19, 20]. In addition, several studies have revealed associations between stress and maladaptive behaviors (e.g., increased alcohol consumption, tobacco smoking, or substance abuse) and increased anxiety or depressive symptoms [21, 22]. Due to such detrimental consequences of chronic stress, it is imperative to prevent them as early as possible, by introducing helpful nonpharmacological stress management interventions [23].

2.3 Impact of chronic stress on memory and cognition

Everyone has an inherited ability to deal with stress. For instance, after a person confronts a stressful event, the "fight-or-flight" response occurs, which is characterized by elevated catecholamine's level. However, in the chronic phase of stress, cortisol levels are usually high and can lead to impaired neurogenesis and cause structural and functional changes in the central nervous system (CNS) (e.g., in the brain areas responsible for short-term memory, cognition, affect, and impulse control) [21, 23]. In addition, sleep deprivation can negatively influence the abilities to learn due to decreased clarity of the thought process, poor creativity, or problem-solving skills, which are often linked with impaired scholarly performance among students [24]. In particular, the rapid eye movement (REM) sleep phase is crucial for processing the information that has been stored in the short-term memory reservoir (e.g., hippocampus) and consolidating the memory traces in the long-term memory reservoir (e.g., the temporal lobes of brain cortex) [24]. Furthermore, a person's working memory can only contain approximately seven units of information, and thus, when a student is under stress, and her/his mind is being occupied with several stressors, the student's learning capabilities can be deteriorated [25]. In addition, since a student's attention is often not focused on the learning task, the relevant memory trace will be difficult to retrieve in the future. Moreover, stress in students has also been found to contribute to avoidant coping behavior and depressed mood [26]. In this light, the modulation of stress response seems to be particularly important in students, who are exposed to chronic stressors. It should be noted that high levels of the perceived stress and the inefficient adaptation to stressors have been correlated with increased rates of anxiety and depression [23, 27]. Unfortunately, in the case of chronic stress, a desynchronization of the HPA axis contributes to various stress-related conditions and impaired cognitive performance [23, 27].

2.4 Stress perception: different intellectual and emotional aspects

In general, stress can be caused by challenge stressors (e.g., that allow someone to have sufficient motivation to accomplish a certain task) and threat stressors (e.g., that evoke fear, such as a signal of imminent danger) [28]. In fact, all stimuli that are perceived as harmful can have devastating effects on one's psychosomatic health [27]. For instance, if a given situation is perceived as a threat, the organism's response is identical, regardless of whether the stressor is a wide animal ready to attack or an upcoming exam. Thus, a person's specific perception and interpretation of given circumstances, regardless of their real danger, represent a key factor indicating how much stress the person is actually experiencing [28]. Furthermore, stress may also steam from situations that are subjectively viewed as positive. For instance, some students may have positive feelings about their assignments and like being busy, yet they may be under considerable stress that they are not fully aware of having. In contrast, a situation is considered to be stressful, when students think that they do not have the abilities or sufficient resources to deal with it [28]. On the other hand, a higher level of one's confidence can modify the perception of stressors, so that a person's appraisal (e.g., intellectual and emotional) of the stressful situation can alter her/his level of subsequent stress-induced response [28].

2.5 Stress-related maladaptive behaviors: common presentations and long-term risks

In essence, if a situation is viewed through the lens of negative emotions, the perceived stress level is higher, compared to observing the identical situation, from the perspective of positive emotions or mental connotations [23, 26]. In addition, verbal complaining and "ruminating" about the difficulties can perpetuate and "disseminate" stress, so every negative emotional response to a similar stressor becomes incorporated into the brain's neural networks [23, 26]. This, in consequence, may become the automatic response to such a stressor in the future, leading to an undesirable habit formation [18, 27]. There are some dangerous habits that university students are especially prone to acquire during examination sessions (e.g., frequent lack of sleep, which can adversely affect their physical, mental, and emotional health) [24, 26]. Unquestionably, restful sleep is necessary for proper mental hygiene and the immune system functioning [26, 29]. Fortunately, it appears that by proactive recognition of the stressful situations, and modification of the stress response effects, students could possibly avoid maladaptive coping behaviors and learn helpful stress reduction interventions (e.g., at the beginning of their academic career), in order to protect their psychophysical health in the future. Some other common habits that students often acquire include excessive drinking of coffee and other beverages, containing a high content of caffeine or similar stimulants (e.g., which can elevate blood pressure and heart rate or exacerbate anxiety) [26]. An analysis of other risk behaviors that students often demonstrate while under stress (e.g., tobacco smoking and alcohol or substance abuse) causing potential detrimental health consequences is beyond the scope of discussion in this chapter.

2.6 The key role of appraisal of the stressors

Stress reflects a bi-directional process, which consists of the creation of stressors by the environment and the individual's response to them. As a consequence, when there is a real or imagined imbalance between demands and resources, in which the demands outweigh resources, a person experiences stress [23, 27]. During this process, a cognitive appraisal is an initial step in the coping mechanism, which varies individually. It occurs when a person knows the reason why a given interaction creates stress [21, 23, 30]. It should be underscored that both the past experiences and the present events influence the way a person reacts to a current situation [21, 23, 30]. Also, it is important to point out that the stress reaction takes place after a certain meaning has been attached to a current situation, evoking an emotional response [21, 23, 30]. As a consequence, cognitive appraisal influences how a person will cope with a given event and how she/he will most likely react to analogical circumstances in the future [21, 23, 30]. According to a current model of stress, the primary appraisal of a stressful situation relates to the initial perception of the stressor (e.g., as negative, positive, or neutral), and the secondary appraisal refers to the coping strategies and resources (e.g., how to overcome or adapt to the stressor) [21, 23, 30]. At this point, an individual's coping approach can be positive (e.g., addressing a stressor as a challenge) or negative (e.g., viewing a stressor as a threat, especially if an adverse outcome is expected, which is associated with anxiety, anger, or fear) [21, 23, 30]. In addition, the repeated negative appraisal may lead to maladaptive behaviors and long-term negative consequences [21, 23, 30]. Overall, it appears that modifying the perception of stressors can help students to enhance their learning skills and academic achievements [28, 31]. For instance, assessing stressful situations as being challenging (and thus apprised as helpful) rather than as being threatening (and thus apprised as harmful) changes the stress physiology [32]. In particular, if the students perceived certain stressors as motivating them to overcome some obstacles, their learning skills and academic performance were positively correlated with the increased motivation [32]. Conversely, if the students perceived a dangerous situation (e.g., in which the demands were exceeding their resources), their motivation to learn was decreased, leading to impaired scholarly performance [33].

2.7 Coping with stress: important considerations regarding the student population

It should be highlighted that coping is the process of confronting adversities, in an attempt to overcome them or to adapt to the stressful situations [34]. "Positive coping" includes some basic knowledge of factors that underlie personal coping strategies, which are related with the individual's strengths and effective coping techniques, and offers meaningful solutions to ineffective or even harmful stereotypical behaviors [35]. In essence, coping with stress relates to the way how an individual is able to achieve the balance between different life demands and the ability to deal with them. In fact, daily stress is an inevitable and natural part of everybody's life. However, extreme, chronic, or psychological stress can cause adverse health consequences and poor academic performance for every university student [34]. Therefore, there is a growing need to implement feasible stress management intervention programs in the academic setting [35]. Two main coping styles, which are being applied to deal with the ongoing demands, include problem-focused (e.g., that consists of defining problems, generating solutions, and evaluating results) and emotion-focused (e.g., that occurs when a person feels helpless upon confronting the stressful events) methods. The most effective and available stress management approaches for students include relaxation techniques and goal-oriented, positive coping strategies [34–37].

2.8 Interrelations between stress, coping strategies, academic performance, and quality of life: lessons learned from recent research studies

Unquestionably, effective coping strategies are critically important for reducing elevated stress levels among students. In general, successful coping involves managing the interactions between the environment, and the perceived stress levels, where the accompanying emotions are essential parts of this process [23, 30]. Since stress is multifactorial and impacts each person in a different way, a diverse spectrum of coping methods is required [23, 38]. Therefore, providing "well-targeted" tools, necessary to effectively cope with different stressors, is critically important to students, who are under stress. It should be pointed out that on the one hand, short-term stress can play a role of the positive motivator for learning [21, 23]. On the other hand, however, excessive or long-term stress can adversely influence the learning process and deteriorate academic performance [39]. Furthermore, a plethora of stressors, especially in students, who use poor coping techniques, can adversely influence many aspects of their health and scholarly performance [40]. For instance, the prevalence of stress, anxiety, and depression in nursing students was recently explored, and correlations between ineffective coping methods (e.g., avoidance, denial, and substance abuse) and high-risk lifestyles (e.g., in terms of busy study/work schedule, family obligations, poor support systems) were found in those students, who had significantly elevated scores in the depression, anxiety, and distress categories [41]. Furthermore, in a study investigating relations between stress and quality of life (QOL), among nursing students in Norway, one-third of the students reported moderate to high levels of experienced stress, which were impaired QOL [42].

3. Relaxation techniques: nonpharmacological interventions to reduce stress

According to the National Center for Complementary and Alternative Medicine (NCCAM), meditation is a mind-body process, which has been scientifically explored as an intervention to reduce stress [43]. It is a cognitive practice, focused on calming the mind and observing intrusive thoughts, without judging them [44]. In this state of consciousness, the mind is focused on the moment-to-moment experience of one's internal (e.g., thoughts, feelings, and sensations) and external (e.g., events or situations) environment [33]. Individuals who focus their attention on "here and now" and become fully aware (mindful) of their thoughts' processes and emotions are able to create calm, relaxed, and balanced psychophysical condition [43]. Studies have revealed that many people, who have been practicing meditation (even for a short time), have decreased their perceived stress levels, improved health status, and increased QOL [44, 45]. However, classical meditation programs are usually long or expensive and, thus, inconvenient or unavailable for a majority of students. This inspired a new research direction, aimed at exploring whether or not similar benefits can be achieved via shorter-time interventions [46]. For instance, a brief meditation training program (that also incorporated therapeutic breathing), which investigated the effects of this technique on perceived stress, anxiety, and negative emotions, has revealed that the healthy participants experienced significant reductions in negative affect, distress, and anxiety [46]. A similar study has revealed that participation in a single-paced breathing meditation training session resulted in improved QOL and reduced perceived stress levels [47]. Research aimed at exploring stress reduction should combine a few stress management strategies that can be effective in different contexts, among various populations of students [33]. As an illustration of this concept, one of the online stress management programs (e.g., Stress-Free Now) has incorporated meditation and therapeutic breathing. This study was examining the program's effectiveness in decreasing stress and improving psychological well-being by exploring the effects of a 2-month online stress reduction program in three groups, including two intervention groups (that participated in the online program and were receiving a different stress management technique every week, based on mindfulness meditation, visualization, and therapeutic breathing) and one control group [33]. The results of this study have revealed that the online stress reduction program, which incorporated diversified activities, such as mindfulness, relaxation, and meditation techniques, was effective in decreasing the perceived stress levels and improving well-being, among the participants in two intervention groups [33].

3.1 Deep diaphragmatic breathing: a "spotlight" on a "portable intervention"

Relaxation technique, such as deep diaphragmatic breathing (DDB), is feasible and can be practiced anywhere. In essence, DDB includes controlled deep (abdominal) breathing that enables the individual to enter a relaxed state, in an effortless manner. Simultaneously, this simple technique has been found to be very effective in stress reduction among students [48]. In addition, some relaxation techniques have been revealed to reduce stress levels, even after a single session [19]. Therefore, a proposed "portable intervention" for an effective coping with stressors should be universal and safe strategy for numerous university students. An early introduction of this simple and helpful technique can result in desirable health-related habits and long-term beneficial psychophysical conditions.

Conflict of interest

There is no "conflict of interest" to declare.

Author details

Katarzyna (Kate) Rygiel
Department of Family Practice, Medical University of Silesia (SUM), Zabrze, Poland

*Address all correspondence to: kasiaalpha@yahoo.co.uk

References

[1] Marine A, Ruotsalainen J, Serra C, Verbeek J. Preventing occupational stress in healthcare workers. Cochrane Database of Systematic Reviews 2006, Issue 4. Art. No.: CD002892

[2] Kabat-Zinn J. Full Catastrophe Living: Using the Wisdom of your Body and Mind to Face Stress, Pain and Illness. New York: Delta Trade Paperbacks; 2005

[3] Kabat-Zinn J, Massion AO, Kristeller J, et al. Effectiveness of a meditation-based stress reduction program in the treatment of anxiety disorders. The American Journal of Psychiatry. 1992;**149**:936-943

[4] Kabat-Zinn J, Lipworth L, Burney R. The clinical use of mindfulness meditation for the self-regulation of chronic pain. Journal of Behavioral Medicine. 1985;**8**:163-190

[5] Kabat-Zinn J, Lipworth L, Burney R, Sellers W. Four-year follow-up of a meditation program for the self-regulation of chronic pain: Treatment outcome and compliance. The Clinical Journal of Pain. 1987;**2**:159-173

[6] Kabat-Zinn J, Wheeler E, Light T, et al. Influence of a mindfulness-based stress reduction intervention on rates of skin clearing in patients with moderate to severe psoriasis undergoing phototherapy (UVB) and photochemotherapy (PUVA). Psychological Medicine. 1998;**60**:625-632

[7] Davidson RJ, Kabat-Zinn J, Schumacher J, Rosenkranz M, Muller D, Santorelli SF, et al. Alterations in brain and immune function produced by mindfulness meditation. Psychosomatic Medicine. 2003;**65**(4):564-570

[8] Schenstrom A, Ronnberg S, Bodlund O. Mindfulness-based cognitive attitude training for primary care staff: A pilot study. Complementary Health Practice Review. 2006;**11**:144-152

[9] Shapiro SL, Schwartz GE, Bonner G. Effects of mindfulness-based stress reduction on medical and premedical students. Journal of Behavioral Medicine. 1998;**21**:581-599

[10] Perciavalle V, Blandini M, Fecarotta P, et al. The role of deep breathing on stress. Neurological Sciences. 2016;**38**(3):451-458. DOI: 10.1007/s10072-016-2790-8

[11] Wright LD. Meditation: A new role for an old friend. American Journal of Hospice & Palliative Medicine. 2006;**23**(4):323-327

[12] Miller JJ, Fletcher K, Kabat-Zinn J. Three-year follow-up and clinical implications of a mindfulness meditation-based stress reduction intervention in the treatment of anxiety disorders. General Hospital Psychiatry. 1995;**17**:192-200

[13] Titlebaum H. Relaxation. Complementary Health Practice Review. 1998;**4**:123-148

[14] Ma X, Zi-Qi Y, Zhu-Qing G, et al. The effect of diaphragmatic breathing on attention, negative affect and stress in healthy adults. Frontiers in Psychology. 2017;**8**:874. DOI: 10.3389/fpsyg.2017.00874

[15] Palmer S. Occupational stress. Health and safety practitioners. 1989;**7**(8):16-18

[16] McEwen BS, Stellar E. Stress and the individual. Mechanisms leading to disease. Archives of Internal Medicine. 1993;**153**(18):2093-2101

[17] McEwen BS, Wingfield JC. What is in a name? Integrating homeostasis,

allostasis and stress. Hormones and Behavior. 2010;**57**(2):105-111

[18] Ganzel BL, Morris PA, Wethington E. Allostasis and the human brain: Integrating models of stress from the social and life sciences. Psychological Review. 2010;**117**(1):134-174

[19] Cohen S, Janicki-Deverts D, Miller GE. Psychological stress and disease. JAMA. 2007;**298**(14):1685-1687

[20] Lucini D, Di Fede G, Parati G, et al. Impact of chronic psychosocial stress on autonomic cardiovascular regulation in otherwise healthy subjects. Hypertension. 2005;**46**:1201-1206

[21] Juster RP, McEwen BS, Lupien SJ. Allostatic load biomarkers of chronic stress and impact on health and cognition. Neuroscience & Biobehavioral Reviews. 2010;**35**(1):2-16

[22] Kanji N, White A, Ernst E. Autogenic training to reduce anxiety in nursing students: Randomized controlled trial. Journal of Advanced Nursing. 2006;**53**(6):729-735

[23] Tonhajzerova I, Mestanik M. New perspectives in the model of stress response. Physiological Research. 2017;**66**(Supplement 2):S173-S185

[24] Maquet P. The role of sleep in learning and memory. Science. 2001;**294**(5544):1048-1052

[25] Ormrod JE. Human Learning. 4th ed. Upper Saddle River, NJ: Pearson Education, Inc.; 2004

[26] Dyson R, Renk K. Freshman adaptation to university life: Depressive symptoms, stress, and coping. Journal of Clinical Psychology. 2006;**62**(10):1231-1244

[27] Karatsoreos IN, McEwen BS. Psychobiological allostasis: Resistance, resilience and vulnerability. Trends in Cognitive Sciences. 2011;**15**(12):576-584

[28] Largo-Wight E, Peterson PM, Chen WW. Perceived problem solving, stress, and health among college students. American Journal of Health Behavior. 2005;**29**(4):360-370

[29] Glaser R, Kiecolt-Glaser JK. Stress-induced immune dysfunction: Implications for health. Nature Reviews. Immunology. 2005;**5**:243-251

[30] Lazarus RS, Folkman S. Stress, Appraisal and Coping. New York: Springer; 1984

[31] Rausch SM, Gramling SE, Auerbach SM. Effects of a single session of large group meditation and progressive muscle relaxation training on stress reduction, reactivity, and recovery. International Journal of Stress Management. 2006;**13**(3):273-290

[32] LePine JA, LePine MA, Jackson CL. Challenge and hindrance stress: Relationships with exhaustion, motivation to learn, and learning performance. Journal of Applied Psychology. 2004;**89**(5):883-891

[33] Morledge TJ, Allexandre D, Fox E, et al. Feasibility of an online mindfulness program for stress management – A randomized controlled trial. Annals of Behavioral Medicine. 2013;**4**:137-148

[34] Gibbons C. Stress, coping and burn-out in nursing students. International Journal of Nursing Studies. 2010;**47**(10):1299-1309

[35] Jones M, Johnston D. Is the introduction of a student-centered, problem-based curriculum associated with improvements in student nurse well-being and performance? An observational study of effect. International Journal of Nursing Studies. 2006;**43**:941-952

[36] Peterson U, Berstrom G, Samuelson M, et al. Reflecting peer-support groups in the prevention of stress and burnout:Randomized control trial. Journal of Advanced Nursing. 2008;**63**(5):506-516

[37] Yearwood E, Riley JB. Curriculum infusion to promote nursing student well-being. Journal of Advanced Nursing. 2010;**66**(6):1356-1364

[38] Weiss M, Nordlie JW, Siegel EP. Mindfulness-based stress reduction as an adjunct to outpatient psychotherapy. Psychotherapy and Psychosomatics. 2005;**74**:108-112

[39] Wichianson JR, Bughi SA, Unger JB, et al. Perceived stress, coping, and eating in college students. Stress and Health. 2009;**25**(3):235-240

[40] Deary IJ, Watson R, Hogston R. A longitudinal cohort study of burnout and attrition in nursing students. Journal of Advanced Nursing. 2003;**43**(1):71-81

[41] Chernomas W, Shapiro W. Stress, depression, anxiety among undergraduate nursing students. International Journal of Nursing Education Scholarship. 2013;**10**:1-12

[42] Kleiveland B, Natvig GK, Jepsen R. Stress, sense of coherence and quality of life among Norwegian nurse students after a period of clinical period. PeerJ. 2015;**3**:74-82

[43] The National Center for Complementary and Alternative Medicine (NCCAM). 2012. Available from: www.nccam.nih.org [Accessed on: 20 December 2018]

[44] Lazar SW, Kerr CE, Wasserman RH, et al. Meditation experience is associated with increased cortical thickness. NeuroReport. 2005;**16**(17):1893-1897

[45] Oman D, Beddoe AE. Health interventions combining meditation with learning from spiritual exemplars: Conceptualization and review. Annals of Behavioral Medicine. 2005;**29**:S126

[46] Lane JD, Seskevich JE, Pieper CF. Brief mediation training can improve perceived stress and negative mood. Alternative Therapies in Health and Medicine. 2007;**13**(1):38-44

[47] Prasad K, Wahner-Roedler D, Cha S, et al. Effect of a single-session meditation training to reduce stress and improve quality of life among health care professionals: A "dose-ranging" feasibility study. Alternative Therapies in Health and Medicine. 2011;**17**(3):46-49

[48] Inanlu M, Baha R, Seyedfatemi N, et al. Coping strategies among nursing students in Hayat. Iranian Journal of Nursing and Midwifery Research. 2012;**18**:66-75

Chapter 6

Calmness Conquers Anxiety: What Language Tells Us about Mind and Body Control

Heli Tissari

Abstract

This chapter is fully based on linguistic data representing Early Modern and Present-day English, including early English printed books and contemporary online texts. The main bulk of the data was collected with the search term *calmness*. The data indicates that it is important for people to experience control of their emotions and behavior and that they understand emotional calmness in terms of the kinds of tranquility that they see in nature, for example, when the sea is still. The connection between people and nature seems therefore to be strong. However, the data also suggest that calmness does not just naturally occur in people but has to be achieved through active work and that ideas concerning the nature of such work differ from one context, period, and location to another.

Keywords: body, control, linguistics, mind

1. Introduction

The English noun *calmness* covers a surprisingly wide range of phenomena from nature, mathematics, and music to action, body, and states of the body, including death. More generally, the topic of calmness relates, for example, to the trends of medicalization and mindfulness. People seek calmness by shutting out various kinds of noise: it can be external or internal noise. However, it is interesting how little my data say about drugs considering, for instance, Aldous Huxley's novel *Brave New World* where a drug called *soma* provides a solution to human anxiety. This parallels the extent to which antidepressants offer a solution to many contemporary problems.

My original interest in the noun *calmness* had to do with emotions since I had written many studies concerning the linguistics of emotions, beginning from my PhD thesis on love [1]. I had the following kinds of questions: How often does the noun *calmness* refer to the control of emotions and in which contexts do people use it? Who is characterized as *calm* and how does that person achieve calmness? In this chapter, I deal with these questions on the basis of a comparison between Early Modern and Present-day English. Most of my Early Modern data come from a database called *Early English Books Online* (EEBO, 1473–1700). I used the *WebCorp* tool to collect Present-day English online data [2]. These sources provided me with hundreds of examples of how the noun calmness had been used.

1.1 On calmness of the mind, Western culture, and cognitive linguistics

Calmness as the control of emotions relates to at least two key ideas: One is that people can learn to control their emotions. The other is that this leads to a state of relative peace and happiness, which is worth attaining. Sorabji summarizes ancient ideas about these matters by suggesting that a transition occurred from Stoic agitation to Christian temptation [3]. Among the Roman philosophers, one that was interested in tranquility of the mind was Seneca [4]. Nowadays, people often associate calmness of the mind with meditation and mindfulness.

I associate the noun *calmness* with the relationship between the body and the mind from the perspective of a cognitive linguist. The pioneering cognitive linguists Lakoff and Johnson have strongly criticized what they consider the Cartesian dualism of Western thought; they emphasize that such dualism fails to understand that the mind and body work together and depend on each other [5, 6].

It is possible to see Western thought from another angle as well. Brosché has noticed that Cartesian dualism does not agree with the Hebrew thought represented by the Old Testament in the Christian Bible. In his view, there is thus no reason to claim that Christianity should adhere to such a dualism [7].

Many American cognitive linguists seem to lean toward Buddhism as a source of enlightenment on the relationship between body and mind. Varela, Thompson, and Rosch explain such ideas in detail in their book on human experience [8]. Their views resemble those of the 17th century philosopher Spinoza's, who in his turn is admired by a currently active, famous neuroscientist. This is how Damasio summarizes Spinoza's wisdom:

"... I assimilate the notion of spiritual to an intense experience of harmony, to the sense that the organism is functioning with the greatest possible perfection. The experience unfolds in association with the desire to act towards others with kindness and generosity. Thus to have a spiritual experience is to hold sustained feelings of a particular kind dominated by some variant of joy, however serene." [9].

1.2 On the method used in this study

In this study, I have applied the corpus linguistic method to some corpora, a database and the Internet. Corpus linguistics is based on the idea that it is possible to store large, well-planned selections of linguistic materials electronically and that those materials can then be analyzed with the help of the computer. The programs used to analyze linguistic corpora assist in making simple searches for word forms but can also grow into complex modeling of textual structures.

Here, I have simply searched for words that begin with the stem *calm**, mostly for the noun *calmness* but also for some other words such as the adjective and noun *calm* with no suffix. Apart from the above-mentioned EEBO and the Internet—which cannot be, strictly speaking, considered linguistic corpora—I have used four small corpora that represent Early Modern English (1450–1700) and Present-day English (1991).

In this way, I acquired a dataset of hundreds of instances where someone had used words denoting calmness. This chapter delineates how they had used them; it sketches the meaning of *calm(ness)* in these data. Several methods could have been used to achieve this aim, ranging from lexicographical methods used by dictionary makers to semantic methods used by university scholars. I will return to a brief discussion of such methods soon. Suffice it here to say that this chapter focuses on who or what is characterized as calm and in what sense.

1.2.1 More on the data

To continue with EEBO, its home page tells us that it "contains page images of virtually every work printed in England, Ireland, Scotland, Wales, and British North America and works in English printed elsewhere from 1473–1700" [10]. The materials for this study were collected as early as in 2004, when the University of Helsinki offered us a trial period for using EEBO. I then found 448 instances of the noun *calmness*.

What strikes the analyst at once is that almost all the examples of the noun *calmness* in EEBO are from the 17th century. This raises the questions whether it was a particularly popular word at the time, whether many people wrote about this particular topic then, or whether the database gives us a skewed idea of the matter, for one reason or another. A simple explanation could be that the number of printed books was very much on the rise in the 17th century as compared to the previous ones.

In addition to the examples from EEBO, this chapter deals with data collected from the Early Modern English part of the *Helsinki Corpus of English Texts* (HC, 1500–1710) and the *Corpus of Early English Correspondence Sampler* (CEECS, 1418–1680). Scholars have written several introductions to Early Modern English; one of them is by Nevalainen [11]. The Early Modern English part of the HC consists of selected texts representing a number of text types common to the period, while the CEECS data consists of letters, as suggested by the name of the corpus [12, 13]. These corpora are small in comparison to several Present-day English corpora, let alone the Internet. The Early Modern English part of the HC comprises 551,000 words and the CEECS 450,000 words.

The data on Present-day English were mainly collected with the help of a search program called WebCorp that is currently hosted by Birmingham City University. It was collected in 2006 when I worked as a fellow at the Helsinki Collegium for Advanced Studies. The program provided me with 682 occurrences of the word *calmness* in 116 different Internet addresses. These data are somewhat skewed in that they include a book titled *Calmness* that was written by bishop Shenouda III of the Coptic church already in 1989 and amended in 1997. It contains as many as 213 occurrences of the word form *calmness* [14]. This of course needs to be taken into account when evaluating the findings. It is unlikely that Christian uses of the word *calmness* comprise about a third of them. However, that this book occurs in the data reminds us of the important fact that the English language is used all over the world by various kinds of people and that when we search for English words online, we also encounter uses that are not typical of native speakers.

On top of the Internet materials, the Present-day data consulted in this chapter comprise two one-million-word corpora, the *Freiburg-Brown Corpus of American English* (FROWN) and the *Freiburg-LOB Corpus of British English*, which both represent the year 1991 [15, 16]. These corpora were modeled after the pioneering 1960s corpora that represented American and British English: the *Brown University Standard Corpus of Present-Day American English* (usually simply referred to as the *Brown Corpus*), and the *Lancaster-Oslo-Bergen Corpus* (often referred to as the *LOB Corpus*), respectively.

Table 1 shows the sizes of the corpora and the numbers of instances of the *calm* words that were found in them. We can see that the *calm* words are more frequent in the Present-day than Early Modern materials but that there are nevertheless hundreds of examples from both periods.

1.2.2 On semantic analysis

To conclude the introduction, let us briefly consider ways of analyzing linguistic meaning, as suggested earlier. Since the 1960s, many linguists have been inspired by

Data source	Size in words	Hits	N/100,000
EEBO	(Exact size unknown)	448	(Unknown)
HC, Early Modern	551,000	5	1
CEECS	450,000	4	1
Early Modern total	—	457	—
WebCorp	(Exact size unknown)	682	(Unknown)
FLOB	1,000,000	44	4.4
FROWN	1,000,000	33	3.3
Present-day total	—	759	—

Table 1.
The data on calmness.

the idea that concepts such as word meanings do not have distinct boundaries but overlap with one another. Around 20 years later, this view was labeled prototype semantics. In 1997, Geeraerts wrote a book on how historical changes in word meanings can be discussed in terms of prototype semantics [17]. This study was inspired by prototype semantics although I ended up considerably simplifying the presentation of my findings. My first figures had far too many overlapping meanings to make sense to the viewer.

A development relatively simultaneous to the birth of prototype semantics in linguistics was the growing enthusiasm in the nature of metaphors that culminated in the idea that metaphors play a key role in our understanding of abstract concepts [5, 6]. Metaphor can be seen to play a key role in our understanding of calmness because people see correspondences between calmness in nature and calmness in humans. However, this chapter will not delve into that aspect of calmness.

Notably, many cognitive linguists are nowadays attracted by the idea that form and function go hand in hand and that what we need to do, above all, is to pay attention to structures that reoccur in language. This idea was epitomized, among others, by Goldberg who named a new type of grammar *construction grammar* [18]. However, it is also embraced through the use of other terms such as *frequency*, *entrenchment* and *salience*, which furthermore emphasize language use [19]. Of all these concepts, it is mainly language use that plays a role in this chapter because it is based on data that reflect how people use the studied words, notably in situations where they are not prompted to reflect on their linguistic meaning.

I have focused on cognitive linguistics here because I have profiled as a cognitive linguist in my career and applied both prototype semantics and conceptual metaphor theory to my previous data [1]. However, while prototype semantics hovers in the background in this chapter, the presentation of the meaning of *calmness* is not rigidly prototype semantic. As already mentioned, when I first illustrated my data as clusters of overlapping meanings, the images became too crowded because I found so many subcategories of meaning. The overall picture was fascinating but confusing. The various senses of the noun *calmness* covered many kinds of things related to humans, their bodies and their activities, such as emotions and the will, the intellect, literary and verbal expression, music and society. These findings were driven by the research question who and what calmness is associated with. Many various kinds of things were characterized as calm.

Having noticed that it would be difficult to produce a brief, coherent description of all aspects of calmness in the data, I decided to aim at a more general description in this chapter. It includes a number of examples followed by two simple figures that summarize the data. However, extra information is provided in the appendix. As I mentioned before, metaphors will not play a role in the chapter. It will nevertheless include comments on some other characteristics of the noun *calmness*, the primitive *calm*, and its further derivations that will help us understand what it means when someone or something is characterized as calm.

2. Where do we find calmness?

This section will begin by focusing on the four linguistic corpora. It will explain in what kind of contexts the substantive *calm* and its derivatives occur. To put it differently, this section will first zoom in on some detail that can be detected in the smaller sets of data, and then zoom out on findings in EEBO and the Internet. The first focus on the substantive *calm* can be justified by noting that the longer noun *calmness* is derived from it, and secondary in that sense.

To be more precise, it is difficult to say which occurred first in the English language, the noun *calm* or the verb *to calm*. It is likely that the noun preceded the verb because the compilers of the *Oxford English Dictionary* date it slightly earlier. However, the temporal difference between the first quote of the noun in 1393 and the first quote of the verb in 1399 is small. [20, 21] It only gives us a hint of what happened in spoken English.

2.1 Small corpora

2.1.1 The Early Modern corpora

The Early Modern English corpora attested only a small number of occurrences of the noun *calm* and its derivatives: 5 in HC and 4 in CEECS. These were more frequent in FROWN and FLOB where they occurred 33 and 44 times, respectively. It is impossible to claim anything statistically significant as regards differences between the two periods represented by these data, but these corpora nevertheless give us a glimpse of how the words were and are used.

Let us begin with a royal example from the 16th century and a second one that has to do with the art of dying:

1. And then hir majesty began to be more *calm* than befor, and, as I conceaved, redyar to quallefy hir displesur and hir opinion. (CEECS 1586: William Cecil)

2. [He] spoke of his Conversion to God as a thing now grown up in him to a setled and *calm* serenity. (HC: Burnet: *Some Passages of the Life and Death of the Right Honourable John, Earl of Rochester*)

CEECS provides us with two examples of the noun, spelled *calme*, one example of the verb *to calm*, and one example of the adjective *calm*. Both occurrences of the noun concern seafaring. They occur in passages describing the safe journey of a ship from one harbor to another. The other two occurrences concern the queen's attitude changing from suspicious to favorable. Although all these occurrences of the words primarily convey an idea of tranquility, they also strongly denote favorable conditions. In other words, the writers are not only interested in whether the sea or queen is calm but also in the mindset of the seafarers and the recipients of the letters. It is natural that such connotations appear exactly in correspondence whose aim is to report information about circumstances in one place to a recipient located in another place.

In HC, the use of the word *calm* and its derivatives is clearly different from that in CEECS. It contains one occurrence of the form *calmys* that refers to the behavior of the sea. All the other uses somehow relate to people's mental states. The only occurrence of the noun form *calmness* occurs in a passage discussing a situation where a woman wishes that a man would control his jealousy and listen to her patiently. The adjective *calm* occurs three times, twice in a biography and once in a comedy. The comedy again deals with jealousy, albeit the jealous person is now a woman, while the biography explains how a dying person is reconciled with God before death occurs.

To sum up how the *calm* words behave in the Early Modern data, they apply both to nature and to people. These two are unlikely to be completely separate phenomena—rather, they overlap in that when the sea is calm, the seafarers' and their senders' minds are calm as well. These data also suggest a synonym to *calmness*, *serenity*.

2.1.2 The Present-day English corpora

To move on to the Present-day English corpora, the noun *calm* and its derivatives appear 44 times in the FLOB corpus. The noun itself only occurs once, and the same applies to the longer form *calmness*. The adverb *calmly* occurs most frequently, 15 times, albeit the difference between the adverb and the adjective *calm* is minimal, the latter occurring 14 times. The verb to *calm*, including its reflexive form *to calm oneself*, also follows very closely with its 13 occurrences. The reflexive form is in fact particularly interesting, since it suggests that calmness has to do with self-control. Furthermore, the verb occurs in the phrase *to calm down*, as in example (3). It gives calmness a downward direction, which corresponds with the waves of the sea sinking to form an even surface of water. However, arguably a person is more responsible for calming down than the sea is.

3. "Now, now. *Calm down*." Rose spoke patiently as a nurse to a child. (FLOB: K K01: 11)

4. She took it *calmly*. (FLOB: K K05: 25)

Example (4) illustrates how the *calm* words often describe reactions to incidents, the other possibility being that calmness is a long-term attitude or emotional state. These by no means exclude each other. If a person is able to face sudden negative information calmly, it is likely that s/he has a calm attitude toward life in general. It should also be mentioned that at least 8 of the 44 occurrences of the *calm* words relate to people's way of speaking.

As to the FROWN corpus, it contains 33 occurrences of the noun *calm* and its derivatives. The most frequent is the adjective *calm*, which yields 17 hits, more than half of the data. It is followed by the verb *to calm* (7 hits), the adverb *calmly* (6), and lastly, the noun *calm* itself (3). The longer noun *calmness* does not appear in this corpus at all; neither does the reflexive verb form *to calm oneself*. The verb is used, among other things, to discuss situations where someone or something creates a calm state, as in example (5). The adjective *calm* is, for instance, combined with the verb *keep* in order to suggest the continuation of a state, as in example (6).

5. As I reflected on the most turbulent years of my life, that psalm *calmed* my memory, bringing peace and closure. (FROWN: F F16: 10)

6. No ... no ... *keep calm* ... It was only a play. (FROWN: G G24: 8)

Seen together, the two corpora suggest a central use of the *calm* words, exhortations to stay or become calm, which often appear in the form of formulaic expressions (*calm down, keep calm*). Considering that people exhort one another to calmness, calmness does not only concern an individual's inner experience but is very intersubjective—a social matter, to put it differently. It is important for groups of people that their members are calm, able to control themselves.

2.2 The bigger data

When I collected data from EEBO and the Internet, I only focused on the noun *calmness*. There were two main reasons for this. The first one was that I had also analyzed data on two nouns that are similar to it in form, *happiness* and *sadness* [22, 23]. The other was that it was possible to find plenty of data by searching for this word form only. Moreover, based on my previous research, I could expect that the noun *calmness* would be more likely to be used in metaphorical expressions than the corresponding verb and adjective and that it would have more potential senses [1]. To verify such hypotheses would nevertheless require a separate study. The analysis consisted of categorizing the occurrences of *calmness* according to who or what attested calmness.

2.2.1 EEBO

Let us begin the discussion of the bigger sets of data from EEBO, which represents the earlier period. There I found 448 instances of the noun *calmness* after removing items that occurred twice in the same form. The analysis is not deep in the sense that I did not attempt to find the original sources and to peruse them to understand the contexts where the noun occurred. Consequently, I also allowed for some room for uncertainty in the analysis, including an open category in the Excel table where I put all the instances I was uncertain about. These comprised 41 items. The aim here is to draw a general picture of the data rather than discussing the data in intricate detail.

In most cases in EEBO, calmness was attributed to someone's *mind* (54 occurrences). It could also be attributed to their *spirit* (38) or *conscience* (21). The following seats of calmness could be included in the same series: *affections* (1), *brain* (1), *breast* (6), *heart* (6), *humor* (1), *judgment* (1), *nature* (1), *passions* (3), *reason* (7), *soul* (16), *temper* (10), *thoughts* (2), *virtue* (2), *understanding* (1), *will* (1), and *wisdom* (1). All of these relate in one way or another to the functions of the human mind (example 7), although it is possible to make further distinctions between such realms as emotion, reason, and spirituality. Furthermore, such a categorization is strictly speaking an anachronism because Early Modern people did not understand these concepts exactly as we do. For example, the noun *emotion* was not in wide use at the time when the EEBO data were written [24]. Instead, other words were used to discuss what we now categorize under that umbrella term.

7. We should bear all things with steady *calmness* and composedness of mind (Barrow 1685: *Of contentment, patience, and resignation to the will of God*).

If the above group was accepted as representing the mind, it would be possible to parallel it with a group representing calmness of the body, and even to suggest that EEBO represents a dualistic worldview. Note, however, that the abovementioned *breast* and *heart* suggest some overlapping of these two groups. In addition, EEBO suggests that calmness can characterize the entire *body* (4 occurrences), gestures, and ways of expressing oneself, including tone of voice (22 occurrences; example 8), *face* (6 occurrences), *eyes* (2), *brow* (1), *looks* (1), and *act(ion)* (7).

8. she told me with much grace and *calmness* (Boyle, *Earl of Orrery 1676: Parthenissa, that most fam'd romance the six volumes compleat*)

It is nevertheless not entirely clear that the EEBO data would convey a dualistic worldview. To return to the previous, can the breast and heart be separated from the body even if they are symbols rather than literal parts of the body? Would a calmness of the breast or heart not be reflected on the outside of the body, as the way a person behaves and looks like? In addition, calmness is associated with hearing, talking and ways of writing in EEBO, at least 7 times. In other words, it has to do with interaction. Calmness applies both to individuals and groups of people; it is a "social" word.

To continue with this theme, 111 occurrences of *calmness* in EEBO relate to people who are referred to with the pronouns *I* (13 times), *we* (9), *s/he* (56), *you* (6), and *they* (27). Here, I have also counted references with names under personal pronouns (example 9). The pronoun *it* only occurs once.

9. Dr. Norton is a Man of great gravity, *calmness*, sound Principles, of no Faction, an excellent Preacher (Baxter 1696: *Reliquiæ Baxterianæ*)

The social and societal occurrences of *calmness* also include calmness applied to *life* (1 occurrence) and *death* and ways of dying (3; example 10) on the one hand, and *reign* (3), *church and state* (1), *world* (1), *peace* (1), *empire* (1), and the *commonwealth* (1) on the other.

10. he abundantly enjoyed ... that happy *calmness* of death, which the Emperor Augustus was wont to pray for (Pierce 1671: *A collection of sermons upon several occasions*).

Calmness is also seen in nature, and people wish for calmness in nature. The noun *calmness* occurs in contexts where people discuss the *elements* (1 times), *air* (7; example 11), the *climate* (1), weather (8), and various spaces and locations, which need not be geographical: *heaven* (5), the *firmament* (1), and above all, water and the sea (19).

11. one Great sign of an Earthquake is excessive *Calmness* of the Air (Watson 1682: *Religion our true interest, or, Practical notes upon the third chapter of Malachy the sixteen, seventeen and eighteen verses*).

Furthermore, the EEBO data contain conceptual associations of calmness to the blood of Christ (1 times), *face of things* (1) *that condition* (1; this has to do with a person's position in society), *anything in this life* (1; example 12), *set forms* (1; this relates to prayer), and the metaphorical *sea of love* (1). In other words, this noun also belongs to rather abstract and general contexts.

12. nor is there anything in this life that can pretend to *calmness* and security (Lipsius 1670: *A discourse of constancy in two books chiefly consisting of consolations against public evils*).

To conclude on the EEBO data, in spite of the possibility to use the noun *calmness* in abstract and even vague senses, it suggests that calmness was something fairly concrete and observable, and not only in nature, but in the way other people appeared and behaved. Although the first two senses of the noun *calmness* in the *Oxford English Dictionary* describe nature [25], these data give no reason for us to assume that such senses would have been most salient to Early Modern speakers of English.

2.2.2 WebCorp

Next, I will discuss the data that were collected with the help of the WebCorp program. It consisted of 682 occurrences of the noun *calmness*. It was challenging to categorize and interpret these data, because the search result could be a short advert, for example. Sometimes, the same clause occurred several times in the data. To arrive at Figure 682, I pruned the data, leaving out doublets and web addresses.

The noun *mind* and the adjective *mental* outstood in the WebCorp data, with 51 occurrences (example 13), even though the mind did not play exactly as significant a role in these data as in the EEBO data. The following words that were associated with calmness may also be included in this set: *character* (2 occurrences), *head* (1), (a person's) *state* (3), *spirit* (4), *soul* (4), *temperament* (1), *thoughts* (5), and *inner being* (1). Emotions were represented in these data also by the words *anger* (2 times; it can be calmed), *emotions* (1), *feelings* (1), *love* (1), and *heart* (7).

13. system positively generating quietness and *calmness* in your emotional mind (http://www.yogawithsaeed.co.uk/p3a_physio.html; last accessed 2009-27-11).

It is difficult to see the WebCorp data as attesting a dualist understanding of calmness in a human being that would separate the mind from the body or vice versa. It contains the explicit claim that the body and mind should be in balance. The word pair *body and mind* occurs twice, and the noun *body* 5 times. The data include explanations of how calmness concerns the electric system of the body (2 occurrences), *senses* (2), *breath* (5), *nerves* (6), and the *central nervous system* (1). People's calmness is reflected in their behavior and actions (3 times), *features* (3), *movement* (2; example 14), manner of using the sword (8; example 15), and speech and writing (11).

14. stillness of the senses and *calmness* of movement (http://www.tasbeha.org/content/hh_books/Calmness; last accessed 2019-02-08).

15. If the return of the sword to front center is lively, relaxed, and instantaneous, this represents the imperceptible movement in stillness known as seishi, or living *calmness*. (http://www.unofficial.ki-society.org/VKS/vks19970330.txt; last accessed 2009-27-11)

The WebCorp data also attest religious sentiments. They refer to the Virgin Mary (2 times), other saints (7, example 16), God (1), Satan (1), angels (1), Jesus (2), and a *monastery* (1). These correspond to references to particularly calm and exemplary people in EEBO.

16. God looked upon the *calmness* of His servant (http://www.kosovo.com/news/archive/2005/October_15/2.html; last accessed 2006-01-30).

To continue, like the EEBO data, the WebCorp data also attribute calmness to people: the first person *I* (11 times), *you* (68), *we* (37), *s/he* (130), *they* (48), and even to *everyone* (1). Potentially relevant to this group are also contexts which address the recipient not directly with the pronoun *you* but with referring to something that is theirs, for example, *your life* or *your body and mind*. Example (17) discusses the addressee's mind and body, and themselves, as a potential location of calmness.

17. Daily practice will calm down your mind. This *calmness* will influence your inner being, your body, your circumstances, and the people you meet. It will transform you into a peacefulness and *calmness* generator. (http://www.successconsciousness.com/index_000068.htm; last accessed 2019-02-08).

A single expression that should be mentioned because it occurs 7 times is *state of cessation*. It refers to a state which can be reached through Buddhist meditation (example 18).

18. The Amitabha Buddha who was, and is, revered and praised by Buddhists around the world radiates indefinite light and life from this "state of cessation". This state is a continuous process of *calmness*. (http://www.buddhanet.net/cbp2_f6.htm; last accessed 2019-02-08).

The WebCorp data also suggest that speakers of Present-day English see calmness in *country life* (1 occurrence), and *music* (12). They would like to experience it even in the *city* (1 times). These people associate calmness with *inexperience* (1 times) and the Christian's journey to heaven (1). Moreover, the noun calmness occurs as a mathematical concept (16 times), and it is used in contexts referring to *science* (1), *form* (4), and spaces (9). Example (19) was not among my WebCorp data but illustrates well how *calmness* is discussed in mathematics papers.

19. The paper deals with the calmness of a class of multifunctions in finite dimensions. Its first part is devoted to various conditions for *calmness*, which are derived in terms of coderivatives and subdifferentials. The second part demonstrates the importance of *calmness* in several areas of nonsmooth analysis. (http://portal.acm.org/citation.cfm?id=589266; last accessed 2019-02-08).

In nature, calmness appears in animals (2 times, example 20 talks about rats), *air* (1), roots of a tree (1), and water (2). Calmness in nature as a general concept is discussed 10 times. In addition, the WebCorp data contain 4 references to the *calmness* (balance) of *everything*.

20. Note that while moderate depigmentation tends to correlate with *calmness*, extreme depigmentation can correlate with neurological problems (Grandin 1998), as well as vision and hearing impairments. (http://www.ratbehavior.org/CoatColor.htm; last accessed 2019-02-08).

3. Discussion

This section continues to discuss the central senses of the nouns *calm* and *calmness* in Early Modern English before comparing the two varieties and drawing more general conclusions. It should be taken into account that although I use the terms Early Modern and Present-day English, the data representing these varieties are limited. Toward the end of this section, I will move on to discuss calmness of the mind. One question that can be asked is if it is a virtue rather than an emotional state.

3.1 Central meanings of the noun *calmness*

3.1.1 Early Modern English

The current data suggest that in Early Modern English, calmness was, above all, a person's state. It could be rephrased, for example, as the tranquility radiating from people and their behavior. It had subcategories relating to people's mind and emotions, their life and actions, and their death. Death could be discussed separately since it is likely that discussions of calm death have to do with the art of dying which involves the ability to prepare for one's departure. It may also be assumed that Christianity affected Early Modern English speakers' ideas of how people should think, talk, and act in their lives and in moments preceding their deaths. At the same time, it is important to remember that calmness and tranquility were not purely Christian ideals but that many ideas concerning them were rooted in Antique philosophy and literature. This is all the more so in these data since the learned people who wrote books in those days had studied Latin and Greek. However, the CEECS data also remind us that discussions containing *calm* words could be rather pragmatic and concern people's reactions to incidents in their everyday lives. They were not only used when discussing philosophy or religion.

I am reluctant to separate any of the central senses of the noun *calmness* from the others as regards Early Modern English. **Figure 1** shows the meaning of *calmness* in terms of three concentric circles. The outer circle that surrounds it all is tranquility in nature, the middle one is peaceful cohabitation in human societies, and the innermost and most central sense refers to the calmness of individual people. This underlines the interaction of all these senses: individuals contribute to society and society is located in and surrounded by nature. It is good to notice that people had not yet tamed nature to the extent that has happened since then. A sea journey, for example, involved a greater risk than it would involve for us now (excepting extreme cases such as refugees crossing the Mediterranean Sea), and it was more likely to make a person even consider the art of dying.

It is even possible to consider the meaning of *calmness* in EEBO in terms of percentages, focusing on the mind–body distinction. If we compare references to the mind, intellect, character, and will (33%) with references to the body (3%), it looks like the focus of the meaning was on the mind. However, it is also possible to subsume references to people, their emotions, their literary and verbal expression, and actions as references to the body (33%). In that case, the noun refers to the body more frequently than the mind (36% vs. 33%). A reasonable compromise would be to assume that what is discussed is interaction between these two. More information is given in **Table A1** in the appendix.

3.1.2 Present-day English

In Present-day English, as represented by the WebCorp data, the noun *calmness* appears to have two main meanings that could be separated from each other in a dictionary: a more general sense of tranquility and a more specific sense in mathematics. As in Early Modern English, the noun *calmness* frequently characterizes people and their actions, but its central senses could be grouped in a somewhat different way. Two things appear to belong to the core of the idea of calmness: self-control and spirituality. Setting mathematical references aside, the most central senses of the noun *calmness* could thus be titled self-control and spiritual peace of the mind. These two senses overlap since it is often suggested that spirituality, for example, meditation, helps people gain self-control. It even happens that religious websites claim that the ideas presented there are backed up by science. It is surprising how central a place spirituality takes in Present-day English. The data contain both references to Christian saints and monasteries and Eastern meditation. It nevertheless has to be taken into account that the websites included in the data may not represent mainstream thinking, nor have they always been written by native speakers of English.

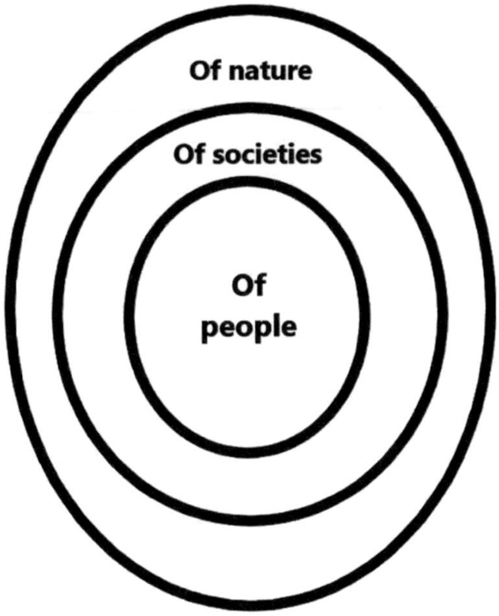

Figure 1.
Calmness in the Early Modern English data.

Something else still remains to be mentioned. Also, in Present-day English, the noun *calmness* refers furthermore to tranquility of nature and, more generally, the world surrounding the writers of the texts. It can be seen to form the background to the two central senses. It covers, for example, ruminations on how to escape noise in the city and how peaceful it is in the countryside, as well as descriptions of various physical spaces such as hotel rooms. Taken further, this framework could be seen to include references to political peace and even those to mathematical balance.

Again, percentages of senses in the WebCorp can be considered as well. The striking finding then becomes that calmness is associated with people, via pronouns or nouns such as *person*, in almost 44% of the data. The mind, intellect and character play a minor role compared to that (10.4%). References to the body are particularly infrequent (2.6%). Associations to religion and spirituality are in fact more frequent (5%). **Figure 2** is correct insofar as people's calmness is understood as their self-control. The body plays a key role insofar as such self-control can be read from the way they behave and carry themselves. The former is assumed here because self-control has become something that can be advertised, bought, and taught (cf. Section 3.1.3.). The latter may be assumed implicitly since the corpus data include exhortations to people to calm down. However, further research would be in place to understand this further. It could be that the mind–body dualism has faded into the background and that people now focus more on the calm person as a whole. Two hits that refer to the calmness of body and mind hint to such a conclusion. More information can be seen in **Table A2** in the appendix.

3.1.3 A comparison between the two varieties

There is something that clearly distinguishes the Early Modern data from its Present-day English counterpart in this study that has only been briefly mentioned so far. Many of the websites in the WebCorp data are commercial. Calmness is sold to people. Adverts suggest that people can buy tranquility of mind in the form of recordings that they can listen to, or beautiful tourist sites, for instance. This difference might not be as accentuated if the Present-day English data were collected somewhere else than the Internet.

Clearly, the meaning of *calmness* in Early Modern English resembles that in Present-day English. Both varieties underline the role of individual human beings and their ability to control themselves and their behavior. Simultaneously, clear differences exist. The Early Modern English data is more specific about which aspects of people and their behavior can be calm. It also lacks references to religions other than Christianity while the Present-day English data suggest that calmness can be reached through Eastern meditation and martial arts. The Present-day English data hardly touch upon the art of dying, although they discuss Heaven. Surprisingly enough, the Early Modern English data also emphasize communication skills more. One potential explanation is that they focus more on cohabitation and collaboration, while the Present-day English data focus on individuals, their experience of internal well-being and how they appear to us on the outside. Similarly, the Early Modern English data put more weight on the state and its ruler. What they lack are references to scientific studies addressing, for example, human physiology; neither do they mention music nor mathematics, as the Present-day English data.

Let us return a little to the linguistic corpora. It may be added that the use of such phrases as *keep calm* and *calm down* seems to be typical of Present-day rather than Early Modern English. It seems that speakers of Early Modern English observed each other's calmness while speakers of Present-day English actively exhort each other to be calm. Notably, neither data include recorded conversations. While part of the Early Modern letters may come close to Early Modern spoken English, the Present-day English data contain imaginary conversations from novels. How these differ from each other could be studied further. It would also be interesting to ask which period allowed or allows more divergence from the norm in terms of how calm people should be.

When it comes to the percentages of different associations in the data, the most striking finding is that calmness is so simply and directly attributed to people in the Present-day English data. This may reflect the disappearance of a culture where calmness was analyzed in detail in terms of the mind and body, but it may also tell us that calmness has become something that is expected of people. In that case, the development of the calm words would parallel that of the adjective *happy* which nowadays tends to be relatively neutral. It is as if the assumption is that most people are relatively happy [23, 26].

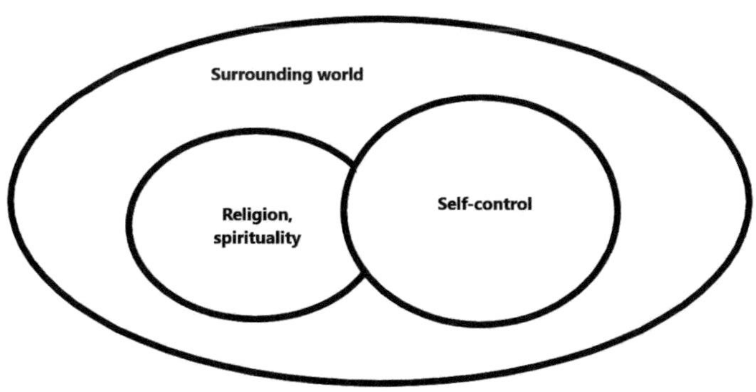

Figure 2.
Calmness in the Present-day English data.

3.2 On calmness of the mind

Lastly in this section, I will focus on the concept of calmness, or tranquility, of the mind which plays an important role in the findings. One question of interest is how people achieve or at least attempt to achieve such mental peace.

3.2.1 Calmness of the mind in the Early Modern data

The Early Modern data suggest that people aimed at calmness through reasoning and through controlling their emotions. The idea was not to let one's passions take over. Instead, people wanted to act and speak in a steady, stable manner regardless of circumstances. This was especially expected of leaders such as monarchs. It is this ideal that binds together discussions of firmness of character, judgment, wisdom, and eventually also the art of dying.

Another way to acquire calmness was to turn to God in order to be reconciled with God. Such a reconciliation provided a person with a clean conscience which in its turn led to calmness. This was particularly important at the hour of death.

Moreover, it pays to note that the Early Modern period was a stormy one in terms of politics and economy and that people extended their travels further and further around the globe. The data reflect this through referring to wars and seafaring. We may surely assume that such outer circumstances affected people's experience of calmness or lack of it regardless of how high their ideals were. Explorers reported of calm, paradisiacal conditions in places far away from their countries of birth.

3.2.2 Calmness of the mind in the Present-day English data

Moving on to the time of the Internet, people nowadays seek calmness in quiet environments, religion, and various techniques of mind and body control and meditation. It is interesting to consider how their experience and activities differ from those of their Early Modern predecessors in this respect. More and more people live in noisy cities and yearn after the peace of the countryside or even a monastery instead of dreaming of conquering new continents. At the same time, perhaps more than ever, people are regarded as organisms or machines that can be controlled if their workings are understood. People consider the matter in terms of biology, medicine, and even systems research. In addition to self-control, people are interested in ways to relax.

In both periods, some people stand out as models of mental calmness. However, it is somewhat surprising that in these data, Present-day English authors go further backwards in time to find such role models. The Early Modern texts mention contemporary people and some people that had passed away relatively recently, whereas the Internet data discuss the Virgin Mary, saints of old, and Jesus. To exaggerate a little, calmness seems to be associated with something that is remote, be it a person or a place.

3.2.3 Calmness of the mind as a virtue

My original interest in calmness is related to my interest in what language tells us about emotions. While these data suggest that calmness has to do with the control of emotions, it can also be approached from another angle. It can be seen as a virtue. This particularly applies to the Early Modern data which contain a couple of direct references to virtue, in addition to a plethora of comments suggesting that people should seek understanding, use reason and judgment, and control their emotions and behavior, even at the hour of death. To recapitulate, calmness of the mind is a rational virtue in the Early Modern data, but not only that: it is also a religious and

DOI: http://dx.doi.org/10.5772/intechopen.86138

social virtue. It is considered good to be in good terms with both God and people: "There is no pillow as soft as a clear conscience." In addition, a virtuous Early Modern monarch was capable of maintaining calmness in a country, which in turn led to calmness and tranquility in individual subjects' lives.

It is not quite so clear if calmness is a virtue in our times. What is clear is that many people search for calmness. However, they do not necessarily seek to be virtuous; instead, they may seek inner calmness that involves a good feeling in general and, in particular, a feeling that they are in control of what is happening to them. Maybe calmness comes closer to happiness and satisfaction in Present-day than Early Modern English. In addition, it is more closely tied to this moment rather than the future, the future including an expectation of eternal life in the Early Modern data. However, if calmness has become the expected of state of people in the way happiness appears to be, then it can be a virtue in that sense, meaning that people know they should be calm. This in turn would be a cause of why people feel bad if they do not feel calm and are willing to learn how to become calm. This could then lead them to commercial websites on the one hand, and to spirituality on the other hand.

Here we might return to the thought that Damasio quoted from Spinoza, namely that spirituality is intense harmony experienced by a person whose mind and body function in an ideal manner [9]. Damasio appears to consider such a harmony virtuous, but even if he quotes an Early Modern thinker, his understanding of spirituality fits our times. To specify, he sees the human being as a system that can function in an optimal way, rather than seeing it in relation to an invisible other, or an otherworldly existence more generally.

Lastly, if we only consider social interaction, calmness is certainly a virtue in both periods. When people live together and collaborate, it tends to be desirable that they all remain more or less calm and can express themselves in a clear, peaceful manner instead of letting their emotions take control. If emotions were allowed to rule, they could, in extreme cases, make people's lives particularly difficult. They could also paralyze their experiencers, making them unable to contribute to the common good. Seen from this angle, it is not always a priority how calmness is achieved. In addition, it can be a virtue to make another person calm.

4. Conclusion

This chapter has dealt with the English nouns *calm* and *calmness* and some other words that can be derived from the same stem. It has considered data from the Early Modern and Present-day English periods. The sample of around a thousand occurrences of these words suggests that both inner peace and outer peace were and are important to people in both periods but that they were and are associated with slightly different things. Data from both periods suggest that self-control helps us to achieve calmness, but it is not exactly the same concept. The Early Modern data emphasizes rationality, firmness of character, and the ability to express oneself in a good, constructive manner, and contains references to Christianity. The Present-day English data lean more toward techniques of controlling one's body and mind and of meditation.

This piece of research could be developed not only by collecting more data but also by delving deeper into the original texts, other contemporary thought and further research on similar topics. It has nevertheless already given us an idea of how *calmness* is represented in selected Early Modern and Present-day English texts and how linguists can model concepts. Sometimes, these concepts can be central to society's functioning; this could even be claimed of *calmness* even if it is not a word frequently in use in political discussions.

If these findings were taken over to social and political discussions, we might consider questions such as:

Is calmness of the body and mind a goal in itself or a means to an end? Or is it a byproduct of something else?

Does it matter how people achieve calmness of the body and mind? Should we evaluate how people attempt to achieve it?

Does everyone have a right to calmness of the body and mind? What does it mean in a situation where such calmness is also strongly commercialized?

Is it important that people act calm and stay calm in all situations? Are there any situations when they can be allowed to be anxious or angry, to raise their voices and shout, and even make trouble?

Is it more important to feel calm or to be able to control oneself? Does it depend on the situation?

A. Appendix

Category: Calmness of ...	Percentage of the data
Nature and the environment	9
Time	3.1
People	25
Mind	27
Intellect	2.7
Character	2.7
Will	0.2
Emotions	0.9
Body	3.1
Literary and verbal expression	4.7
Actions and behavior	2.5
Life and death	0.9
A geographical area	0.9
The conscience (+ 1 hit: Christ's blood)	4.9
Other things such as set forms	1.1
Unclear cases	11

Table A1.
Categories of calmness in EEBO.

Category: Calmness of ...	Percentage of the data
Environment	4.1
People	44
Mind	8.8
Intellect	1
Character	0.6
Emotions	1.8
Body and mind	0.3

Category: Calmness of ...	Percentage of the data
Body	2.6
Literary and verbal expression	1.6
Actions and behavior	1.9
Life and death	1
Religious people, God	5
Mathematical objects	2.3
Music	1.8
Others such as form	0.6
Unclear cases	23

Table A2.
Categories of calmness in WebCorp.

Author details

Heli Tissari
Department of English, Stockholm University, Sweden

*Address all correspondence to: heli.tissari@english.su.se

References

[1] Tissari H. LOVEscapes: Changes in Prototypical Senses and Cognitive Metaphors Since 1500 [thesis]. Helsinki: Société Néophilologique; 2003. p. 470

[2] WebCorp Live: Concordance the web in real-time [Internet]. 1999-2019. Available from: http://www.webcorp.org.uk/live/ [Accessed: 02 February 2019]

[3] Sorabji R. Emotion and Peace of Mind: From Stoic Agitation to Christian Temptation. Oxford: Oxford University Press; 2002. p. 499. DOI: 10.1093/acprof:oso/9780199256600.001.0001

[4] Motto A. Seneca Sourcebook: Guide to the Thought of Lucius Annaeus Seneca in the Extant Prose Works. Amsterdam: Adolf M. Hakkert; 1970

[5] Lakoff J, Johnson M. Metaphors we Live by. Chicago: The University of Chicago Press; 1980

[6] Lakoff J, Johnson M. Philosophy in the Flesh: The Embodied Mind and its Challenge to Western Thought. Chicago: The University of Chicago Press; 1999

[7] Brosché F. Helhetssynen återupptäckt: Den kristna skapelsetrons helhetssyn på människan och bejakelse av många slags helande. Stockholm: EFS; 1985

[8] Varela F, Thompson E, Rosch E. The Embodied Mind: Cognitive Science and Human Experience. Cambridge, Ma: The MIT Press; 1995

[9] Damasio A. Looking for Spinoza: Joy, Sorrow and the Feeling Brain. Orlando: Harcourt; 2003

[10] EEBO Early English Books Online: What is Early English Books Online? [Internet]. 2003-2019. Available from: https://eebo.chadwyck.com/about/about.htm [Accessed: 02 February 2019]

[11] Nevalainen T. Introduction to Early Modern English. Edinburgh: Edinburgh University Press; 2006

[12] Nurmi A. Manual for the Corpus of Early English Correspondence Sampler CEECS. Helsinki: Department of English, University of Helsinki; 1998. Available from: http://clu.uni.no/icame/manuals/CEECS/INDEX.HTM [Accessed: 11 February 2019]

[13] Kytö M. Manual to the Diachronic Part of the Helsinki Corpus of English Texts: Coding Conventions and Lists of Source Texts. 3rd ed. Helsinki: Department of English, University of Helsinki; 1996. Available from: http://clu.uni.no/icame/manuals/HC/INDEX.HTM [Accessed: 11 February 2019]

[14] Calmness by H. H. Pope Shenouda III [Internet]. 1997. Available from: http://tasbeha.org/content/hh_books/Calmness/ [Accessed: 02 February 2019]

[15] Hundt M, Sand A, Siemund R. Manual of Information to accompany The Freiburg—LOB Corpus of British English ('FLOB'). Freiburg: Albert-Ludwigs-Universität Freiburg, Englisches Seminar; 1998. Available from: http://clu.uni.no/icame/manuals/FLOB/INDEX.HTM [Accessed: 11 February 2019]

[16] Hundt M, Sand A, Skandera P. Manual of Information to Accompany the Freiburg—Brown Corpus of American English ('Frown'). Freiburg: Albert-Ludwigs-Universität Freiburg, Englisches Seminar; 1999. Available from: http://clu.uni.no/icame/manuals/FROWN/INDEX.HTM [Accessed: 11 February 2019]

[17] Geeraerts D. Diachronic Prototype Semantics: A Contribution to Historical Lexicology. Oxford: Clarendon; 1997

[18] Goldberg A. Constructions: A Construction Grammar Approach to

Argument Structure. Chicago: The University of Chicago Press; 1995

[19] Dąbrowska E, Divjak D, editors. Handbook of Cognitive Linguistics. Berlin: De Gruyter Mouton; 2015. p. 716

[20] Calm N. OED/The Oxford English Dictionary [Internet]. 2019. Available from: http://www.oed.com/ [Accessed: 03 February 2019]

[21] Calm V. OED/The Oxford English Dictionary [Internet]. 2019. Available from: http://www.oed.com/ [Accessed: 03 February 2019]

[22] Tissari H. On the concept of sadness: Looking at words in contexts derived from corpora. In: Lewandowska-Tomaszczyk B, editor. Corpus Linguistics, Computer Tools, and Applications: State of the Art. Frankfurt am Main: Peter Lang; 2008. pp. 281-308

[23] Tissari H. Happiness and joy in corpus contexts: A cognitive semantic analysis. In: Tissari H, Pessi AB, Salmela M, editors. Happiness: Cognition, Experience, Language. Helsinki: Helsinki Collegium for Advanced Studies, University of Helsinki; 2008. pp. 144-174. Available from: www.helsinki.fi/collegium/journal/volumes/volume_3/

[24] Tissari H. Current emotion research in English linguistics: Words for emotions in the history of English. Emotion Review. 2017;**9**(1):86-94. DOI: 10.1177/1754073916632064

[25] Calmness N. OED/The Oxford English Dictionary [Internet]. 2019. Available from: http://www.oed.com/ [Accessed: 08 February 2019]

[26] Heikkinen K, Tissari H. *Gefeoh* and *geblissa* or happy birthday! On old English *bliss* and modern English *happy*. In: Raumolin-Brunberg H, Nevala M, Nurmi A, Rissanen M, editors. Variation Past and Present: Varieng Studies on English for Terttun Nevalainen. Helsinki: Société Néophilologique; 2002. pp. 59-76

Chapter 7

Stress, Hypertension and Yoga

Surendra Shripati Wadikar

Abstract

Stress and stress-related disorders are emerging as a major health challenge. In the classical stress concept, stress can be broadly defined as an actual or anticipated disruption of homeostasis by certain physical and psychological events that are known as 'stressors'. Prolonged exposure to stress can lead to a destructive, self-perpetuating cascade of neuroendocrine, metabolic and neuropsychological alterations that play an important role in the development and progression of cardio-vascular disease (CVD) like hypertension. Dysregulation of stress system is causally linked to pathogenesis of essential hypertension, which involves over activity of hypothalamic-pituitary-adrenal axis (HPA) and sympathoadrenal system (SAS) and resetting of baroreceptors as the underlying pathophysiological mechanisms. Evidence suggests that regular practice of yogasanas and pranayama appears to cause down-regulation of the HPA axis and the sympathetic nervous system (SNS), increases vagal activity, improves baroreceptor sensitivity, and thereby helps to reduce blood pressure. Although the exact mechanism of beneficial effects of yoga are not known, evidence suggests that yogic intervention may be acting through multiple mechanisms simultaneously influencing diverse neural structures involved in the regulation of the neuroendocrine and the cardiovascular response to stress to cause neurohumoral modulations resulting in alleviation of stress and improvement in cardiovascular indices.

Keywords: stress, hypertension, hypothalamic-pituitary-adrenal axis, sympathoadrenal system, baroreceptors, yoga

1. Introduction

Fast pace of life, growing aspirations of people, peer pressure and collapsing social support institutions like family, are affecting peoples' health in modern society. Stress and stress-related disorders are emerging as a major health challenge across the globe. Stress is perceived as an event or experience that invoke a range of unpleasant emotions like uneasiness, nervousness, anxiety, and fear. More scientifically speaking stress is a state of disharmony or threatened homeostasis provoked by psychological, environmental, and/or physiological factors called 'stressors'. Stress is often implicated in the pathogenesis of non-communicable diseases like hypertension, coronary heart disease, depression, and obesity. Evidence suggests that dysregulation of stress system is causally linked to the pathogenesis of essential hypertension, with over activity of Hypothalamic-pituitary-adrenal axis (HPA) and Sympathoadrenal System (SAS) and resetting of baroreceptors as the underlying pathophysiological mechanisms.

Non-pharmacological interventions such as relaxation techniques in the form of yoga and meditation are slowly gaining recognition as an adjunctive therapy in case

IntechOpen

of stress-related health disorders like hypertension, anxiety, and depression. Yoga promises to be one of the best and relatively safest methods to counter stress. The most popularly used yoga intervention techniques include yogasanas (yoga postures) and pranayama (controlled breathing techniques) and meditation. Asanas and pranayamas reduce stress, relax and revitalise body. Relaxation helps to control anxiety, calms mind and brings down heart rate and blood pressure.

2. Concept of stress, allostasis and allostatic load

All living organisms strive towards a dynamic equilibrium, which is called homeostasis. Homeostasis is maintenance of relative stability of the core parameters required for cell survival [1]. In the classical stress concept, stress can be broadly defined as an actual or anticipated disruption of homeostasis by certain physical and/or psychological events that are known as 'stressors' [2].

Modern concept of stress defines it as a consciously or unconsciously perceived threat to homeostasis [3], which involves specific response of the body that in turn depends on the factors like the nature of the challenge to homeostasis, the perception of the stressor and the ability to cope with it [4]. A new concept called 'allostasis' was introduced to define and explain stress. Accordingly, the term allostasis refers to the process whereby an organism maintains physiological stability by changing parameters of its internal milieu by matching them appropriately to environmental demands [5, 6]. Thus, homeostasis is a process that keeps us alive whilst allostasis is a process that helps us to adapt to the environmental challenges.

Allostatic load (AL) refers to the cumulative effects of chronic and acute stress on the body. It represents the 'wear and tear' the body experiences when repeated allostatic responses are activated during stressful situations [7]. Allostatic overload is the final stage of the progression of allostatic load, whereby the culmination of physiological dysregulations both at the cellular and organ levels leads to disordered, diseased, and deceased endpoints [8].

The concepts of allostasis, allostatic load and overload are to be understood in the context that the physiological systems involved in allostatic responses help us to adapt to challenges imposed by stressors and the dysregulation or overuse of the same systems due to prolonged exposure to stressors can lead to pathological disorders [7]. Thus, allostasis involves health protective adaptive responses to stressors, whereas, allostatic load is the result of the overuse or dysregulation of the systems involved in allostatic responses that leads to pathological disorders, a state referred to as allostatic overload [6].

3. Neurobiology of stress response

The stress response involves multiple organ systems of the body like central nervous system (CNS), autonomic nervous system (ANS), endocrine system, cardiovascular system and immune system [9]. However, individual's response to stressors is conditioned by the genetic, environmental and developmental factors. The collective stress responses are mediated by largely overlapping circuits in the hypothalamus, the limbic cortex, and many neural elements in the brainstem [10]. The brain triggers stress responses that are commensurate with the nature of the stressor. Accordingly, stress regulatory neuro-circuits activated by a particular stressor are crucially dependent on stressor attributes [2].

Depending on their nature, the stressors can be broadly divided into two categories: Physical or Physiological stressors and Psychogenic or Psychological stressors. Stressors that produce actual disturbances of homeostasis are considered as physical stressors, e.g. haemorrhage or infection. Whereas, stressors that threaten the current state and are predicted or anticipated based on prior experiences are considered as psychogenic stressors, e.g. aversive environmental stimuli [11]. Thus, physical stressors represent 'Systemic stressors' which are of immediate survival value and are mainly processed by brainstem and hypothalamic regions [2, 11]. By contrast, 'Psychogenic stressors' represent 'Processive' stressors. They require sequential stimulus assembly and processing of signals from multiple sensory modalities in the forebrain and can occur in anticipation of or in reaction to stressful events prior to initiation of a stress response. They involve the 'Limbic stress pathways' for processing information [12]. The vast majority of decisions regarding the initiation of stress responses seem to be made at the level of limbic structures, which communicate information to subcortical sites positioned to interface with ongoing homeostatic feedback [13]. It is also believed that limbic forebrain regions may also contribute to processing of physical stressors, influencing the autonomic responses to stress and the activation of the HPA-axis [2].

3.1 Brainstem circuitry in stress response

The autonomic nervous system (ANS) provides the immediate response to stressors mainly mediated via brainstem circuitry. The brainstem region receives neuronal inputs carrying signals of homeostatic disturbances involving cardiovascular system (CVS), respiratory system (RS) and visceral organs [14], which cause reflex stimulation of sympathetic response [15]. Reflex sympathetic activation represents the classic 'fight or flight' response to stress [2].

Besides this, signals from medulla and spinal cord are sent to other autonomic regulative sites in the hindbrain, midbrain and forebrain. The complex interplay between these neural structures and the descending signals from the hypothalamus and limbic cortex ultimately modulate the autonomic response to stressors [15].

Homeostatic imbalance also triggers signals to the brainstem leading to activation of the HPA axis. Ascending brainstem pathways project to the paraventricular nucleus of the hypothalamus (PVN). Catecholaminergic projections to the PVN originate in the nucleus of the solitary tract (NTS) and C1-C3 regions and represent a major HPA excitatory pathway, promoting corticotropin releasing hormone (CRH) and thereby, adrenocorticotropic hormone (ACTH) release [16]. NTS projections to PVN also release neuropeptide Y, glucagon-like peptide 1, inhibin β, somatostatin and enkephalin, that can regulate HPA activation [17].

Ascending catecholaminergic pathways mainly mediate systemic-stress responses [14]. However, some non-catecholaminergic NTS cell groups (e.g. glucagon-like peptide 1 neurons) are involved in the generation of HPA responses to both psychogenic and systemic stressors [18]. Thus, NTS appears to be a common site for integration of reactive HPA responses. Neurons throughout NTS are activated by a variety of acute and chronic stressors [19]. In addition to sending projections that target subcortical limbic regions critical for regulating behavioural responses to stress, NTS also receives direct input from the amygdala, the bed nucleus of stria terminalis (BST), and the prefrontal cortex [20]. Thus, NTS is a critical hub for integrating interoceptive and viscero-sensory input with descending affective and cognitive information from the limbic forebrain.

3.2 Hypothalamic nuclei

Paraventricular nucleus of the hypothalamus (PVN) acts as a principal integrator of stress signals and is directly involved in regulating HPA axis and autonomic responses to stressors [2]. As mentioned earlier, the PVN receives its major adrenergic inputs from the A2/C2 regions of NTS, which represents a major HPA excitatory pathway promoting CRH release [16]. The PVN neurons project to the autonomic targets in the brainstem and spinal cord such as the intermediolateral cell column, the parabrachial nucleus, the dorsal motor nucleus of the vagus nerve and the NTS [13]. PVN also receives serotonergic innervation from the median raphe nuclei in the midbrain. Serotonin activates the HPA axis and stimulates ACTH release and secretion of glucocorticoids (GCs) [21].

Many of the hypothalamic regions interact with the limbic inputs and are involved in homeostatic integration. Hypothalamic communications with limbic cortex and their combined downward effect on the HPA and ANS activity modulate responses to stressors with respect to ongoing physiological state.

PVN is heavily innervated by inhibitory GABAergic inputs from limbic regions [22]. Most of these limbic–PVN connections are indirect and are made through the bed nucleus of stria terminalis (BST) and peri-PVN regions of the hypothalamus, enabling it to translate limbic information into modulation of the HPA axis or autonomic activation [23]. While PVN projecting GABAergic neurons from posterior BST nuclei inhibit HPA response to stress, CRH neurons from anteroventral BST nuclei to PVN are responsible for excitation of HPA activity [24].

PVN also receives inhibitory GABAergic innervation from the medial preoptic hypothalamus (mPoA), which receives projections from the hippocampus and the medial nucleus of amygdala (MeA) and is an important site for interaction between limbic inputs and physiological regulatory processes [2].

Lateral hypothalamic neurons are positioned to modulate autonomic and/or HPA tone [2, 25]. The Dorsomedial hypothalamus (DMH) regulates autonomic and perhaps also HPA axis responses to psychogenic stimuli [2]. Suprachiasmatic nucleus (SCN) has effect on the diurnal variations and basal HPA activity and autonomic responses to psychogenic stressors [26]. SCN innervates peri PVN regions, where it interacts with the signals from limbic cortex.

3.3 Limbic stress circuits

The interface between the incoming sensory information about the stressors and the appraisal process is formed by limbic brain structures. Both psychogenic and physical stimuli are processed in multiple limbic forebrain structures, including the amygdala, the hippocampus and the prefrontal cortex [2]. These regions receive associational information from subcortical and cortical areas involved in higher-order sensory processing and memory and also ascending inputs from sites involved in attention and arousal. Limbic structures do not communicate directly with the primary stress effector systems. Instead, they send signals to the subcortical relay sites, which in turn interface with the primary stress effector neurons in the PVN, caudal medulla and spinal cord [14]. Usually, there is interaction between the outputs from the stress-excitatory structures (central (CeA) and medial (MeA) nuclei of amygdala and infralimbic cortex) and stress-inhibitory regions (hippocampus, prelimbic cortex), so that local integration of limbic information occurs before relaying it to the primary stress effector sites [14]. Downward signals from these limbic regions modulate the activity of the HPA axis and probably also autonomic responses to stress [2].

3.3.1 Amygdala

Studies suggest that the Central nucleus of amygdala (CeA) and the BST coordinate to orchestrate both acute and chronic responses to various kinds of threatening stimuli and are involved in the control of fear and anxiety [27]. CeA is primarily involved in behavioural, autonomic and endocrine responses to stress [10]. The medial nucleus of amygdala (MeA) and basolateral nucleus of amygdala (BLA) are preferentially activated by psychological stressors [11, 25]. There is a two-way neural communication between amygdala and the dorsal raphe nucleus and catecholaminergic nuclei in the brainstem. CeA sends inputs to CRH neurons in the PVN both directly and through the bed nucleus of the stria terminalis and mediates the adrenocortical response to somatosensory stimuli [2, 10].

3.3.2 Hippocampus

The hippocampus inhibits the HPA axis activity. It also influences autonomic tone. Hippocampus has no major direct projections to the brainstem, but its action on autonomic function might be routed through NTS-projecting regions of the medial prefrontal cortex (mPFC) [2].

3.3.3 Prefrontal cortex (PFC)

Prefrontal cortex (PFC) is critical to develop appropriate responses to environment changes, enabling behavioural plasticity [28]. The prelimbic medial PFC (mPFC) preferentially inhibits HPA axis response to psychogenic stressors and, like the hippocampus it is involved in response termination [2]. The infralimbic PFC is involved in initiating autonomic and HPA responses to psychogenic stimuli. The infralimbic cortex is selectively involved in stress induced cardiovascular regulation, perhaps through modification of the baroreflex activity. As a result of its interconnections with the hippocampus and the amygdala, the prefrontal cortex is positioned at the top of the response initiation hierarchy and might be a principal limbic coordinator of physiological reactivity [2].

3.4 Circumventricular organs (CVO)

PVN projections from subfornical organ (SFO) are angiotensinergic and also promotes CRH secretion and biosynthesis [29]. This pathway may be involved in fluid/electrolyte balance stress induced stimulation of HPA-axis activity via activation of the angiotensin II type-1 receptor [30]. There are projections from organum vasculosum of the lamina terminalis (OVLT) to the anteroventral preoptic nucleus, DMH and preautonomic PVN. These pathways are believed to be responsible for initiating cardiovascular response to stress [31].

4. Primary mediators of stress response

The body's responses to stressors are mediated by an intricate stress system, which includes the hypothalamic–pituitary–adrenal (HPA) axis and the sympathoadrenal system (SAS), which consists of sympathetic nervous system (SNS) and adrenomedullary system (AS) [32]. The hormones of HPA axis and catecholamines released by SAS are the primary mediators of the stress response [33].

As mentioned earlier the paraventricular nucleus of hypothalamus (PVN) plays a major role in stress response. Stress induced activation of the parvocellular neurons of the PVN causes the release of CRH and Arginine vasopressin (AVP) and initiates the endocrine response to stressors. CRH controls ACTH release from the anterior pituitary gland [10]. AVP is co-localised with CRH in parvocellular neurons of PVN. In the anterior pituitary, AVP potentiates the effect of CRH on ACTH release [34]. Reciprocal connections exist between CRH neurons in PVN and noradrenergic neurons in the locus ceruleus (LC); hence, they stimulate each other in a positive feedback fashion [33]. CRH serves as a neurotransmitter that mediates sympathetic arousal, providing a link between the adrenocortical and autonomic branches of the stress response. The locus ceruleus-norepinephrine system (LNE) controls the stress-induced stimulation of the sympathoadrenal system (SAS) [10]. ACTH is the key regulator of glucocorticoid secretion from the adrenal cortex. Glucocorticoid hormones, mainly cortisol in humans, and cortisone in animals, are the final effectors of the hypothalamic-pituitary-adrenal axis (HPA) axis, which mediate the response of the organism to stressors [10].

5. Acute vs. chronic stress response: protection vs. damage

The first phase of the acute stress response involves activation of sympathoadrenal system (SAS), which results in a typical 'fight-or-flight' responses. These are rapid but short-term physiological adaptations, so as to meet the challenge imposed by a stressful event. It is mediated by the release of catecholamines like norepinephrine (NE). Whereas, the secondary phase involves the hormonal mechanism (hypothalamic-pituitary-adrenal axis) considered sluggish compared to the synaptic mechanisms that activate the SAS, but resulting in an amplified and protracted secretory response involving stress hormones like CRH, ACTH and glucocorticoids (GCs), mainly cortisol in human beings (long-lasting response). Cortisol in turn has effects all over the body including brain [13].

In acute stress response, the action of SAS and HPA axis mediators is protective in nature and is geared to enable the individual to adapt to stressors. However, chronic exposure to stressors results in over-activation and or dysregulation of SAS and HPA-axis to induce a chain reaction of deleterious effects on the biological systems involved in stress response, which eventually leads to stress-related disorders [35]. Stress induced brain changes further diminish the body's ability to cognitively process and physiologically respond to stressors [36]. In chronic stress, prolonged and synergistic effects of the stress hormones and pro-inflammatory cytokines adversely affect multiple interconnected organ systems (autonomic, neuroendocrine, immune and cardiovascular systems) involved in stress response, which finally results in various pathological conditions [8].

6. Aetiology of essential hypertension

Essential hypertension is a multifactorial disorder with a strong genetic predisposition. Multiple studies have suggested involvement of many factors in the genesis of essential hypertension. The principal factors among them are: increased activity of SNS including renal SNS; over activity of renin-angiotensin-aldosterone system (RAAS); positive sodium imbalance; low levels of vasodilators, like nitric oxide (NO), prostacyclin (PGI2), and the natriuretic peptides; high levels of vasoconstrictors like endothelin 1 (ET 1); structural and functional vascular defects; increased activity of vascular growth factors; and obesity [37]. In recent studies, oxidative stress, endothelial dysfunction, vascular remodelling and decreased vascular compliance are implicated as the primary antecedents, which may be involved in the development of essential hypertension [38].

7. Role of stress in pathogenesis of essential hypertension

Due to the complexity of the mechanisms controlling blood pressure regulation and involvement of many interconnected regulatory organ systems, with various endogenous and exogenous factors interacting with these regulatory systems, the exact cause of essential hypertension is still not known [39].

Although stress is clearly implicated in the aetiology of essential hypertension, the relationship between a psycho-physiological construct like stress and the physical manifestation of essential hypertension is not simple or direct. It is quite likely that multiple etiologic pathways as well as the variety of intervening variables exist that lead to the onset of essential hypertension. However, psychological stress has been considered to be one of the major risk factors for essential hypertension [40–42].

7.1 Cardiovascular reactivity and essential hypertension

There have been many studies which suggest that, the exaggerated cardiovascular response (CVR) to life stressors appear to play a key role in the stress–hypertension relation [43, 44]. It has been suggested that, heightened cardiovascular reactivity could reflect sympathetic hyper responsivity or enhanced vagal withdrawal during stress, whereas poorer cardiovascular recovery could be due to prolonged sympathetic activation, diminished vagal tone, or attenuated or delayed vagal rebound following the termination of stress [45]. It is believed that increased cardiovascular reactivity and poor cardiovascular recovery could indicate autonomic dysregulation of cardiovascular system, which may be contributing in the pathogenesis of essential hypertension [46].

7.2 Chronic stress and essential hypertension

Evidence suggests that chronic exposure to psychosocial stress leads to the onset of essential hypertension via stress response, which includes the affective, cognitive, behavioural, and physiological alterations. Stress induced increased sympathetic activity, decreased vagal activity, reduced baroreflex gain, over activity of the hypothalamic-pituitary-adrenal (HPA) axis and endothelial dysfunction as a long-term consequence, cause increase in blood pressure and heart rate by affecting central and peripheral regulation of the CVS [47].

There is a mount of evidence linking chronic stress with essential hypertension. Clinical and epidemiological studies indicate that chronic psychological stress can lead to essential hypertension [48, 49]. Many workers in their studies have found that individuals exposed to chronic stress show persistent hypertension [40, 50, 51]. Various population studies have demonstrated that psychosocial stress is associated with an increased risk of hypertension [52, 53]. Studies have also found that stress induced alterations in blood pressure persist even after the end of exposure to stressors [54, 55].

7.3 Possible mechanisms leading to essential hypertension

7.3.1 Increased activity of sympathetic nervous system

Chronic exposure to stressors leads to dysregulation of autonomic nervous system and increase in the activity of HPA axis. Dysregulation of ANS causes increase in the activity of sympathetic nervous system (SNS), which further augments the activity of HPA axis [56]. Activation of SNS leads to enhanced release of NE, Nitric oxide (NO) and Neuropeptide Y (NPY) from sympathetic nerve terminals [57].

Stimulation of sympathetic nervous system is a pathophysiological hallmark of essential hypertension, and especially, hypertension attributable to chronic mental stress [40, 58, 59]. Increased SNS activity leads to the development of hypertension by several mechanisms like peripheral vasoconstriction, increased cardiac contraction, renal sodium and water retention, baroreflex dysfunction, and vascular damage [60, 61]. Chronic sympathetic stimulation causes left ventricular hypertrophy and dysfunction, and arterial remodelling [62]. Repeated stress-induced vasoconstriction may also result in vascular hypertrophy, leading to progressive increases in peripheral resistance and blood pressure [63].

NE and NPY modulate the release of pro-inflammatory cytokines, such as Interleukin-6 (IL-6), C-reactive protein (CRP), and tumour necrosis factor (TNF) [52]. These cytokines in turn cause inflammation and endothelial dysfunction and lead to development of hypertension [64].

The mechanisms underlying dysregulation of sympathetic nervous system activity involve impairment in sympathetic restraint due to alterations in arterial and cardio-pulmonary baroreflexes and central/peripheral chemoreflexes or error in the processing of reflex signals in brainstem cardio vascular centre [65]. Resetting of the baroreflex to a higher pressure and reduced baroreflex sensitivity are important mechanisms underlying essential hypertension [66, 67]. Resetting of baroreflex can be at afferent, central or efferent level [68]. Afferent component can be altered by defective mechanosensitive transduction in case of decreased vascular compliance and loss of coupling of vessel wall stretch to baroreceptors [67]. Prolonged stimulation of CNS via baroreceptor afferents may result in remodelling of the neural networks involved in the processing of baroreceptor signals. CNS 'rewiring' may be contributing to the resetting, adaptation, and post excitatory depression of the baroreceptors. This resetting in CNS could be due to decreased responsiveness of the medullary autonomic regulatory centres to baroreceptor signalling. Central resetting of baroreceptors causes sympathetic activity to 'escape' the inhibitory effect of baroreflex [69]. Evidence also shows that angiotensin II, aldosterone and reactive oxygen species (ROS) may be involved in the centrally mediated changes in baroreflex efferent activity, which contribute to sympathetic over activity in hypertension [69].

Sympathetic outflow also affects renal regulation of blood pressure. Stimulation of the renal sympathetic outflow is thought to be a common final pathway in the pathogenesis of essential hypertension in chronic stress [51, 52]. The activation of renal sympathetic nerves underlines the concurrent 'neural', 'renal', and 'sodium' mechanisms leading to the development of hypertension. Stimulation of renal sympathetic nerves is believed to have direct and indirect effects (through RAAS) on renal 'pressure-natriuresis' mechanism inducing sodium and water retention, causing volume expansion and increased blood pressure [70].

7.3.2 Over activity of HPA axis

Dysregulation of HPA activity due to stress especially psychogenic stress, causes marked enhancement in basal HPA tone causing enhanced CRH and AVP synthesis [71], increase in the baseline glucocorticoid secretion, adrenal hypertrophy [72], down regulation of glucocorticoid receptors (GR) in feedback regions, such as hippocampus and prefrontal cortex [71], enhancement of cortisol response to stressors [73], blunting of glucocorticoid negative feedback effect [74], and increased anxiety and depression [75].

Activation of HPA axis involves increased secretion of CRH and AVP in the hypothalamus. AVP in turn potentiates CRH activity [76]. CRH stimulates production of ACTH by the anterior pituitary gland. ACTH then acts on the adrenal glands to cause release of glucocorticoids (GCs), mainly cortisol and mineralocorticoids (MRs). In addition to being a principal regulator of the HPA axis, CRH also causes stimulation of SNS activity [77]. Glucocorticoids stimulate biosynthesis, secretion and release of catecholamines (CA) by sympathetic nerves and adrenal medullary cells [78], and enhance vasoconstrictor effects of angiotensin-II and catecholamines and it has also been implicated in endothelial dysfunction [79]. Thus, synergistic and prolonged actions of CRH, glucocorticoids and catecholamines cause central and autonomic dysregulation of cardiovascular system, which eventually leads to hypertension.

7.3.3 Renin-angiotensin-aldosterone system (RAAS)

Renin–angiotensin-aldosterone system (RAAS) plays an important role in the development of stress induced hypertension [80, 81]. Angiotensin II is the main effector of RAAS, which increases blood pressure by various mechanisms including, increase in the sympathetic outflow from the brain, constriction of resistance vessels, stimulation of aldosterone secretion, increase in renal tubular sodium reabsorption directly and indirectly, stimulation of thirst, and release of AVP hormone [38]. Angiotensin II modulates 'pressure natriuresis' mechanism in the kidneys and contribute to the development of RAAS-dependent blood pressure dysregulation in hypertension [82].

Evidence suggests that activation of angiotensinergic pathways in the central nervous system (CNS) plays a critical role in the development of hypertension by circulating angiotensin II or aldosterone [10]. Most of the actions of angiotensin II are mediated by angiotensin II type 1 receptors (AT1), which are expressed in a number of brain regions like, circumventricular organs (CVOs), hypothalamus, brainstem and parts of limbic cortex associated with the emotional stress response like, the amygdala, bed nucleus of stria terminalis (BST) and other limbic regions [83]. Projections from limbic regions extend to the areas involved in autonomic control of blood pressure, namely, circumventricular organs (CVOs) including Subfornical organ (SFO) and organum vasculosum of the lamina terminalis (OVLT) [84]. Angiotensinergic sympatho-excitatory neurons in CVO project to the paraventricular nucleus (PVN), and the PVN neurons in turn project to the rostral ventrolateral medulla (RVLM) in the brainstem or directly to the intermediolateral cell column in the spinal cord [85]. Circulating angiotensin II or angiotensin II released from nerve terminals bind to AT1 receptors and cause activation of presympathetic neurons thereby increasing SNS activity and blood pressure [86]. Thus, circulating angiotensin II acts as a major signal to the CNS that contributes to the development of hypertension. Angiotensin II not only exerts the central effects mentioned above to increase sympathetic outflow, but also has direct effects on postganglionic fibres to enhance the release of catecholamines [87].

Angiotensin II also promotes vasoconstriction [88], and is a potent stimulus for pro-inflammatory and pro-oxidative events leading to endothelial dysfunction, vascular remodelling and eventual development of hypertension [89, 90]. Angiotensin II exerts vascular damage by generation of reactive oxygen species (ROS) and stimulation of redox-dependent signalling pathways [91].

7.3.4 Immune dysfunction and inflammation

Psychological stress can affect immune function by activating sympathoadrenal system (SAS) as well as the HPA axis to release catecholamines (adrenaline and noradrenaline), ACTH, and glucocorticoids (cortisol). These stress hormones in turn induce immune modulation leading to production of pro-inflammatory cytokines, including C-reactive protein (CRP), tumour-necrosis factor (TNFα), Interleukin-6 (IL-6), Interleukin-1 (IL-1β), Interleukin-2 (IL-2), and the transcription factor of nuclear factor kappa B (NF-κB) [92]. Immune modulation can also occur directly through the binding of the stress hormones to their receptors on the surface of the immune cells as almost all immune cells express receptors for one or more of the stress hormones [93].

Various studies suggest that hypertension is a state of chronic low grade inflammation, that is characterised by the infiltration of immune cells into the interstitium of affected organs, (mainly kidneys, blood vessels, brain and heart), where they release pro-inflammatory cytokines and promote oxidative stress, which then leads to dysfunction of these organs, causing hypertension and eventual end-organ damage [94, 95]. Thus, inflammation in the kidneys, vessels, and CNS plays a major role in the pathogenesis of hypertension [96].

Evidence shows that hypertensive patients have increased levels of circulating monocytes, lymphocytes and pro-inflammatory cytokines, such as tumour necrosis factor α (TNF-α), interleukin (IL) 6 and C-reactive protein [97]. Vascular inflammation is characterised by an accumulation of macrophages, monocytes, dendritic cells, B and T lymphocytes; moreover, increased expression of pro-inflammatory cytokines and cell adhesion molecules in different layers of the vascular wall induce extracellular matrix deposition, smooth muscle hypertrophy, and endothelial dysfunction, contributing to the development and maintenance of arterial hypertension [98]. Immune cells and cytokines stimulate formation of reactive oxygen species (ROS) by vascular smooth muscle cells and endothelial cells, which in turn causes endothelial dysfunction and hypertension [95].

Several studies show that hypertension is associated with accumulation T cells, monocyte/macrophages and dendritic cells in the kidneys. Cytokines secreted by innate and adaptive immune cells, as well as renal epithelial cells, modulate the expression and activity of sodium transporters along the nephron, leading to defective pressure natriuresis, sodium and water retention, and hypertension [95, 99]. Cytokines produced by T cells, especially IL −17 A, play an important role in pathogenesis of hypertension due to renal inflammation. Renal inflammation, immune cell infiltration, and augmented angiotensin II activity blunt pressure dependent natriuresis and cause hypertension [100].

The central nervous system (CNS), the sympathetic nervous system (SNS), and the immune system are interconnected in the physiological modulation of hemodynamic and immune activity [101]. Inflammatory cells and cytokines can impair central autonomic control of blood pressure regulation [102]. CNS can serve as both a target for inflammatory cells in hypertension and as a mediator of inflammation through its communication with the immune system. Angiotensin II is a key contributor to these processes in the setting of hypertension. Angiotensin II causes T cell activation and vascular inflammation especially in CVO region of the brain and leads to hypertension [103].

7.3.5 Oxidative stress and endothelial dysfunction

There is increasing evidence that oxidative stress is strongly associated with essential hypertension [104]. Many studies have shown that chronic psychological stress promotes oxidative stress throughout the body [105, 106]. Oxidative stress occurs when there is over production of oxidant agents, reactive oxygen species (ROS) that overwhelm the cellular antioxidant defence system. Oxidative stress causes endothelial dysfunction and thus contributes to the development of hypertension [107].

Endothelial dysfunction involves alteration of the endovascular lining of blood vessels that is characterised by a pro-thrombotic, pro-inflammatory, and pro-constrictive phenotype [107]. An imbalance in the homeostasis of the endothelial derived relaxing factors like NO and prostacyclin (PGI2) and endothelial derived constricting factors like endothelin 1 (ET 1) and angiotensin II, is a major feature in endothelial dysfunction, that leads to functional changes in the microvasculature with a predominant and deleterious constrictive tone, which causes increased peripheral resistance and hypertension [108].

Reactive oxygen species (ROS) and reactive nitrogen species (RNS) have an important role in the homeostasis of the vascular wall, hence they are implicated in the pathogenesis of hypertension [109]. The most important ROS within the vasculature include the superoxide anion, hydrogen peroxide, hydroxyl radical and RNS being peroxynitrite. Physiologically, ROS generation is tightly regulated by endogenous cellular antioxidants, which include superoxide dismutase (SOD), catalase, thioredoxin, glutathione, and antioxidant vitamins [110]. In hypertension, there is a mismatch between ROS production and protective antioxidant mechanisms in the cells, leading to a state of oxidative stress [111].

Oxidative stress may contribute to the development and/or maintenance of hypertension via numerous mechanisms. ROS such as superoxide combines with nitric oxide (NO), to form peroxynitrite. This reduces bioavailability of NO causing impaired endothelial derived vasodilation [112]. Free radical induced generation of lipid peroxidation products, such as F2-isoprostanes have vasoconstrictor effect and thus can modulate the vascular tone [113]. Superoxide leads to oxidation of tetrahydrobiopterin (BH4), which promotes endothelial nitric oxide synthase (eNOS) uncoupling and causes further production of ROS [114]. ROS also adversely affects blood vessels leading to structural remodelling and vascular dysfunction [115]. When produced in excess, ROS has many deleterious effects that results in endothelial dysfunction, increased vascular contractility, vascular remodelling, vascular inflammation, growth of vascular smooth muscle cells and apoptosis, lipid peroxidation and deposition of extracellular matrix proteins, all the major processes involved in pathogenesis of hypertension [116, 117].

Evidence also suggests an interrelationship between immune response and oxidative stress. Oxidative stress induced immune activation mechanism have been proposed in the pathogenesis of hypertension [95, 118]. It has been proposed that oxidative stress-induced ROS causes production of 'isoketals' by fatty acid oxidation, which serve as autoantigens [119]. Autoantigens then cause T cell proliferation and increased production of pro-inflammatory cytokines such as chemokine (C-C motif) ligand 2 (CCL2), IL-1, IL-6, IL-17A, and TNF α in the kidneys, blood vessels and other tissues [89, 120]. These inflammatory mediators along with catecholamines and other blood pressure elevating hormones mutually exert their actions to cause vascular and renal dysfunction, which ultimately results in development of hypertension [119].

7.4 Mediators of inflammation and endothelial dysfunction: a possible causative link between stress and pathogenesis of essential hypertension

Chronic inflammation and endothelial dysfunction play a crucial role in the development and progression of essential hypertension [121–123]. Prolonged exposure to stress generates, on the one hand, a state of chronic inflammation, which adversely affects the health and integrity of the endothelium [124]; and, on the other hand, activation of the HPA axis and the SNS, which produce mediators that directly affect the organ systems involved in blood pressure regulation [125]. Some of the mediators which may be central to the inflammatory mechanisms contributing to the pathogenesis of hypertension are listed below.

7.4.1 Immune cells

As mentioned earlier infiltration of immune cells into the interstitium of kidneys, brain, heart, and blood vessels and release of cytokines cause inflammation and leads to the development of hypertension. It has been found that the number of circulating 'immunosenescent' pro-inflammatory CD8+ T cells is increased in hypertensive patients. These cells produce pro-inflammatory cytokines like IFN-γ and TNF-α, and the cytotoxic molecules, granzyme B and perforin [126]. These cells also express mineralocorticoid receptors, which play a major role in development of systemic hypertension by promoting production of IFN-γ [127]. It has been shown that IL-17A, produced by CD4+ T cells and γ/δ T cells, plays a critical role in hypertension [128, 129]. Clinical and experimental hypertension is associated with raised serum IgG, IgA or IgM antibodies produced by B cells [130]. Autoantibodies that are agonistic to angiotensin type 1 receptor (AT1 R) are found to be present in hypertensive patients [131, 132]. Monocytes and macrophages have been implicated in various models of experimental hypertension [133, 134]. They accumulate in the perivascular tissue, adventitia and kidneys [135] and promote the release of pro-inflammatory mediators and free radicals via NADPH oxidase 2 (NOX 2) to cause inflammation [136] Studies indicate that Dendritic cells (DCs) play a role in the development of hypertension. DCs in hypertensive animals produce an increased amount of superoxide and cytokines (IL-1ß, IL-6, IL-23), which affects T cell polarisation into the inflammatory phenotype [137].

7.4.2 Cytokines

Cytokines produced by immune cells have deleterious inflammatory effects on the kidneys, blood vessels, heart and brain. IL-17A contributes to angiotensin II (Ang II)-induced renal injury and modulates the expression of renal sodium transporters affecting pressure natriuresis [138, 139]. Interferon Gamma (IFN-γ) produced by TH1 cells, CD8+ T cells (TC1 cells) and natural killer T cells, affect local renin-angiotensin system and along with IL-17A, it is found to alter the expression of renal sodium transporters in proximal and distal tubules to directly affect pressure-natriuresis mechanism [139]. Tumour Necrosis Factor-α (TNF-α), produced by T cells, macrophages, and endothelial cells, decrease the renal tubular expression of eNOS affecting NO production, which leads to sodium retention [140, 141]. Interleukin 6 (IL 6) produced by dendritic cells, macrophages, monocytes, and TH1 cells is considered to be a major signal to promote polarisation of CD4+ T cells to produce IL-17A [138]. IL-17A is implicated in the angiotensin induced hypertension [142].

Studies also show that IL-17A causes vascular dysfunction by increasing superoxide production and reduced NO production by impairing eNOS activity [94, 128, 138]. TNF-α affects endothelial eNOS expression, affecting production of NO by endothelial cells [143]. TNF-α also activates NF-κB and NADPH oxidase [143], which causes induction of oxidative stress and overexpression of both chemokines and adhesion molecules [144]. IFN-γ causes superoxide production via upregulation of the expression and activity of NADPH oxidases in human aortic smooth muscle cells [145]. It acts directly on vascular smooth muscle cells to induce their proliferation and apoptosis [146]. IL-6 mediates elevation of superoxide production and endothelial impairment by affecting NO-cGMP pathway [147]. IL-6 has also been reported to play a role in vascular smooth muscle cells migration and proliferation causing vascular medial hypertrophy [148].

7.4.3 Corticotropin-releasing hormone (CRH)

Besides being produced in nervous system, CRH is also an autocrine and paracrine mediator in tissues like endothelium. In vitro studies show that CRH dose-dependently induces the release of endothelin-1 (ET-1) [149], causes increase in reactive oxygen species (ROS) content, increased catalase activity, and peroxynitrite levels as well as a decrease in the activity of endothelial nitric oxide synthase (eNOS) and nitric oxide (NO) production [150]. It also cause increased vascular permeability, and cytokine release further affecting vascular health [151].

7.4.4 Glucocorticoids (GCs)

Circulating high level of GCs in hypertensive patients are believed to cause overproduction of ROS and reduced availability NO in the vascular endothelium. The GC-induced decrease in NO availability may elicit vascular endothelial dysfunction, leading to hypertension. GCs are also believed to stimulate release of vasoconstrictor endothelin 1 (ET 1) and increase vascular tone [56].

7.4.5 Endothelin 1 (ET 1)

ET-1 are powerful vasoconstrictor peptides produced by variety of tissues including vascular endothelium, heart, and kidney epithelial cells. The synthesis of ET-1 is stimulated by angiotensin II, AVP, norepinephrine, glucocorticoids, hypoxia, shear stress, lipoproteins, oxidative stress [152] and of particular interest, by acute mental or physical stress [153]. Studies have shown that ET-1 at the central level plays an essential role in the cardiovascular sympathetic response to stress [154]. Besides its vasoconstrictive action, ET-1 causes fibrosis of the vascular wall, mitotic stimulation of vascular smooth muscle, increased production of ROS (superoxide) and is pro-inflammatory [155]. ET 1 contributes to the development of inflammatory mechanisms by activating transcription factor-κB, and by increasing production of pro-inflammatory cytokines like, TNFα, IL-1, and IL-6. ET 1 also induces cyclooxygenase-2 (COX-2) expression and prostaglandin E2 (PGE 2) release by mitogen-activated protein kinase (MAPKs) and NF-κB. Cyclooxygenase-2 is involved in the development of vascular inflammation [156].

7.4.6 Angiotensin II and aldosterone

Angiotensin II induces an inflammatory response in the kidneys, heart and vasculature by increasing the expression of pro-inflammatory chemokines, and also causes T cell mediated inflammation [157]. Angiotensin II is one of the major vasoactive peptides involved in the regulation and activation of NAD(P)H oxidase, a major source of ROS in the vascular wall, and thus, it contributes to the production of ROS in vascular smooth muscle cells and endothelial cells [110]. Through ROS generation, angiotensin II exerts several deleterious vascular effects, including functional and structural changes, which results in hypertension [158]. Angiotensin II also promotes endothelial dysfunction through cyclooxygenase-2 (COX-2) activation, which generates vasoactive thromboxane A2 and ROS [159].

Aldosterone has been reported to exert mineralocorticoid receptor mediated pro-inflammatory effects in vessels, heart and kidneys [64]. It induces inflammation by stimulating the formation of reactive oxygen species such as superoxide and hydrogen peroxide [160]. In the heart, aldosterone can increase vascular expression of intracellular adhesion molecule-1 (ICAM-1), monocyte chemotactic protein-1 (MCP-1), osteopontin, and COX-2, to cause inflammation [161]. In the kidneys, aldosterone has been shown to cause inflammation by leukocyte infiltration and elevation of osteopontin, IL-6, IL-1β, and MCP-1 levels [162].

7.4.7 Reactive oxygen species (ROS) and reactive nitrogen species (RNS)

ROS/RNS are strongly implicated in the pathogenesis of hypertension by causing oxidative stress, endothelial dysfunction and inflammation. ROS are derived from oxygen reduction which produces, through several steps, important intermediate products: superoxide anion, hydrogen peroxide, and hydroxyl radical [104] Some of the enzymes involved in ROS generation are: nitric oxide synthase, peroxidases, NADPH oxidase, NADPH oxidase isoforms (NOX), xanthine oxidase (XO), lipoxygenases (LOXs), glucose oxidase, and cyclooxygenases (COXs) [163]. RNS derives from nitric oxide (NO) that is generated by the NADPH-dependent enzyme nitric oxide synthase [164]. NO is a free radical but is relatively stable. NO is able to form other nitrogen reactive intermediates (nitrate, peroxynitrite, and 3-nitrotyrosine), which affect cell functions [165].

ROS are potent modulators of vascular contraction, dilatation, and structural remodelling by processes such as reducing bioavailability of NO by superoxide anion ($O2^-$), generation of vasoconstrictor lipid peroxidation products (F2-isoprostanes), depletion of tetrahydrobiopterin (a key cofactor for NO synthase), activation of pro-inflammatory transcription factors, stimulation of growth factor production, and induction of fibrosis through activation of matrix metalloproteinase [166]. These processes induce increased intracellular calcium, activation of growth and inflammatory signalling pathways, and increased extracellular matrix deposition, leading to endothelial dysfunction, increased vascular smooth muscle reactivity, and vascular remodelling [167]. All of these factors contribute to the development of hypertension.

8. How does stress cause hypertension?

The answer to this question is not simple or straight forward. However, it is evident from the above discourse that stress, especially chronic psychological stress directly affects neuro-endocrinal control of blood pressure regulatory systems and contribute to the development and progression of essential hypertension. Central to the pathogenesis of hypertension is the over activity of SNS and HPA axis. Increased sympathetic outflow and HPA system hyperactivity act synergistically to potentiate the actions of each other and results in a cascade of deleterious effects on the various inter-connected organ systems involved in blood pressure regulation. Principle among these organs are kidneys, brain, heart and blood vessels, which may suffer eventual structural and functional deterioration. The consequences of these effects are baroreflex dysfunction, stimulation of RAAS activity, activation of immune cells, oxidative stress and endothelial dysfunction. The end result of these effector mechanisms is manifested in several different ways affecting the target organs; in kidneys, altered pressure dependent natriuresis leading to sodium retention and fluid volume expansion, in blood vessels, vascular inflammation, increased vascular contractility, vascular remodelling and arterial stiffness all causing increased peripheral resistance, and in heart, cardiac injury, fibrosis of heart and cardiac hypertrophy. Combination of all these factors eventually lead to the development of essential hypertension.

9. Yoga as a therapeutic intervention for the management of essential hypertension

Yoga is an ancient Indian discipline designed to bring balance and health to the physical, mental, emotional, and spiritual dimensions of the individual [168]. Numerous studies have shown yoga to have beneficial effects on cardio-vascular indices in hypertensive patients. The exact underlying mechanisms of the beneficial effects of yoga in hypertension still remain elusive. However, there is a reason to believe that yoga may be having multiple and simultaneous effects on diverse neuro-endocrine regulatory structures to cause neurohumoral modulation resulting in alleviation of stress and improvement in cardiovascular behaviour. Thus, yoga seems to have beneficial effects in essential hypertension by two-way action of simultaneously influencing blood pressure regulatory mechanisms as well as stress regulatory mechanisms.

Various neurophysiological mechanisms have been proposed in previous studies to explain the beneficial effects of yoga therapy in hypertension. Following sections describe some of the possible neuro-endocrine mechanisms underlying the beneficial effects of yoga in essential hypertension.

9.1 Down-regulation of HPA axis and SNS activity

There is increasing evidence that yoga appears to have widespread beneficial effects on the cardiovascular response to stress in healthy and hypertensive individuals through down-regulation of the HPA axis and the sympathetic nervous system (SNS) [168, 169].

In various studies, it has been found that regular practitioners of yoga asanas showed a significant reduction in the blood levels of adrenaline, noradrenaline and plasma rennin activity [170, 171]. The attendant reduction in catecholamines and cortisol, decline in cardiovascular reactivity, enhancement of mood and well-being, and alleviation of perceived stress may result in positive downstream effects on metabolic and hemodynamic profiles [168, 171, 172]. Yoga thus significantly decreases heart rate and systolic and diastolic blood pressure probably by its quietening effect on HPA axis and SNS activity [168, 171, 173].

Down regulation of HPA axis and SAS by yoga may be brought by the actions of yoga on different neural structures involved in stress response and cardiovascular regulation. It has been proposed that yoga may be acting at the level of the paraventricular nuclei (PVN) of the hypothalamus, which is a principal integrator of stress signals involved in regulating HPA axis and autonomic responses to stressors. Evidence suggests that the yogic practices probably inhibit the activity of PVN with the resultant decrease in ACTH release from anterior pituitary which in turn decreases the synthesis of cortisol from the adrenal glands [174]. Cortisol also tends to activate phenyl ethanolamine-*N* -methyl transferase (PNMT) required for conversion of norepinephrine to epinephrine. Consequent to sympathetic inhibition and a decrease in PNMT, catecholamine formation decreases. The decreased levels of corticosteroids and catecholamines are known to decrease stress responses [174, 175].

Yoga may also be causing inhibition of the posterior hypothalamus to decrease sympathetic activity and thus, may restore autonomic balance between sympathetic and parasympathetic limbs to alleviate stress [174–176].

Yoga may also be acting at the level of limbic cortex and/or higher cortical centres to modulate autonomic response to stress. It has been proposed that regular practice of yoga results in modulation of autonomic response such that there is a predominant parasympathetic effect and reduced sympathetic tone, which causes reduction in heart rate and blood pressure. Furthermore, it is suggested that this modulation of autonomic balance may be mediated through the limbic system and higher cortical areas resulting in the inhibition of posterior nuclei of hypothalamus leading to decreased discharge through descending autonomic fibres [176–178].

Studies have also shown that regular practice of yoga is associated with the reduction in the basal cortisol and catecholamine secretion, decrease in sympathetic activity with the corresponding increase in parasympathetic activity [179]. It is believed to be due to the alleviation of stress by yoga. Stress relieving effect of yoga may be due to modulation of limbic signals, which may alter sympathetic activity and hormonal response during stress via hypothalamus [180, 181]. Yoga might also be involved in upregulation of hippocampal 5HT1A receptors leading to decrease in cortisol levels and thus helping to relieve stress [179].

In a study, which assessed the effect of yoga based guided relaxation on autonomic variables, it was found that there was a decrease in heart rate and skin conductance levels along with the decrease in power of the low frequency component of heart-rate variability and increase in the power of high frequency component, which could be attributed to decreased sympathetic tone after guided relaxation [182]. In other studies involving yoga intervention in depressed patients, significant reductions in low-frequency heart rate variability (HRV); a sign of sympathetic nervous system activation, was noted following yoga intervention [168, 183].

Regular practice of slow pranayamic breathing is also known to reduce sympathetic nerve traffic and increase parasympathetic activity [184, 185]. One of the long-term effects of pranayamic breathing is the improvement in autonomic function. Specifically, with slow breathing pranayama there is a noted increase in parasympathetic activity and a decrease in sympathetic dominance [177, 184]. Short-term effects of slow pranayamic breathing include increased galvanic skin resistance, decreased heart rate, decreased blood pressure and increased amplitude of theta waves indicating increased parasympathetic activity. Both the short term and long-term effects of pranayamic breathing indicate a dynamic alteration of the autonomic system tilting the balance in favour of parasympathetic dominance [184, 186]. It is proposed that slow deep pranayamic breathing shifts the autonomic balance to parasympathetic dominance by two mechanisms: (1) Inflation of lungs above tidal volume during pranayama stimulates stretch receptors in the lungs. Stimulation of stretch receptors increases the frequency and duration of inhibitory neural signals that are known to elicit synchronisation of neural activity in the cardio-respiratory centre in the brainstem [187] and CNS especially hypothalamus [188]. Synchronisation within the hypothalamus and the brainstem [189] may be responsible for inducing the parasympathetic response [190] during breathing exercises. (2) Pranayama also causes stretching of connective tissue (fibroblasts) localised around the lungs. Hyperpolarisation is generated in the stretched lung fibroblasts, which induces generation of slower brain wave activity and parasympathetic shift of ANS [184]. Hyperpolarisation affects the autonomic nervous system by modulating neuronal excitability [191], resting membrane potential [187], and generating rhythmic brain activity [188].

9.2 Increased vagal activity

It is proposed that by stimulating the vagus nerve activity, yoga may enhance parasympathetic output and thereby shift the autonomic balance from primarily sympathetic to parasympathetic that may buffer the effects of stress leading to positive changes in the cardiovascular, neuroendocrine, and metabolic responses to stress with the resultant decrease in heart rate and blood pressure [172].

It has been proposed that the positive effects of yoga may be mediated by increased vagal activity and consequent reduction in cortisol. This may likely happen via stimulation of dermal and/or sub dermal pressure receptors that are innervated by vagal afferent fibres, which ultimately project to the limbic system and also hypothalamic structures involved in regulating cortisol secretion. These pathways are supported by anatomical studies indicating that baroreceptors and mechanoreceptors within the dermis (i.e. Pacinian corpuscles) are innervated by vagal afferent fibres. Yoga may thus increase vagal activity via stimulation of pressure receptors and cause decrease in cortisol levels [192]. Vagal stimulation promotes down regulation of the hypothalamic-pituitary-adrenal (HPA) axis and the sympathetic nervous system (SNS) [168, 172]. As a result there is a decrease in the release of cortisol and catecholamines leading to reduction in the heart rate and systolic and diastolic blood pressure [193].

In addition, tactile sensory stimulation is conducted through the vagal afferents directly to medulla oblongata in the nucleus of the solitary tract (NTS). Axons from NTS then project to the dorsal motor nucleus of the vagal nerve and the PVN neurons containing oxytocin that mainly influence the NTS regulation of the heart rate and indirectly the blood pressure [194]. Initial studies indicate stress-reducing effects of oxytocin in humans, as increased levels of oxytocin serve to suppress both sympathetic arousal and HPA) axis responses to stress [195]. Many studies in humans found support for a negative relationship between basal plasma oxytocin levels and norepinephrine, blood pressure, and heart rate [196].

In studies employing 'Sudarshan Kriya Yoga', a yogic breathing technique, it was found that physiological responses to stress improved through mechanisms involving both afferent vagal activity (altering CNS behaviours) and efferent vagal activity, as well as through decreased chemoreflex sensitivity and improved baroreflex response [197, 198]. In another study it was found that long term practice of yogic breathing enabled body to tolerate exercise induced higher levels of carbon dioxide by decreasing chemoreflex sensitivity mediated via vagus nerve [199]. It has been proposed that adaptation of peripheral/central chemoreceptors to chronic carbon dioxide retention or adaptation of pulmonary stretch receptors to a habit of slow respiration may increase vagal afferent discharge to the brainstem centre NTS. Vagal nerve afferents synapse in the medulla on the nucleus tractus solitarius (NTS), which in turn communicates to the thalamic nuclei via parabrachial nucleus (leading to modulatory effects on cerebral cortex) and the limbic system. Through the limbic system directly or indirectly through subcortical areas, the neuroendocrine outputs are then modulated, resulting in the reduction of cortisol and increase in oxytocin, and prolactin secretion. These vagal effects are physically and emotionally calming and help in alleviation of stress [200, 201].

9.3 Restoration of baroreflex sensitivity

The arterial baroreflex acts to buffer acute changes in blood pressure by reciprocal modulation of sympathetic and parasympathetic activity that controls the heart and vasculature [202]. Baroreflex sensitivity indicates cardiovagal adaptability allowing greater responsiveness and sensitivity to changing environmental demands [172]. Vagal stimulation increases heart rate variability (HRV) and baroreflex sensitivity [203]. HRV is a cyclic variation in the beat-to-beat interval that results from the tonic firing of cardiac-vagal efferents originating in the medulla. High HRV and baroreflex sensitivity are generally considered to indicate cardiovagal adaptability and sympathovagal balance [203].

Yoga breathing exercises and postures are known to have immediate beneficial effects on heart rate variability and baroreflex sensitivity with reductions in heart rate and blood pressure [171, 172, 182, 204]. These effects are thought to reflect direct stimulation of the vagal nerve [171, 172].

Practice of yogic postures has been shown to restore baroreflex sensitivity leading to blood pressure reduction [171]. It is suggested that strong mechanical pressure at the neck by some yogasanas like 'halasana' and 'sarvangasan' can increase arterial pressure (locally) so as to stimulate carotid baroreceptors to activate baroreceptor reflex mechanism leading to reduction in the heart rate and fall in the blood pressure via parasympathetic stimulation as in relaxation technique [205].

In a study conducted in the patients of essential hypertension (EH), it was found that at the end of 3 weeks of yoga course, the head-up and head-down tilt yogasanas restored baroreflex sensitivity to normal and reduced blood pressure significantly. It was suggested that once the sensitivity of baroreceptor mechanism was restored, it corrected all other neurohormonal malfunctioning, which was evident from the reduction in sympathetic activity, blood catecholamines, plasma rennin activity [171].

In another study exploring the effects of aerobic exercise training and yoga, on the baroreflex sensitivity in sedentary, healthy, normotensive elderly persons, it was found that, after 6 weeks of yoga training, the heart rate decreased in yoga group [204]. There was increased alpha-index at High Frequency (HF) reflecting parasympathetic activity but alpha-index at mid frequency (MF) (reflecting sympathetic activity as well) was not increased. However, short-duration aerobic training did not modify the alpha-index at MF or at HF in aerobic group [204].

Besides yogasanas, yogic breathing is also known to increase baroreflex sensitivity. In a study investigating the effect of a single session of slow breathing (6 breaths/minute) in healthy subjects, there was increased baroreflex sensitivity and reduction in chemoreflex sensitivity [206]. This seemed to occur through a relative increase in vagal activity and a corresponding decrease in sympathetic activity. The increase in tidal volume could be responsible for these autonomic changes through a reduction in sympathetic activity or via the Hering-Breuer reflex. Reduced sympathetic activity may be linked to a reduction of chemoreflex overactivity due to the reciprocal influences of the baroreflex and chemoreflex [207].

In yet another study on the patients of essential hypertension, slow breathing increased baroreflex sensitivity and reduced sympathetic activity and reduced chemoreflex activity, suggesting a potentially beneficial effect of yogic breathing technique in hypertension [208]. It has been proposed that slow breathing may enhance baroreflex sensitivity through increased vagal activity and decrease in sympathetic activity. Besides this, slow breathing may also cause increase in tidal volume and activate Hering–Breuer reflex, an inhibitory reflex triggered by lung stretch receptors and mediated by vagal afferents, which may increase baroreflex sensitivity. It has been also suggested that slow breathing may increase oxygen absorption that follows increased tidal volume, this may cause reduction in chemoreflex sensitivity, which in turn may result in increased baroreflex sensitivity via their reciprocal relationship [206–208]. It has also been proposed that, the nucleus tractus solitarius (NTS) acts as an integrating centre for baroreflex, chemoreflex and Hering-Breuer reflex and plays an important role in the effect of breathing on cardiovascular modulation and blood pressure reduction. However, the exact mechanism of such integration is not clear [209].

9.4 Action of yoga on GABA

GABA is essential as a negative regulator of neuronal excitability in the PVN, thus mediating the amplitude and the duration of the stress response [210]. One of the major mechanisms responsible for inhibition of HPA axis is the direct neural inhibition of PVN neurons by the neurotransmitter GABA [210, 211]. The neurocircuitry data suggest that GABA-containing pathways might comprise a key component of the abnormalities in the HPA axis seen in human stress pathology [12]. It is suggested that impaired GABAergic control of PVN neurons may contribute to the elevated sympathetic drive in hypertension [212].

Yoga may be modulating HPA axis and SNS response at the level of PVN by its effect on GABA system. It has been shown that practice of yoga asanas results in significant increase in brain GABA levels especially in thalamus [213]. It is suggested that increase in brain GABA levels following yogic intervention may be due to the ability of yoga practices to increase the activity of parasympathetic nervous system (PNS) by stimulating vagal afferents [213, 214]. Inhibitory influences from thalamus over the stress axis probably may be acting by way of BST-GABAergic inputs to PVN [215].

Thus, the beneficial effects of yoga appear to be mediated through several mechanisms including down regulation of HPA axis and sympathoadrenal system, stimulation of vagus to shift the autonomic balance towards parasympathetic dominance, enhancement of baroreflex sensitivity, and increase in brain GABA levels so as to inhibit PVN, the integrator area of stress signals.

10. Conclusion

Stress disturbs homeostasis of the body, which results in a series of neuroendocrine and behavioural responses aiming to cope with the challenges evoked by the stressors. However, chronic exposure to stressors can turn the protective adaptive responses into self-perpetuating vicious cycle of deleterious effects on various systems of the body, including cardiovascular, renal, immune, and nervous system, which finally culminates into pathological conditions like essential hypertension. Yogic intervention exerts its beneficial effects by acting through several different mechanisms and modulates neuro-endocrine control of stress response and cardiovascular behaviour. Thus, yoga has two-way action, at one level it tones down neuro-humoral response to stress and at another level, it brings about improvement in the cardiovascular indices in essential hypertension.

Conflict of interest

The author declares that he does not have any conflict of interest.

Author details

Surendra Shripati Wadikar
Department of Physiology, Topiwala National Medical College, Mumbai, India

*Address all correspondence to: surenin18@gmail.com

References

[1] Day TA. Defining stress as a prelude to mapping its neurocircuitry: No help from allostasis. Progress in Neuro-Psychopharmacology & Biological Psychiatry. 2005;**29**:1195-1200

[2] Ulrich-Lai YM, Herman JP. Neural regulation of endocrine and autonomic stress responses. Nature Reviews. Neuroscience. 2009;**10**:397-409

[3] Goldstein DS, McEwen B. Allostasis, homeostats, and the nature of stress. Stress. 2002;**5**:55-58

[4] Goldstein DS. The Autonomic Nervous System in Health and Disease. New York, NY: Marcel Dekker, Inc.; 2001

[5] Sterling P, Eyer J. Allostasis: A new paradigm to explain arousal pathology. In: Fisher S, Reason JT, editors. Handbook of Life Stress, Cognition, and Health. Chichester: Wiley; 1988. pp. 629-649

[6] McEwen BS, Wingfield JC. The concept of allostasis in biology and biomedicine. Hormones and Behaviour. 2003;**43**(1):2-15

[7] McEwen BS. Protective and damaging effects of stress mediators. The New England Journal of Medicine. 1998;**338**:171-179

[8] Juster R-P, McEwen BS, Lupien SJ. Allostatic load biomarkers of chronic stress and impact on health and cognition. Neuroscience and Biobehavioral Reviews. 2010;**35**:2-16

[9] Chrousos GP. Stress and disorders of the stress system. Nature Reviews. Endocrinology. 2009;**5**(7):374-381

[10] Carrasco GA, Van de Kar LD. Neuroendocrine pharmacology of stress. European Journal of Pharmacology. 2003;**463**:235-272

[11] Dayas CV, Buller KM, Crane JW, Xu Y, Day TA. Stressor categorization: Acute physical and psychological stressors elicit distinctive recruitment patterns in the amygdala and in medullary noradrenergic cell groups. The European Journal of Neuroscience. 2001;**14**:1143-1152

[12] Herman JP, Cullinan WE. Neurocircuitry of stress: Central control of the hypothalamo–pituitary–adrenocortical axis. Trends in Neurosciences. 1997;**20**(2):78-84

[13] Godoy LD, Rossignoli MT, Delfino-Pereira P, Garcia-Cairasco N, de Lima Umeoka EH. A comprehensive overview on stress neurobiology: Basic concepts and clinical implications. Frontiers in Behavioral Neuroscience. 2018;**12**:127

[14] Herman JP, Figueiredo H, Mueller NK, Ulrich-Lai Y, Ostrander MM, Choi DC, et al. Central mechanisms of stress integration: Hierarchical circuitry controlling hypothalamo-pituitary-adrenocortical responsiveness. Frontiers in Neuroendocrinology. 2003;**24**:151-180

[15] Iversen S, Iversen L, Saper CB. In: Kandel ER, Schwartz JH, Jessell TM, editors. Principles of Neural Science. New York: Mc-Graw Hill; 2000

[16] Plotsky PM, Cunningham ET Jr, Widmaier EP. Catecholaminergic modulation of corticotropin-releasing factor and adrenocorticotropin secretion. Endocrine Reviews. 1989;**10**:437-458

[17] Larsen PJ, Tang-Christensen M, Holst JJ, Orskov C. Distribution of glucagon-like peptide-1 and other preproglucagon-derived peptides in the rat hypothalamus and brainstem. Neuroscience. 1997;**77**:257-270

[18] Kinzig KP, D'Alessio DA, Herman JP, Sakai RR, Vahl TP, Figueiredo HF, et al. CNS glucagon-like peptide-1 receptors mediate endocrine and anxiety responses to interoceptive and psychogenic stressors. The Journal of Neuroscience. 2003;**23**:6163-6170

[19] Flak JN, Solomon MB, Jankord R, Krause EG, Herman JP. Identification of chronic stress-activated regions reveals a potential recruited circuit in rat brain. The European Journal of Neuroscience. 2012;**36**:2547-2555

[20] Myers B, Scheimann JR, Franco-Villanueva A, Herman JP. Ascending mechanisms of stress integration: Implications for brainstem regulation of neuroendocrine and behavioural stress responses. Neuroscience and Biobehavioral Reviews. 2017;**74**(Pt B):366-375

[21] Lowry CA. Functional subsets of serotonergic neurones: Implications for control of the hypothalamic-pituitary-adrenal axis. Journal of Neuroendocrinology. 2002;**14**:911-923

[22] Park JB, Skalska S, Son S, Stern JE. Dual GABAA receptor-mediated inhibition in rat presympathetic paraventricular nucleus neurons. Journal of Physiology. 2007;**582**:539-551

[23] Crestani CC, Alves FH, Gomes FV, Resstel LB, Correa FM, Herman JP. Mechanisms in the bed nucleus of the stria terminalis involved in control of autonomic and neuroendocrine functions: A review. Current Neuropharmacology. 2013;**11**:141-159

[24] Dong HW, Petrovich GD, Watts AG, Swanson LW. Basic organization of projections from the oval and fusiform nuclei of the bed nuclei of the stria terminalis in adult rat brain. The Journal of Comparative Neurology. 2001;**436**:430-455

[25] Cullinan WE, Herman JP, Battaglia DF, Akil H, Watson SJ. Pattern and time course of immediate early gene expression in rat brain following acute stress. Neuroscience. 1995;**64**:477-505

[26] Kalsbeek A, La Fleur S, Van Heijningen C, Buijs RM. Suprachiasmatic GABAergic inputs to the paraventricular nucleus control plasma glucose concentrations in the rat via sympathetic innervation of the liver. The Journal of Neuroscience. 2004;**24**:7604-7613

[27] Ahrens S, Wu MV, Furlan A, Hwang G-R, Li B, et al. A central extended amygdala circuit that modulates anxiety. The Journal of Neuroscience. 2018;**38**(24):5567-5583

[28] Ridderinkhof KR, Ullsperger M, Crone EA, Nieuwenhuis S. The role of the medial frontal cortex in cognitive control. Science. 2004;**306**:443-447

[29] Krause EG, Melhorn SJ, Davis JF, Scott KA, Li YM, de Kloet AD, et al. Angiotensin type 1 receptors in the subfornical organ mediate the drinking and hypothalamic-pituitary-adrenal response to systemic isoproterenol. Endocrinology. 2008;**149**:6416-6424

[30] James H, Jessica M, Sriparna G, Brittany S, Aynara W, et al. Regulation of the hypothalamic-pituitary-adrenocortical stress response. Comprehensive Physiology. 2016;**6**:603-621

[31] Johnson A, Cunningham J, Thunhorst R. Integrative role of the lamina terminalis in regulation of cardiovascular and body fluid homeostasis. Clinical and Experimental Pharmacology & Physiology. 1996;**23**:183-191

[32] VanItallie TB. Stress: A risk factor for serious illness. Metabolism. 2002;**51**(6 Suppl 1):40-45

[33] Connor TMO', O'Halloran DJ, Shanahan F. The stress response and the hypothalamic-pituitary-adrenal axis: From molecule to melancholia. QJM: An International Journal of Medicine. 2000;**93**:323-333

[34] Steckler T, Kalin NH, Reul JMHM, editors. Handbook of Stress and Brain Part 1: The Neurobiology of Stress. 1st ed. Amsterdam, The Netherlands: Elsevier B.V. publication; 2005. p. 209

[35] Lupien SJ, Ouellet-Morin I, Hupbach A, Walker D, Tu MT, et al. Beyond the stress concept: Allostatic load—A developmental biological and cognitive perspective. In: Cicchetti D, Cohen DJ. editors. Handbook Series on Developmental Psychopathology. New Jersey, USA: John Wiley and Sons Inc.; 2006. p. 784

[36] McEwen BS. Allostasis, allostatic load, and the aging nervous system: Role of excitatory amino acids and excitotoxicity. Neurochemical Research. 2000;**25**:1219-1231

[37] Calhoun DA, Bakir SE, Oparil S. Etiology and pathogenesis of essential hypertension. In: Crawford MH, DiMarco JP, editors. Cardiology. London: Mosby International; 2000. pp. 3.1-3.10

[38] Oparil S, Zaman MA, Calhoun DA. Pathogenesis of hypertension. Annals of Internal Medicine. 2003;**139**:761-776

[39] Larkin KT. Stress and Hypertension: Examining the Relation between Psychological Stress and High Blood Pressure, Chapter 4-Stress and Essential Hypertension. New Haven and London: Yale University Press; 2005. pp. 92-126

[40] Esler M, Eikelis N, Schlaich M, Lambert G, Alvarenga M, Dawood T, et al. Chronic mental stress is a cause of essential hypertension: Presence of biological markers of stress. Clinical and Experimental Pharmacology & Physiology. 2008;**35**:498-502

[41] Matthews KA, Katholi CR, McCreath H, Whooley MA, Williams DR, Zhu S, et al. Blood pressure reactivity to psychological stress predicts hypertension in the CARDIA study. Circulation. 2004;**110**:74-78

[42] Gasperin D, Netuveli G, Dias-da-Costa JS, Pattussi MP. Effect of psychological stress on blood pressure increase: A meta-analysis of cohort studies. Cadernos de Saúde Pública. 2009;**25**:715-726

[43] Lovallo WR, Gerin W. Psychophysiological reactivity: Mechanisms and pathways to cardiovascular disease. Psychosomatic Medicine. 2003;**65**(1):36-45

[44] Treiber FA, Kamarck T, Schneiderman N, Sheffield D, Kapuku G, Taylor T. Cardiovascular reactivity and development of preclinical and clinical disease states. Psychosomatic Medicine. 2003;**65**(1):46-62

[45] Mezzacappa ES, Kelsey RM, Katkin ES, Sloan RP. Vagal rebound and recovery from psychological stress. Psychosomatic Medicine. 2001;**63**:650-657

[46] Manuck SB. Cardiovascular reactivity in cardiovascular disease: "Once more unto the breach". International Journal of Behavioral Medicine. 1994;**1**:4-31

[47] Lucini D, Norbiato G, Clerici M, Pagani M. Hemodynamic and autonomic adjustments to real life stress conditions in humans. Hypertension. 2002;**39**:184-188

[48] Flaa A, Eide IK, Kjeldsen SE, Rostrup M. Sympathoadrenal stress reactivity is a predictor of future blood pressure: An 18-year follow-up study. Hypertension. 2008;**52**(2):336-341

[49] Harshfield GA, Dong Y, Kapuku GK, Zhu H, Hanevold CD.

Stress-induced sodium retention and hypertension: A review and hypothesis. Current Hypertension Reports. 2009;**11**(1):29-34

[50] Timio M, Saronio P, Verdura C, Schiaroli M, Timio F, Monarca C. A link between psychosocial factors and blood pressure trend in women. Physiology & Behavior. 2001;**73**:359-363

[51] Pickering TG. Reflections in hypertension: Work and blood pressure. Journal of Clinical Hypertension (Greenwich, Conn.). 2004;**6**:403-405

[52] Liu Y-Z, Wang Y-X, Jiang C-L. Inflammation: The common pathway of stress-related diseases. Frontiers in Human Neuroscience. 2017;**11**(316)

[53] Hu B, Liu X, Yin S, Fan H, Feng F, Yuan J. Effects of psychological stress on hypertension in middle-aged Chinese: A cross-sectional study. PLoS One. 2015;**10**(6)

[54] Bobrovskaya L, Beard D, Bondarenko E, Mi B, Jobling P, Walker F, et al. Does exposure to chronic stress influence blood pressure in rats? Autonomic Neuroscience. 2013;**177**:217-223

[55] Jr M, Le KM, Haines WR, Gan Q, Knuepfer MM. Hemodynamic response pattern predicts susceptibility to stress-induced elevation in arterial pressure in the rat. American Journal of Physiology. Regulatory, Integrative and Comparative Physiology. 2001;**281**:R31-R37

[56] Golbidi S, Frisbee JC, Laher I. Chronic stress impacts the cardiovascular system: Animal models and clinical outcomes. American Journal of Physiology. Heart and Circulatory Physiology. 2015;**308**:H1476-H1498

[57] Pongratz G, Straub RH. The sympathetic nervous response in inflammation. Pongratz and Straub Arthritis Research & Therapy. 2014;**16**:504

[58] Esler M, Lambert E, Schlaich M. Point counterpoint: Chronic activation of the sympathetic nervous system is the dominant contributor to systemic hypertension. Journal of Applied Physiology. 2010;**109**:1996-1998

[59] DiBona GF, Esler M. Translational medicine: The antihypertensive effect of renal denervation. American Journal of Physiology Regulatory Integrative and Comparative Physiology. 2010;**298**:R245-R253

[60] Fink GD. Sympathetic activity, vascular capacitance, and long-term regulation of arterial pressure. Hypertension. 2009;**53**:307-312

[61] Joyner MJ, Charkoudian N, Wallin BG. A sympathetic view of the sympathetic nervous system and human blood pressure regulation. Experimental Physiology. 2008;**93**:715-724

[62] Brook RD, Julius S. Autonomic imbalance, hypertension, and cardiovascular risk. American Journal of Hypertension. 2000;**13**:112S-122S

[63] Light KC. Environmental and psychosocial stress in hypertension onset and progression. In: Oparil S, Weber MA, editors. Hypertension: A Companion to Brenner and Rector's the Kidney. Philadelphia: WB Saunders; 2000. pp. 59-70

[64] Dinh QN, Drummond GR, Sobey CG, Chrissobolis S. Roles of inflammation, oxidative stress, and vascular dysfunction in hypertension. BioMed Research International. 2014;**2014**:406960

[65] Guyenet PG. The sympathetic control of blood pressure. Nature Reviews. Neuroscience. 2006;7:335-346

[66] Dampney RAL. Resetting of the baroreflex control of sympathetic vasomotor activity during natural behaviors: Description and conceptual model of central mechanisms. Frontiers in Neuroscience. 2017;**11**:461

[67] Kougias P, Weakley SM, Yao Q, et al. Arterial baroreceptors in the management of systemic hypertension. Medical Science Monitor. 2010;**16**:RA1-RA8

[68] Barrett C, Malpas SC. Problems, possibilities, and pitfalls in studying the arterial baroreflexes influence over long-term control of blood pressure. American Journal of Physiology. Regulatory, Integrative and Comparative Physiology. 2005;**288**:R837-R845

[69] Albaghdadi M. Baroreflex control of long term arterial pressure. Revista Brasileira de Hipertensao. 2007;**14**(4):212-225

[70] Coffman TM, Crowley SD. Kidney in hypertension, Guyton redux. Hypertension. 2008;**51**:811-816

[71] Gomez et al. Hypothalamic-pituitary-adrenal response to chronic stress in five inbred rat strains: Differential responses are mainly located at the adrenocortical level. Neuroendocrinology. 1996;**63**:327-337

[72] Ulrich-Lai YM. Chronic stress induces adrenal hyperplasia and hypertrophy in a subregion-specific manner. American Journal of Physiology. Endocrinology and Metabolism. 2006;**291**:E965-E973

[73] Akana SF. Feedback and facilitation in the adrenocortical system: Unmasking facilitation by partial inhibition of the glucocorticoid response to prior stress. Endocrinology. 1992;**131**:57-68

[74] Mizoguchi K. Chronic stress attenuates glucocorticoid negative feedback: Involvement of the prefrontal cortex and hippocampus. Neuroscience. 2003;**119**:887-897

[75] Willner P. Chronic mild stress (CMS) revisited: Consistency and behavioural-neurobiological concordance in the effects of CMS. Neuropsychobiology. 2005;**52**: 90-110

[76] Scantamburio G, Ansseau M, Legros JJ. Role of the neurohypophysis in psychological stress. Encephale. 2001;**27**:245-259

[77] Willenberg HS, Bornstein SR, Hiroi N, et al. Effect of a novel corticotropin-releasing-hormone receptor type 1 antagonist on human adrenal function. Molecular Psychiatry. 2000;**5**:137-141

[78] Pilipović I, Radojević K, Perišić M, Leposavić G. Glucocorticoid catecholamine interplay within the composite thymopoietic regulatory network. Annals of the New York Academy of Sciences. 2012;**1261**:34-41

[79] Murphy MO, Cohn DM, Loria AS. Developmental origins of cardiovascular disease: Impact of early life stress in humans and rodents. Neuroscience and Biobehavioral Reviews. 2017;**74**(Pt B):453-465

[80] Groeschel M, Braam B. Connecting chronic and recurrent stress to vascular dysfunction: no relaxed role for the renin-angiotensin system. American Journal of Physiology. Renal Physiology. 2011;**300**:F1-F10

[81] Liu F, Havens J, Yu Q, Wang G, Davisson RL, Pickel VM, et al. The link between angiotensin II-mediated anxiety and mood disorders with NADPH oxidase-induced oxidative stress. International Journal of Physiology, Pathophysiology and Pharmacology. 2012;**4**:28-35

[82] Hall JE, Brands MW, Henegar JR, Angiotensin II. Long-term arterial

pressure regulation: The overriding dominance of the kidney. Journal of the American Society of Nephrology. 1999;**10**(suppl 12):S258-S265

[83] Herichova I, Szantoova K. Renin-angiotensin system: Upgrade of recent knowledge and perspectives. Endocrine Regulations. 2013;**47**:39-52

[84] Sunn N, McKinley MJ, Oldfield BJ. Circulating angiotensin II activates neurones in circumventricular organs of the lamina terminalis that project to the bed nucleus of the stria terminalis. Journal of Neuroendocrinology. 2003;**15**:725-731

[85] Cato MJ, Toney GM. Angiotensin II excites paraventricular nucleus neurons that innervate the rostral ventrolateral medulla: An in vitro patch-clamp study in brain slices. Journal of Neurophysiology. 2005;**93**:403-413

[86] Chen Q, Pan HL. Signaling mechanisms of angiotensin II-induced attenuation of GABAergic input to hypothalamic presympathetic neurons. Journal of Neurophysiology. 2007;**97**:3279-3287

[87] Dendorfer A, Thornagel A, Raasch W, Grisk O, Tempel K, Dominiak P. Angiotensin II induces catecholamine release by direct ganglionic excitation. Hypertension. 2002;**40**:348-354

[88] Evans RG, Head GA, Eppel GA, Burke SL, Rajapakse NW. Angiotensin II and neurohumoral control of the renal medullary circulation. Clinical and Experimental Pharmacology & Physiology. 2010;**37**:e58-e69

[89] Guzik TJ, Hoch NE, Brown KA, McCann LA, Rahman A, Dikalov S, et al. Role of the T cell in the genesis of angiotensin II induced hypertension and vascular dysfunction. The Journal of Experimental Medicine. 2007;**204**:2449-2460

[90] Virdis A, Neves MF, Amiri F, Viel E, Touyz RM, Schiffrin EL. Spironolactone improves angiotensin-induced vascular changes and oxidative stress. Hypertension. 2002;**40**(4):504-510

[91] Touyz RM. Reactive oxygen species and angiotensin II signaling in vascular cells—Implications in cardiovascular disease. Brazilian Journal of Medical and Biological Research. 2004;**37**:1263-1273

[92] Miller AH, Maletic V, Raison CL. Inflammation and its discontents: The role of cytokines in the pathophysiology of major depression. Biological Psychiatry. 2009;**65**:732-741

[93] Sanders VM, Kavelaars A. Adrenergic regulation of immunity. In: Ader R, editor. Psychoneuroimmunology. 4th ed. Vol. 1. New York: Elsevier/Academic; 2007. pp. 63-83

[94] Norlander AE, Madhur MS, Harrison DG. The immunology of hypertension. The Journal of Experimental Medicine. 2018;**215**:21-33

[95] McMaster WG, Kirabo A, Madhur MS, Harrison DG. Inflammation, immunity, and hypertensive end-organ damage. Circulation Research. 2015;**116**(6):1022-1033

[96] Rodríguez-Iturbe B, Pons H, Quiroz Y, Johnson RJ. The immunological basis of hypertension. American Journal of Hypertension. 2014;**27**(11):1327-1337

[97] Cachofeiro V, Miana M, Heras N, et al. Inflammation: A link between hypertension and atherosclerosis. Current Hypertension Reviews. 2009;**5**:40-48

[98] Guzik TJ, Touyz RM. Oxidative stress, inflammation, and vascular aging in hypertension. Hypertension. 2017;**70**(4):660-667

[99] Norlander AE, Madhur MS. Inflammatory cytokines regulate renal sodium transporters: How, where, and why? American Journal of Physiology. Renal Physiology. 2017;**313**:F141-F144

[100] Franco M, Tapia E, Bautista R, Pacheco U, Santamaria J, Quiroz Y, et al. Impaired pressure natriuresis resulting in salt-sensitive hypertension is caused by tubulo-interstitial immune cell infiltration in the kidney. American Journal of Physiology. Renal Physiology. 2013;**304**:F982-F990

[101] Elenkov IJ, RI W, Chrousos GP, Vizi S. The sympathetic nerve—An integrative interface between two supersystems: The brain and the immune system. Pharmacological Reviews. 2000;**52**:595-638

[102] Paton JF, Waki H. Is neurogenic hypertension related to vascular inflammation of the brainstem? Neuroscience and Biobehavioral Reviews. 2009;**33**:89-94

[103] Marvar PJ, Thabet SR, Guzik TJ, Lob HE, McCann LA, Weyand C, et al. Central and peripheral mechanisms of T-lymphocyte activation and vascular inflammation produced by angiotensin II-induced hypertension. Circulation Research. 2010;**107**:263-270

[104] Sorriento D, De Luca N, Trimarco B, Iaccarino G. The antioxidant therapy: New insights in the treatment of hypertension. Frontiers in Physiology. 2018;**9**:258

[105] Wang L, Muxin G, Nishida H, Shirakawa C, Sato S, Konishi T. Psychological stress-induced oxidative stress as a model of sub-healthy condition and the effect of TCM. Evidence-based Complementary and Alternative Medicine. 2007;**4**(2):195-202

[106] Miller GE, Chen E, Parker KJ. Psychological stress in childhood and susceptibility to the chronic diseases of aging: Moving toward a model of behavioral and biological mechanisms. Psychological Bulletin. 2011;**137**:959-997

[107] González J, Valls N, Brito R, Rodrigo R. Essential hypertension and oxidative stress: New insights. World Journal of Cardiology. 2014;**6**(6):353-366

[108] Bleakley C, Hamilton PK, Pumb R, Harbinson M, McVeigh GE. Endothelial function in hypertension: Victim or culprit? The Journal of Clinical Hypertension. 2015;**17**(8):651-654

[109] Paravicini TM, Touyz RM. Redox signaling in hypertension. Cardiovascular Research. 2006;**71**:247-258

[110] Virdis A, Duranti E, Taddei S. Oxidative stress and vascular damage in hypertension: Role of angiotensin II. International Journal of Hypertension. 2011;**2011**:916310

[111] Landmesser U, Harrison DG. Oxidative stress and vascular damage in hypertension. Coronary Artery Disease. 2001;**12**(6):455-461

[112] Touyz RM, Schiffrin EL. Reactive oxygen species in vascular biology: Implications in hypertension. Histochemistry and Cell Biology. 2004;**122**:339-352

[113] Cracowski JL, Durand T, Bessard G. Isoprostanes as a biomarker of lipid peroxidation in humans: Physiology, pharmacology and clinical implications. Trends in Pharmacological Sciences. 2002;**23**:360-366

[114] Vaziri ND, Ni Z, Oveisi F, Trnavsky-Hobbs DL. Effect of antioxidant therapy on blood pressure and NO synthase expression in hypertensive rats. Hypertension. 2000;**36**:957-964

[115] Zalba G, San Jose G, Moreno MU, Fortuno MA, Fortuno A, Beaumont FJ, et al. Oxidative stress in arterial hypertension: Role of NAD(P) H oxidase. Hypertension. 2001;**38**:1395-1399

[116] Schiffrin EL. Beyond blood pressure: The endothelium and atherosclerosis progression. American Journal of Hypertension. 2002;**15**:115S-122S

[117] Grossman E. Does increased oxidative stress cause hypertension? Diabetes Care. 2008;**31**(Supplement 2): S185-S189

[118] Nosalski R, McGinnigle E, Siedlinski M, Guzik TJ. Novel immune mechanisms in hypertension and cardiovascular risk. Current Cardiovascular Risk Reports. 2017;**11**:12

[119] Harrison DG, Guzik TJ, Lob HE, Madhur MS, Marvar PJ, Thabet SR, et al. Inflammation, immunity, and hypertension. Hypertension. 2011;**57**:132-140

[120] Madhur MS, Lob HE, McCann LA, Iwakura Y, Blinder Y, Guzik TJ, et al. Interleukin 17 promotes angiotensin II-induced hypertension and vascular dysfunction. Hypertension. 2010;**55**:500-507

[121] Satou R, Penrose H, Navar LG. Inflammation as a regulator of the renin-angiotensin system and blood pressure. Current Hypertension Reports. 2018;**20**(12):100

[122] De Miguel C, Rudemiller NP, Abais JM, Mattson DL. Inflammation and hypertension: New understandings and potential therapeutic targets. Current Hypertension Reports. 2015;**17**(1):507

[123] Pickering TG. Stress, inflammation, and hypertension. Journal of Clinical Hypertension (Greenwich, Conn.). 2007;**9**(7):567-571

[124] Toda N, Nakanishi-Toda M. How mental stress affects endothelial function. Pflugers Archiv: European Journal of Physiology. 2011;**462**(6):779-794

[125] Black PH. The inflammatory consequences of psychologic stress: Relationship to insulin resistance, obesity, atherosclerosis and diabetes mellitus, type II. Medical Hypotheses. 2006;**67**(4):879-891

[126] Youn J-C, Yu HT, Lim BJ, Koh MJ, Lee J, Chang D-Y, et al. Immunosenescent CD8+ T cells and C-X-C chemokine receptor type 3 chemokines are increased in human hypertension. Hypertension. 2013;**62**:126-133

[127] Sun X-N, Li C, Liu Y, Lin-Juan D, Zeng M-R, et al. T-cell mineralocorticoid receptor controls blood pressure by regulating interferon-gamma. Circulation Research. 2017;**120**:1584-1597

[128] Nguyen H, Chiasson VL, Chatterjee P, Kopriva SE, Young KJ, Mitchell BM. Interleukin-17 causes rho-kinase-mediated endothelial dysfunction and hypertension. Cardiovascular Research. 2013;**97**:696-704

[129] Caillon A, Mian MOR, Fraulob-Aquino JC, Huo KG, Barhoumi T, Ouerd S, et al. γδ T cells mediate angiotensin II-induced hypertension and vascular injury. Circulation. 2017;**135**:2155-2162

[130] Chan CT, Lieu M, Toh B-H, et al. Antibodies in the pathogenesis of hypertension. BioMed Research International. 2014;**2014**:504045

[131] Fu ML, Herlitz H, Schulze W, Wallukat G, Micke P, Eftekhari P, et al. Autoantibodies against the angiotensin

receptor (AT1) in patients with hypertension. Journal of Hypertension. 2000;**18**:945-953

[132] LaMarca B, Wallace K, Granger J. Role of angiotensin II type I receptor agonistic autoantibodies (AT1-AA) in preeclampsia. Current Opinion in Pharmacology. 2011;**11**:175-179

[133] De Ciuceis C, Amiri F, Brassard P, Endemann DH, Touyz RM, Schiffrin EL. Reduced vascular remodeling, endothelial dysfunction, and oxidative stress in resistance arteries of angiotensin IIinfused macrophage colony-stimulating factor-deficient mice: Evidence for a role in inflammation in angiotensin-induced vascular injury. Arteriosclerosis, Thrombosis, and Vascular Biology. 2005;**25**(10):2106-2113

[134] Franco M, Martinez F, Quiroz Y, Galicia O, Bautista R, Johnson RJ, et al. Renal angiotensin II concentration and interstitial infiltration of immunecells arecorrelatedwithbloodpressure levels in salt-sensitive hypertension. American Journal of Physiology. Regulatory, Integrative and Comparative Physiology. 2007;**293**(1):R251-R256

[135] Mikolajczyk TP, Nosalski R, Szczepaniak P, Budzyn K, Osmenda G, Skiba D, et al. Role of chemokine RANTES in the regulation of perivascular inflammation, T-cell accumulation, and vascular dysfunction in hypertension. The FASEB Journal. 2016;**30**(5):1987-1999

[136] Shirai T, Hilhorst M, Harrison DG, Goronzy JJ, Weyand CM. Macrophages in vascular inflammation—From atherosclerosis to vasculitis. Autoimmunity. 2015;**48**(3):139-151

[137] Kirabo A, Fontana V, deFaria AP, Loperena R, Galindo CL, Wu J, et al. DC isoketal-modified proteins activate Tcells and promote hypertension. The Journal of Clinical Investigation. 2014;**124**(10):4642-4656

[138] Saleh MA, Norlander AE, Madhur MS. Inhibition of interleukin 17-a but not interleukin-17F signaling lowers blood pressure and reduces end-organ inflammation in angiotensin II induced hypertension. JACC: Basic to Translational Science. 2016;**1**:606-616

[139] Kamat NV, Thabet SR, Xiao L, Saleh MA, Kirabo A, Madhur MS, et al. Renal transporter activation during angiotensin-II hypertension is blunted in interferon-gamma−/− and interleukin-17A−/− mice. Hypertension. 2015;**65**:569-576

[140] Ramseyer VD, Hong NJ, Garvin JL. Tumor necrosis factor α decreases nitric oxide synthase type 3 expression primarily via rho/rho kinase in the thick ascending limb. Hypertension. 2012;**59**:1145.50

[141] Garvin JL, Herrera M, Ortiz PA. Regulation of renal NaCl transport by nitric oxide, endothelin, and ATP: Clinical implications. Annual Review of Physiology. 2011;**73**:359-376

[142] Luther JM, Gainer JV, Murphey LJ, Yu C, Vaughan DE, Morrow JD, et al. Angiotensin II induces interleukin-6 in humans through a mineralocorticoid receptor-dependent mechanism. Hypertension. 2006;**48**:1050-1057

[143] Hot A, Lenief V, Miossec P. Combination of IL-17 and TNF alpha induces a pro-inflammatory, pro-coagulant and pro-thrombotic phenotype in human endothelial cells. Annals of the Rheumatic Diseases. 2012;**71**(5):768-776

[144] Sriramula S, Haque M, Majid DS, Francis J. Involvement of tumor necrosis factor-alpha in angiotensin II-mediated effects on salt appetite, hypertension, and cardiac hypertrophy. Hypertension. 2008;**51**(5):1345-1351

[145] Manea SA, Todirita A, Raicu M, Manea A. C/EBP transcription factors

regulate NADPH oxidase in human aortic smooth muscle cells. Journal of Cellular and Molecular Medicine. 2014;**18**(7):1467-1477

[146] Rosner D, Stoneman V, Littlewood T, McCarthy N, Figg N, Wang Y, et al. Interferon-gamma induces Fas trafficking and sensitization to apoptosis in vascular smooth muscle cells via a PI3K- and Akt-dependent mechanism. The American Journal of Pathology. 2006;**168**(6):2054-2063

[147] Orshal JM, Khalil RA. Interleukin-6 impairs endothelium-dependent NO-cGMP-mediated relaxation and enhances contraction in systemic vessels of pregnant rats. American Journal of Physiology. Regulatory, Integrative and Comparative Physiology. 2004;**286**(6):R1013-R1023

[148] Chava KR, Karpurapu M, Wang D, Bhanoori M, Kundumani-Sridharan V, Zhang Q, et al. CREB-mediated IL-6 expression is required for 15(S)-hydroxyeicosatetraenoic acid-induced vascular smooth muscle cell migration. Arteriosclerosis, Thrombosis, and Vascular Biology. 2009;**29**(6):809-815

[149] Wilbert-Lampen U, Trapp A, Modrzik M, Fiedler B, Straube F, Plasse A. Effects of corticotropin-releasing hormone (CRH) on endothelin-1 and NO release, mediated by CRH receptor subtype R2: A potential link between stress and endothelial dysfunction? Journal of Psychosomatic Research. 2006;**61**(4):453-460

[150] Gougoura S, Liakos P, Koukoulis GN. Effect of CRH on NO bioavailability, ROS production and antioxidant defense systems in endothelial EAhy926 cells. Free Radical Research. 2010;**44**(7):803-812

[151] Yang C, Jiang J. Bilateral regulatory action of corticotropin-releasing hormone on immune-mediated inflammation. Chinese Journal of Traumatology. 2009;**12**(6):350-354

[152] Ayada C, Toru Ü, Korkut Y. The relationship of stress and blood pressure effectors. Hippokratia. 2015;**19**(2):99-108

[153] D'Angelo G, Loria AS, Pollock DM, Pollock JS. Endothelin activation of reactive oxygen species mediates stress-induced pressor response in Dahl salt-sensitive prehypertensive rats. Hypertension (Dallas, Tex.: 1979). 2010;**56**(2):282-289

[154] Garrido MR, Israel A. Role of endothelin in stress-induced hypertension. Journal of Human Hypertension. 2002;**16**(Suppl 1): S29-S33

[155] Sticherling M. The role of endothelin in connective tissue diseases. Rheumatology (Oxford, England). 2006;**45**(Suppl 3):8-10

[156] Kowalczyk A, Kleniewska P, Kolodziejczyk M, Skibska B, Goraca A. The role of endothelin-1 and endothelin receptor antagonists in inflammatory response and sepsis. Archivum Immunologiae et Therapiae Experimentalis. 2015;**63**:41-52

[157] Hoch NE, Guzik TJ, Chen W, Deans T, Maalouf SA, Gratze P, et al. Regulation of T-cell function by endogenously produced angiotensin II. American Journal of Physiology. Regulatory, Integrative and Comparative Physiology. 2009;**296**:R208-R216

[158] Touyz RM, Tabet F, Schiffrin EL. Redox-dependent signalling by angiotensin II and vascular remodelling in hypertension. Clinical and Experimental Pharmacology and Physiology. 2003;**30**(11):860-866

[159] Griendling KK, Minieri CA, Ollerenshaw JD, Alexander RW.

Angiotensin II stimulates NADH and NADPH oxidase activity in cultured vascular smooth muscle cells. Circulation Research. 1994;**74**(6):1141-1148

[160] Gilbert KC, Brown NJ. Aldosterone and inflammation. Current Opinion in Endocrinology, Diabetes, and Obesity. 2010;**17**(3):199-204

[161] Rocha R, Rudolph AE, Frierdich GE, et al. Aldosterone induces a vascular inflammatory phenotype in the rat heart. American Journal of Physiology: Heart and Circulatory Physiology. 2002;**283**(5):H1802-H1810

[162] Blasi ER, Rocha R, Rudolph AE, Blomme EAG, Polly ML, McMahon EG. Aldosterone/salt induces renal inflammation and fibrosis in hypertensive rats. Kidney International. 2003;**63**(5):1791-1800

[163] Bhattacharyya A, Chattopadhyay R, Mitra S, Crowe SE. Oxidative stress: An essential factor in the pathogenesis of gastrointestinal mucosal diseases. Physiological Reviews. 2014;**94**:329-354

[164] Drew B, Leeuwenburgh C. Aging and the role of reactive nitrogen species. Annals of the New York Academy of Sciences. 2002;**959**:66-81

[165] Ramchandra R, Barrett CJ, Malpas SC. Nitric oxide and sympathetic nerve activity in the control of blood pressure. Clinical and Experimental Pharmacology & Physiology. 2005;**32**:440-446

[166] Hulsmans M, Holvoet P. The vicious circle between oxidative stress and inflammation in atherosclerosis. Journal of Cellular and Molecular Medicine. 2010;**14**(1-2):70-78

[167] Tabet F, Savoia C, Schiffrin EL, Touyz RM. Differential calcium regulation by hydrogen peroxide and superoxide in vascular smooth muscle cells from spontaneously hypertensive rats. Journal of Cardiovascular Pharmacology. 2004;**44**:200-208

[168] Ross A, Thomas S. The health benefits of yoga and exercise: a review of comparison studies. The Journal of Alternative and Complementary Medicine. 2010;**16**(1):3-12

[169] Ramos-Jiménez A, Hernández-Torres RP, Wall-Medrano A. Hatha yoga program determinants on cardiovascular health in physically active adult women. Journal of Yoga Physical Therapy. 2011;**1**(3):103

[170] Jayasinghe SR. Yoga in cardiac health (a review). European Journal of Cardiovascular Prevention and Rehabilitation. 2004;**11**(5):369-375

[171] Selvamurthy W, Sridharan K, Ray US, Tiwary RS, Hegde KS, Radhakrishnan U, et al. A new physiological approach to control essential hypertension. Indian Journal of Physiology & Pharmacology. 1998;**42**(2):205-213

[172] Innes KE, Vincent HK, Taylor AG. Chronic stress & insulin resistance related indices of cardiovascular disease risk, part 2: A potential role for mind body therapies. Alternative Therapies. 2007;**13**(5):44-51

[173] McCaffrey R, Ruknui P, Hatthakit U, Kasetsomboon P. The effect of yoga on hypertensive persons in Thailand. Holistic Nursing Practice. 2005;**19**(4):173-180

[174] Arora S, Bhattacharjee J. Modulation of immune responses in stress by yoga. International Journal of Yoga. 2008;**1**(2):45-55

[175] Gopal A, Mondal S, Gandhi A, Arora S, Bhattacharjee J. Effect of integrated yoga practices on immune

responses in examination stress—A preliminary study. Intrenational Journal of Yoga. 2011;**4**(1):26-32

[176] Mehrotra R, Phadke AV, Kharche JS, Pranita A, Joshi AR. Effect of yoga on anxiety score and resting heart rate in young healthy individuals. National Journal of Integrated Research in Medicine (NJIRM). 2012;**3**(2):142-146

[177] Herur A, Kolagi S, Chinagudi S. Effect of yoga on cardiovascular and mental status in normal subjects above 30 years of age. Al Ameen Journal of Medical Sciences. 2010;**3**(4):337-344

[178] Malhotra V, Malhotra M, Shakuntala VT, Basvarajaih MG. Physiology of anuloma viloma pranayama. Journal of Research Education Indian Medicine. 2008:61-63

[179] Kyizom T, Singh S, Singh KP, Tandon OP, Kumar R. Effect of pranayama & yoga-asana on cognitive brain functions in type 2 diabetes-P3 event related evoked potential (ERP). Indian Journal of Medical Research. 2010;**131**:636-640

[180] Parshad O. Role of yoga in stress management. West Indian Medical Journal. 2005;**11**:711-717

[181] Gupta N, Khera S, Vempati RP, Sharma R, Bijlani RL. Effect of yoga based lifestyle intervention on state and trait anxiety. Indian Journal of Physiology & Pharmacology. 2006;**50**:41-47

[182] Vempati RP, Telles S. Yoga-based guided relaxation reduces sympathetic activity judged from baseline levels. Psychological Reports. 2002;**90**(2):487-494

[183] Shapiro D, Cook IA, Davydov DM, et al. Yoga as a complementary treatment of depression: Effects of traits and moods on treatment outcomes. Evidence Based Complementary & Alternative Medicine. 2007;**4**:493-502

[184] Jerath R, Edry JW, Barnes VA, Jerath V. Physiology of long pranayamic breathing: Neural respiratory elements may provide a mechanism that explains how slow deep breathing shifts the autonomic nervous system. Journal of Medical Hypotheses. 2006;**67**(3):566-571

[185] Sabbah HN, Ilsar I, Zaretsky A, Rastogi S, Wang M, Gupta RC. Vagus nerve stimulation in experimental heart failure. Heart Failure Reviews. 2011;**16**(2):171-178

[186] Pal GK, Velkumary S, Madanmohan. Effect of short-term practice of breathing exercises on autonomic functions in normal human volunteers. Indian Journal of Medical Research. 2004;**120**:115-121

[187] Siegelbaum R, Robinson S. Hyperpolarization activated cation current: From molecules to physiological function. Annual Review of Physiology. 2003;**65**(1):453-480

[188] Roberts L, Greene J. Hyperpolarization-activated current (Ih): A characterization of subicular neurons in brain slices from socially and individually housed rats. Brain Research. 2005;**1040**:1-13

[189] Newberg A, Iversen J. The neural basis of the complex mental task of meditation: Neurotransmitter and neurochemical considerations. Medical Hypotheses. 2003;**61**(2):282-291

[190] Lutz A, Greischar LL, Rawlings NB, Ricard M, Davidson RJ. Long-term meditators self-induce high amplitude gamma synchrony during mental practice. Proceedings of National Academy of Sciences USA. 2004;**101**(46):16369-16373

[191] Migliore M, Messineo L, Ferrante M. Dendritic Ih selectively blocks temporal summation of unsynchronized sistal inputs in CA1 pyramidal neurons. Journal of Computational Neuroscience. 2004;**16**(1):5-13

[192] Field T. Yoga clinical research review. Complementary Therapies in Clinical Practice. 2011;**17**:1-8

[193] Moyer CA, Rounds J, Hannum JW. A meta-analysis of massage therapy research. Psychology Bulletin. 2004;**130**:3-18

[194] Michelini L. Oxytocin in the NTS. A new modulator of cardiovascular control during exercise. Annals of New York Academy of Sciences. 2001;**940**:206-220

[195] Heinrichs M, Baumgartner T, Kirschbaum C, Ehlert U. Social support and oxytocin interact to suppress cortisol and subjective responses to psychosocial stress. Biological Psychiatry. 2003;**54**(12):1389-1398

[196] Grewen KM, Girdler SS, Amico J, Light KC. Effects of partner support on resting oxytocin, cortisol, norepinephrine, and blood pressure before and after warm partner contact. Psychosomatic Medicine. 2005;**67**(4):531-538

[197] Brown RP, Gerbarg PL. Sudarshan Kriya yogic breathing in the treatment of stress, anxiety, and depression: Part II–clinical applications and guidelines. Journal of Alternative and Complementary Medicine. 2005;**11**:711-717

[198] Brown RP, Gerbarg PL. Sudarshan Kriya yogic breathing in the treatment of stress, anxiety, and depression: Part I–neurophysiologic model. Journal of Alternative and Complementary Medicine. 2005;**11**:189-201

[199] Spicuzza L, Gabutti A, Porta C, Montano N, Bernardi L. Yoga and chemoreflex response to hypoxia and hypercapnia. The Lancet. 2000;**356**:1495-1496

[200] Kuntsevich V, Bushell WC, Theise ND. Mechanisms of yogic practices in health, aging, and disease. Mount Sinai Journal of Medicine. 2010;**77**:559-569

[201] Friedman EH, Coats AJ. Neurobiology of exaggerated heart oscillations during two meditative techniques. International Journal of Cardiology. 2000;**73**:199

[202] Simms AE, Paton JFR, Pickering AE. Hierarchical recruitment of the sympathetic and parasympathetic limbs of the baroreflex in normotensive and spontaneously hypertensive rats. Journal of Physiology. 2007;**579**(2):473-486

[203] Pumprla J, Howorka K, Groves D, Chester M, Nolan J. Functional assessment of heart rate variability: Physiological basis and practical applications. International Journal of Cardiology. 2002;**84**(1):1-14

[204] Bowman AJ, Clayton RH, Murray A, Reed JW, Subhan MM, Ford GA. Effects of aerobic exercise training and yoga on the baroreflex in healthy elderly persons. European Journal of Clinical Investigation. 1997;**27**(5):443-449

[205] Robin M. A Handbook for Yogasana Teachers: The Incorporation of Neuroscience, Physiology and Anatomy into the Practice. Arizona, USA: Wheatmark; 2009. p. 582

[206] Bernardi L, Gabutti A, porta C, Spicuzza L. Slow breathing reduces chemoreflex response to hypoxia and hypercapnia, and increase Baroreflex

sensitivity. Journal of Hypertension. 2001;**19**:2221-2229

[207] Bernardi L, Porta C, Spicuzza L, Bellwon J, Spadacini G, Frey AW, et al. Slow breathing increases arterial baroreflex sensitivity in patients with chronic heart failure. Circulation. 2002;**105**:143-145

[208] Joseph CN, Porta C, Casucci G, Casiraghi N, Maffeis M, Rossi M, et al. Slow breathing improves arterial baroreflex sensitivity and decreases blood pressure in essential hypertension. Hypertension. 2005;**46**:714-718

[209] da Justa Pinheiro CH et al. Spontaneous respiratory modulation improves cardiovascular control in essential hypertension. Arquivos Brasileiros de Cardiologia. 2007;**88**(6):576-583

[210] Kovacs KJ, Miklos IH, Bali B. GABAergic mechanisms constraining the activity of the hypothalamo-pituitary-adrenocortical axis. Annals of New York Academy of Sciences. 2004;**1018**:466-476

[211] Jessop DS, Renshaw D, Larsen PJ, Chowdrey HS, Harbuz MS. Substance P is involved in terminating the hypothalamo-pituitary-adrenal axis response to acute stress through centrally located neurokinin-1 receptors. Stress. 2000;**3**:209-220

[212] Li DP, Pan HL. Role of gamma-aminobutyric acid (GABA)a and (GABA)B receptors in paraventricular nucleus in control of sympathetic vasomotor tone in hypertension. The Journal of Pharmacology and Expermental Therapeutics. 2007;**320**(2):615-626

[213] Streeter CC, Whitfield TH, Owen L, Rein T, Karri SK, Yakhkind A, et al. Effects of yoga versus walking on mood, anxiety, and brain GABA levels: A randomized controlled MRS study. The Journal of Alternative and Complementary Medicine. 2010;**16**(11):1145-1152

[214] Lee MS, Huh HJ, Kim BG, et al. Effects of qi-training on heart rate variability. The American Journal of Chinese Medicine. 2002;**30**:463-470

[215] Radley JJ, Sawchenko PE. A common substrate for prefrontal and hippocampal inhibition of the neuroendocrine stress response. The Journal of Neuroscience. 2011;**31**(26):9683-9695

Chapter 8

Stress 0.0. Experimental Program of Meditations for Stress Reduction

José Jesús Vargas Delgado

Abstract

Welcome to the 0.0 Stress program. A practical trip integrator to reduce stress to its minimum expression. In this chapter, we will deepen our transpersonal experiential program, which can be very useful for anyone who experiences any signs or symptoms of stress such as anxiety, irritability, muscular tension, burnout, apathy, restlessness, headache, fatigue, digestive problems, concentration difficulties, worry, overwork, substance abuse, smoking, eating disorders, sleep disturbances, or simply feeling overwhelmed by events. The Stress 0.0 program can also help you deploy your potentials and cope with the stress associated with living with the disease, chronic pain, and ailments such as arthritis, asthma, cancer, fibromyalgia, gastrointestinal disorders, cardiovascular problems, hypertension, and migraine among others many.

Keywords: mindfulness, meditations, mind, stress 0.0 program, health, well-being

1. Introduction

Stress remains, despite the considerable research done around it and anxiety and the numerous approaches outlined to address it and reduce it, an inevitable aspect of our lives. Stress forms and has always been part of the human condition. We are all plunged, without escape, in the uncertainty of each moment, the problems, the disease, the old age, the death, and the impossibility of controlling the events around which our life revolves. And the situation reaches an extreme where we feel isolated and alienated from the natural world, without knowing how to establish contact with others with life intelligence [1].

Technology and an authentic tsunami of information have accelerated, in recent years, the pace and complexity of our daily lives. Electronic devices, email, whatsapp, and social networks keep us connected 24 h a day, 7 days a week, exposing ourselves to a real flood of activities and daily demands. Our brain is overwhelmed by the acceleration of the rhythm of life and an authentic bombardment of information that exposes us to frustration, worry, panic, resistance, self-criticism, self-demand, and patience [1].

Before going deeply into the essence and development of our innovative program, it is convenient to conduct a comparative study of other forms of meditation and your meditation program, analyzing the merits and disadvantages of each of them.

- Primordial sound meditation. It is a technique of meditation focused through mantras, rooted in the Vedic tradition of India. A mantra is the manifestation of a phrase that verbalized, sung or whispered repeatedly helps us reach a state of relaxation and internalization that favors the meditative state. They are not randomly selected phrases, but they are sacred sounds that wise men and masters of antiquity used for their practical meditation, because they possess great harmonizing power. During meditation, it is necessary to repeat this mantra cyclically silently, because it creates a frequency of vibration that allows it to be placed in a place away from the ruminant noise of the mind, reaching the frequency of calm and full consciousness [2].

- Zazen meditation. It means sitting meditation. It is based on non-judgmental observation of breathing and on neutrally observing thoughts and experiences as they emerge and dissolve through the mind and observe related sensory experiences. The essential focus of the breath is in the belly, instead of the nose as in vipassana. The posture is much more demanding in Zen meditation than in Vipassana, with special attention to the raised, non-tense spine, the chin shyly leaning forward and the hands placed in a resting position present on the belly. The eyes should always be open, with a low look, and in vipassana, there are no strict guidelines for the eyes, although it is usual to keep them closed. Zen meditation is recommended for those who already add hours of meditative flight [3].

- Transcendental meditation. Its origin dates back to ancient India and each person is offered ad hoc a personal mantra used for vibrational qualities, to help calm the mind. Although the goal of meditation in both forms is similar, there are quite a few differences, including the mantras themselves, and how they are selected, the instruction of meditation, and the recommended time to meditate [4].

- Metta meditation or benevolent love. Metta meditation, or benevolent love, has its meaning in unconditional goodness and affection. This style of meditation also has its origin in Buddhist teachings, mainly Tibetan Buddhism. As scientific studies show, compassion and kind and loving meditation has proven to be particularly efficient in fostering empathy, positivity, acceptance, and compassion for oneself and others. Anyone with low self-esteem, high levels of self-criticism, and a desire to be more empathic with others can benefit from this practice [2].

- Kundalini meditation. Thanks to this technique one awakens his kundalini energy, located at the base of the spine. When this energy is released, rises, and travels through the spine, it leads to an experience commonly known as awakening kundalini, which ultimately leads to enlightenment. Kundalini meditations may include breathing techniques, mantras, mudras, and chants to harness the power of the unconscious mind. It is an energizing way of awakening the presence of our being [5].

- Chakra meditation. A chakra is an energy center in the body, we have seven of them, and each one located in a different area of the body, and each one associated with a different color, word, sound, and energy purpose. Chakra meditations can be very powerful, especially when they are focused and connected with one element in the physical or emotional body at the same time. Many chakra meditations use sound, specific hand placement, and visualization techniques to connect with the energy nadis and their healing pranic vibration [5].

- Tongle meditation. This type of meditation is Tibetan Buddhist and is characterized in that the person who practices it connects with their own suffering in an effort to fully accept and overcome it. Our culture teaches us to avoid suffering and flee from it, quite the opposite that tonglen meditation does. This kind of meditation teaches you to handle the difficult situations of life, because it allows you to look into the eyes of suffering, developing an attitude of openness, abandoning negativity and victimhood. It is also called giving and receiving meditation and cultivates compassion and empathy through breathing and visualization [4].

In this context, it is not surprising that many people worry or become depressed so much that, in an attempt to recover the lost inner balance, they are forced to request or receive medication. And although this treatment may sometimes be necessary to recover health and well-being, it is also important to cultivate internal self-care resources that help us cope with stress, pain, and disease with heart intelligence [6].

In the chapter, we will describe the transformer program Stress 0.0 that is aimed at anyone who lives with stress, anxiety, pain or illness. In this way, the commitment of integration and internalization of the program in everyday life will not only help you reduce stress and anxiety to the minimum expression, but it will become an inspiring route that can guide you with a clear mind toward achievement of a healthier, fluid, calm, and compassionate life [6].

The four essential pillars of our chapter are the following:

- Compassion about our emotions and stress. The Stress 0.0 program allows, through compassion, to learn to respect the emotions caused by stress, in order to find some relief, accept, and remember important emotional changes in our lives.

- Conscious focus on our body and stress management. Through a state of presence, it allows to learn to focus attention on the observation of the body, and on the bodily sensations, which produces a deactivation of the thoughts that generate stress, and a reset of the "trapped" mind.

- Breathe consciously. With the current pace of life, we are not aware that we perform an incorrect and scattered breath. We usually breathe in an accelerated, superficial, and unconscious way. The appearance of different common health problems in large metropolises, such as stress and anxiety, make breathing exercise even more difficult.

- Observation and understanding of the nature of our mind [7]. Learn to relate with discernment to thoughts that cause stress, or that arise as a result of them. Understand the nature of our mind and cognitive phenomena. We cannot expect to modify the nature of our mind, but we can become observers of the mind and avoid giving it material for its "game" of generating suffering and stress.

We strongly recommend that when you undertake our chapter and this journey of deep understanding, do so sequentially because your organization meets a structured, well established, and effective program. In this way, the focused readings, self-inquiry questions, internalization practices, and conscious action proposals of each day of the program will not only help you reduce the stress and anxiety generated by the challenges that life gives you. Save, but they will also consolidate your own practice. Good trip Stress 0.0.

2. Embrace with compassion to stress

Stress is a topic of great popularity because it affects a large number of people. It consists of the automatic and natural response of our body to situations that are threatening or challenging. In general, we tend to believe that stress is a consequence of circumstances external to us, but in reality, it is born in us, depending on the way we evaluate events or our ability to cope with them. When stress is prolonged or intensified over time, our health, our performance, and even our personal relationships can be affected [6].

One of the most persistent deceptions of the mind is to think that the origin of our dissatisfaction lies outside of ourselves [8].

One of the most effective ways to dissolve stress with self-awareness comes through our ability to accept its presence and be able to embrace our anxiety with compassion and cardiac intelligence. Paul Gilbert defines compassion as the deep awareness of the suffering of oneself and other beings, along with the desire to help avoid it. From this concept, we find self-pity and its effects for stress management. Self-pity implies affection, kindness, and self-understanding when suffering is experienced in a stressful situation, instead of self-criticizing, blaming or denying one's pain. It consists of treating ourselves as we would treat a helpless child, or a very dear friend. The opposite would be destructive and guilty self-criticism [8].

In general, for the great majority of Westerners, it is more difficult to give affection to oneself than to give it to others. The gesture of embracing our stress in a way that projects self-pity is in a complicated situation. But for some people, this practice is practically impossible. Some live it as a weakness or a risk of becoming indolent. Others do not consider themselves worthy to receive affection from others (frequently, because they did not receive it unconditionally in childhood). If this practice is very complicated for us, an effective trick is to start the practice of compassion toward friends and, when we are giving affection to people we want, we can include ourselves in the image and give ourselves affection as well [9].

Kindly embrace your stress through a compassionate gesture over your body to relieve its symptoms.

The practice of compassion that we propose to dissolve stress seeks to regulate stress by activating the satisfaction, calm, and security system. In self-pity, there are certain types of gestures, related to hug and contact, which release oxytocin, that is, that reassure us.

The main triggers of self-pity linked to stress are three [10]:

- Soft body contact.
- Vocalization in soft tone.
- Feeling of warmth on a physical level.

We invite you to start the compassionate gesture that can be very useful to calm down in times of stress, or simply to feel better at any time.

- Put one or two hands on the heart or in the central area of the chest.
- Put one hand on the heart or in the central area of the chest and another on the abdomen.
- Hug yourself and caress your arms.

- Hug yourself and caress your back.
- Put both hands crossed on the lower belly.
- Cross your arms and caress yourself without hugging.
- Slap your shoulder with one hand or another with both.
- Stroking your legs at different levels: twin thighs.
- Cradle your face with both hands open.
- Stroking the back of your hands, rubbing your hands; touch the fingertips of both hands.
- Caress the cheek.
- Stroking the hair of the head.
- Stroke your forehead.

2.1 Practice: embrace with your breath

Put yourself in your meditation posture. Ensures a good rooting sitting in the chair. Notice the vertical elevation of your column. Pick up the chin slightly, allowing the cervical area to stretch gently. Become aware of your body posture, firmness, grace, and subtlety. And now become aware of the breath. Feel how you inhale and exhale, softly and deeply. You watch the air in and out freely [9].

Now your mind will bring to the present and to the screen of your mind as much compassion, kindness, and affection the image of a stressful and complicated situation that you are living.

For this I will count from 5 to 0. And when I reach 0, you will see that image:

5, 4, 3, 2, 1, ... and 0. Look, feel it.

And now send love, affection, light, and compassion to all the stressful situation you have in front of you: people, objects, decoration, environment, sound, environment, expressions, color, ... Feel how you embrace that situation. Help yourself with your breath full of compassion to send affection.

At the end, let the image dissolve through your breath and thank yourself for this experience in which we embrace a stressful situation with compassion [9].

3. The secret of stress 0: impermanence and not true

Any mental or emotional phenomenon, or any stressful phenomenon, if we do not potentiate it (thinking about it, rejecting it or fighting with it) and simply observe it dispassionately, as an external phenomenon that belonged to another person, will disappear.

This is the great secret of emotional management oriented to the dissolution of stress in our being. Any thought or emotion that causes us stress or anxiety, regardless of its content and as terrible as it may seem at the moment, eventually disappears spontaneously in a short time. Of course, it will have intense moments of influence but it has an internal process and has its rhythm from within [7].

It has been proven that there is an internal cycle of emotional tides. The cycle usually extends over a very determined time like the tides in the sea. Specifically every 45–90 min it has been investigated that there is a change in cognitive and emotional tide and also a change in the frequency in the processes that generate stress. That is to say that the mental processes, any thought that we can have on the screen of our being is absolutely impermanent. It has no identity to stay in time. The important thing is not to strengthen it with our attachment or our internal and anxious struggle. Curiously, the more we try to fight with an emotion, a feeling in our body, or a thought, the greater the permanence in our being. In some way, we are altering the nature and life cycle of each thought.

Impermanence. Every 45–90 min there is a cycle change in cognitive and emotional tide.

But the important thing is that when we perceive an intense tide in front of us, we do not try to generate ruminant thoughts about its appearance, nor fight with it. It is a tide of accepting the present moment with a clear mind and observing it in the most dispassionate way possible. We invite you to perceive it as an external phenomenon that belonged to another person because finally the stress will disappear.

Therefore, why do we need to change it for a more positive one? Why do we want to know how that concrete thought originates? Why do we have to fight with that stressful thought or emotion tried to rationalize its dissolution? Why fight with that emotion or feeling that I have settled in a part of my body?

Our goal and our proposal are to wait for them to disappear without getting caught by them. In addition, other characteristics of the nature of our mind are that thoughts, or cognitive phenomena are not true and of course stressful processes are not [2].

Not true [2]. Stressful cognitive and emotional phenomena are not true. What we think is not the external reality, it is not what happens. If we think we are "useless," it does not mean that we are. If we think that the world is "horrible" or that we are unable to "speak in public", or that such a person is "evil" does not mean that it is so, since many other people see it differently. If we can separate reality from our thoughts, we will not act on the basis of the erroneous information that our scattered mind tells us.

3.1 Practice: just watch and breathe

Take conscious contact with your body. Ensures a good rooting sitting in the chair.

Notice the vertical elevation of your column. Pick up the chin slightly, allowing the cervical area to stretch gently. Become aware of your body posture, firmness, grace, and subtlety. And now become aware of the breath. Feel how you inhale and exhale, softly and deeply. You watch the air in and out freely. Anchor your attention in your breathing.

Watch now the process of how your stressful thoughts appear that you are living in this moment in your life. Watch the process of how they stay in your mental space, and how they disappear in a few seconds, without you doing anything.

You just stay. Breathe consciously. You might even perceive on which side of the mind they appear: above, below, on the left or on the right. Do not want to prevent them from appearing, accelerate their course, or want them to disappear. Let them follow their natural process like that of a tide. You just keep and hold it. Breathe consciously. At the end, let the image dissolve through your breath and thank yourself for this experience in which you observe the mind without attachments through conscious breathing.

4. Enlighten your being

When you feel stressed you have a much better chance of focusing on what's going wrong. This is how our brain works under the influence of stress: it looks for threats and usually overvalues them. Bring to your mind the last time you saw someone stressed: did he keep calm if something went wrong, or exaggerate the negative, making a mountain of a grain of sand? Our brain in stressful episodes loves to make hyperbole of the perception of reality. The discursive and narrative mind appears deepening and expanding the difficulties as a gigantic magnifying glass.

It is important that our intention in this path of stress healing is to incorporate a positive attitude of self-care and self-discovery that illuminates our whole being. But it is important an intention of light in everything we are, in our essence. Deep acceptance of our whole being, and of course our stress. You may be going through a phase in your life with many important difficulties and may not even think of anything positive. But I encourage you to try to strive with full acceptance to put the spotlight on your positive things [11].

Deposit your attention on all the good things you have. Enlighten your goodness. To look for the good things in your life is to illuminate each one of your steps with creativity, reminding you as a mantra the infinity of good things that you have in life. Probably if you are going through a time of great stress, you may wear dark glasses that do not allow you to clearly discern the reality, or the sense of the anxiety situation you are experiencing. We enter a phase of negative cyclical thoughts that are fed back (rumination). Our proposal in this process is to put the intention to see things of a different color and not believe at all what our mind tells us at all times. A way of perceiving with life intelligence [12].

Putting the intention in our goodness and in all our positive things is an emotional passport that allows us to enter our program with a creative and high energy attitude. A way of becoming aware of where we are and of our essence as being.

For this I invite you to answer honestly at this time, and realistically, to the following questions:

- How are you in your best moments?
- How are you when you feel relaxed?
- Why do you feel grateful now pampering?
- What makes you happy, now or in the past?
- What excites or excites you?
- What is going well in your life right now?
- What makes you enjoy now or in the past?

The awareness of our goodnesses is a way of realizing the light that our being has and our infinite display of potentials. By making ourselves convenient. And even verbalize them, or write them, we get a process of anchoring, recognition, and materialization of all our infinite goodnesses [13].

4.1 Practice: cradle your stress

Take a high position of dignity and presence. Ensure a good rooting sitting in the chair. Notice the vertical elevation of your column. Pick up the chin slightly, allowing the cervical area to stretch gently. Become aware of your body posture, firmness, grace, and subtlety. And now become aware of the breath. Feel how you inhale and exhale, softly and deeply. You watch the air in and out freely. Anchor your attention in your breathing.

Now we invite you to bring to your mind an image of anxiety that you are living in this moment. Let it appear smoothly. Next you will place your arms and hands as if you were cradling a child. Now deposit that stressful situation in that place and start feeling how you are cradling that situation. Try to feel a lot of love and kindness about the gesture and above all that appears at that moment. Accepting fully. Breathe that gesture very consciously and support that process.

- You can dedicate 20 breaths for each cradled situation.

- You can repeat the process several times, or include new narrative scenarios with the same frequency of the degree of stress experienced.

At the end, let the image dissolve through your breathing and thank yourself for this experience in which you cradled your stress with kindness and deep acceptance [9].

5. The four pillars of your temple: feet, back, hands, and face

Traditionally, the body has been denied in the West, which has given the mind greater preponderance. The mind has been considered as the place where intellectual life and imaginative and narrative life occur. And, of course, it has been thought that the entire process for the dissolution of stress has its focus exclusively on the mind. And for that reason always in the West, it has been thought that the body is simply a vehicle directed by the mind [14].

Oriental culture has always maintained a different position, considering the body as important as the mind for the balance of the individual. Current research supports the hypothesis of the enormous importance of the body in our psyche and in our way of integrating, remembering, and being able to cope with stress and anxiety in a healthy way [15].

It is shown that interoceptive perceptions (bodily sensations) modify our thoughts and emotions in an important way and vice versa. In fact, there are studies that show that, if the usual posture is modified, simply by inserting a pencil in the mouth and introducing the smile, one finds the most fun experiences and narration (for example, reading a comic story) that if not this modification has been made.

The body, our posture, and breathing, therefore, are formed as an essential variable when it comes to emotion and the perception of thoughts that generate stress. From the perspective of mindfulness, which consists in being attentive to the present moment, the body and the breath are keys because they are always in the present. Therefore, they are the preferred anchor points. Emotions and stressful thoughts will not be useful as anchor points because they are found more frequently in the past and in the future, than in the present moment. For all this, directing attention and connection to our body resets the mind allows it to leave the ruminant loops and the processes of stressful thoughts stop. What we usually do is lose ourselves in the stressful thoughts associated with emotions, which generates more emotions in an endless cycle. Diverting the focus of our attention to our body and the bodily sensations of stress-laden emotion allows us to deactivate the associated negative thoughts and soften the nuclear bodily symptoms of stress in emotions. A wise process of integral growth throughout the body [16].

- Feet: first pillar of your temple. When you stand up, be aware of the posture. Perceive the rooting of your body to the earth. Become aware of the firm contact of your plants on the earth and the anchoring it entails. When you are sitting, perceive how your feet are fully connected to the earth. It is a channel of connection with our essence. Feel how they are open and relaxed, which will induce a corresponding psychological sensation.

- Back: second pillar of your temple. Your back should remain straight, but in a comfortable posture. The back determines our emotional level. Imagine that an invisible thread pulls from the crown and lets it wide and open. It is the pentagram of emotions so try to be expansion to hear all the nuances.

- Hands: third pillar of your temple. It is important that they are not tense. Rest comfortably on the legs to avoid discomfort on the shoulders. The tension of the hands is considered an indicator of mental tension and a space of manifestation of stress.

- Face: fourth pillar of your temple. It is important that there is no tension on the face as usual. The forehead, eyelids, and lips should be relaxed, as well as the area where the tongue rests on the palate. All are areas of frequent tension in times of stress.

What posture tends to express your body to life? How could you open up to take different positions? How is stress expressed and manifested in your body in the face of stressful situations? What are the feelings that you have predominantly maintained this last week?

How do they express themselves through your face and body posture? How is the usual posture of your feet, back, hands, and face, in a stressful situation? What could you do to bring more awareness, connection, and unity in your temple in the posture of your hands, back, feet, and spine?

5.1 Practice: breathe with your body

Update your posture and check the conscious presence of your body. Ensure a good rooting sitting in the chair. Notice the vertical elevation of your column. Pick up the chin slightly, allowing the cervical area to stretch gently. Become aware of your body posture, firmness, grace, and subtlety. And now become aware of the breath. Feel how you inhale and exhale, softly and deeply. You watch the air in and out freely. Anchor your attention in your breathing.

Now you are going to shift the focus of your attention to your hands and you are going to start bringing your breath to your hands. It is as if you breathe with them. You can start with a right hand and take three breaths in your right hand. Then change the focus to your left hand and breathe there consciously in three breaths. If your mind gets distracted and goes somewhere else, bring it back gently to the breath and that area with which you are breathing.

Now I invite you, you will shift the focus of your attention to your back, and you will begin to bring your breath to your back. It is as if you breathe with them. You can start with the lower back and take three breaths. Then change the focus to the central area of your spine and breathe there consciously in three breaths. Finally, climb to the upper part of your spine and breathe consciously with that area. You can repeat the complete cycle of hands and back several times. At the end, let the image dissolve through your breathing and thank yourself for this experience in which you consciously breathe with your body [9].

6. Planet 9 "do" and planet 0 "be"

We currently consider that there are two basic ways of functioning of the human mind and that it has a direct impact on our relationship with stress and anxiety. Mode "do" and mode "be," which are characteristic, but not absolutely specific to Western and Eastern thinking, respectively. They are based on totally different premises [13].

- Planet 9 "Do": Western thinking in way of doing, Planet 9, will be based on the belief that happiness is outside of us. We feel that there is something to be achieved: money, power, social or family relationships, recognition work position, success in a project, and we think directly, causally and simply, that when we have it, we will be happy. The history of all those who reside on Planet 9 in the "do" way is the continuous search for goals/objects that we think can make us happy: a university career, a prestigious job, a couple, children, possessions, trips, reputed social position, ... [13].

The problem is that when we get any of these elements, even something as desired as the jackpot of the lottery, studies confirm that, within 6 to 12 months, individuals return to the level of happiness before it was achieved the object. The conclusion is that we are involved in an endless process of pursuit of happiness, but we never reach it in a stable way. Of course, this continuous and insatiable pursuit of objectives is one of the main causes of the enormous stress we are subjected to in today's life. Planet 9 "do" is associated with the vision of the "biographical self," because the objectives we set ourselves are associated with the labels or descriptions of ourselves that we have developed throughout life and with which we identify. The label of 9 as a way of representing "way of doing" [13].

- Planet 0 "Being". Oriental thought is based on the fact that happiness is not outside of us, but within. There is nothing to pursue, nothing to obtain. Just remembering through the cardiac intelligence of our planet "being" Everything is in the present, which is the only important thing, since past and future do not exist. The way to reach this state of mind is through the approach of acceptance, which is considered the main quality that develops with mindfulness. Acceptance is a concept that generally repels Westerners because they confuse it with resignation, a characteristic associated with our Judeo-Christian tradition. But the resignation happens in the future, it would consist in the resignation to act in the future because it will be useless. On the contrary, acceptance always occurs in the present. From planet 0 "Being," we fully accept stress, but we do not resign [13].

It is based on the idea that what is happening in the present, since we cannot change it, we must take it as it has been delivered to it without avoiding or denying it. On planet 0 "being," we propose to dive unconditionally into what the present brings. Accepting the present does not mean that we like what happens, but that we accept that we cannot change it. Become fully aware from which planet you are living every moment and from which planet you are interpreting the stressful processes you are living [13].

6.1 Practice: breathe your song

Find now your attentive posture of formal meditation. Ensure a good rooting sitting in the chair. Notice the vertical elevation of your column. Pick up the chin slightly, allowing the cervical area to stretch gently. Become aware of your body posture, firmness, grace, and subtlety. And now become aware of the breath. Feel how you inhale and exhale, softly and deeply. You watch the air in and out freely.

Now put on a song that you like and listen to it with great attention accompanying while you put your attention on the breath. Try to feel the sounds, the words or the rhythm without thinking about it, as if the music were generated within you, as if you were one with it, as if you were breathing with it. Accompany the rhythm of the song to your breathing, so that the whole song can be heard accompanied by your breathing fully consciously. Breathe the song consciously through your full presence without judgment.

At the end, let it dissolve and rest the process in breathing silently...

Thank yourself for this experience in which we hear conscious of the hand of our breath [9].

7. Experiential sailboat of your breath

If your mind chatter uncontrollably and your feelings spin like a soup in a boil, you must know that you are not alone. In our agitated and demanding modern society, permanently active, constant stimulation, decisions, and challenges provoke thoughts and emotions. And when we are in that anxiety situation, we have much more chance of reacting automatically (and uselessly) to the stressors of life [17].

An excellent way to manage thoughts is to use breathing. Resorting to the full attention of your breath to cope with stress may seem too simple, but I encourage you and invite you to try it before you judge. The calming effect is produced by the use of breathing to anchor you in the present moment [18]. And the more you use your breath to return to the present, the simpler, more transformative and more effective the method will be.

Take a moment to think about an anchor: its function is to prevent the ship from drifting. May your sailboat connect with the earth. The anchor is always prepared on the ship, and every time this sail leaves, the anchor goes with it. When the sailboat has to stop, someone throws the anchor into the water. The anchor is your breath, and it is always on the boat ready to land when you need it. Similarly, wherever you go, your breathing always goes with you and your potentials unfold with your conscious presence [19]. Luckily, you cannot run away from your breath or leave it at home when you go out to spend the day outside. Breathing always goes with you in all your experiences, night and day. What you can forget is to pay attention from time to time to the sensation of breathing. But whenever you want to make an experiential pause, you can focus your attention on the breath as an anchor to return to the here and now of your sailboat and your being.

Breathing is a fascinating facet of the human being, one of those unique functions of our ship, which can be automatic but also, in part, controlled and deliberate. The heartbeat, for example, is different. The heart beats day and night without stopping, but you cannot make it stop beating for even a few seconds; instead, if you can stop breathing [20]. Neither can you for digestion or your immune system. We invite you in times of stress to put all your attention on breathing. A way to connect with the most authentic anchor of your ship and your being.

Watch your breathing very carefully when you speak, and watch your breathing very carefully when you listen. Breathing is automatic and, at the same time, is under control. There are very few functional body functions so automated that you can also control. Almost all relaxation techniques make use of deep breathing. The reason is that breathing is closely linked to the body system responsible for relaxation. The feelings of relaxation almost always arise when you breathe slowly and deeply. Mindfulness about breathing is slightly different. During careful breathing, it is not necessary to control the rhythm or depth of breathing [21]. It is simply about paying attention to the breath as it is, without judging.

Experience great moments of stress to take your breath hand in hand, through your attention, with curious attention, affection, and presence. Observe and experience from within what happens.

7.1 Practice: the helm of your breathing

Connect now with relaxed attention to the awareness of your body. Ensure a good rooting sitting in the chair. Notice the vertical elevation of your column. Pick up the chin slightly, allowing the cervical area to stretch gently. Become aware of your body posture, firmness, grace, and subtlety. And now become aware of the breath. Feel how you inhale and exhale, softly and deeply. You watch the air in and out freely. Anchor your attention in your breathing.

Now you are going to intensify with curiosity the focus of your attention especially to your exhalation. And you are going to start exhaling more deeply than inhalation. It is not necessary that you be too much at the helm of your breath simply a subtle change so that the exhalation is the double time of the inhalation. Perform this process for 20 breaths, and then return to balance the helm of your breath and watch what happens.

Repeat the cycle, and experience the change in your frequency. At the end, let the image dissolve through your breathing and thank yourself for this experience in which the sailboat of your body calms through the extended exhalation [9].

8. The gratitude frame: whisper to your emotions

Surprisingly, the psychological investigations carried out around this phenomenon have concluded that in reality, the level of satisfaction with one's life does not depend so much on the circumstances we live, nor on personality or character [22]. There is a more determining factor in our sense of well-being that we often forget: gratitude.

It is proven that being grateful has many advantages, the most important of all is that: Thankful people are happier especially practical in stressful processes.

We know that the so-called "reality" and how we interpret it are two very different things. What "happens" is not what we perceive, since all the experiences of our life we see through a particular "glasses" that interpret reality to "their way of seeing." First, let us recognize that all of us wear those "glasses of seeing reality," and then, let us assume that in general, these glasses work in a somewhat limited way.

Let us be honest: do we not tend to dismiss all that we can appreciate in our lives? [23]. Do we not have a strange facility to put our attention on what is inconvenient to us?

This trend is reflected even in the media, which constantly affect tragedies, problems, and catastrophes, almost completely ignoring the beautiful aspects of life that we can appreciate.

To begin to recognize the abundance of gratifying aspects that exist in our lives, we have to realize and recognize you in a very common automatism in us: "Not knowing how to receive." We do not know how to take everything that life offers us for free, we do not think we deserve to receive what is given to us "just because," without having to fight with blood, sweat, and tears for it [24].

We focus on everything we dislike, which could be "better" or otherwise, which leads us to a sea of meaningless complaints, to feel sad and discouraged. Stress scenarios are an absolute example of this process [25].

By expressing and feeling gratitude, we eliminate from our minds the toxic program of complaints. A program that induces us to feel victims of the stressful circumstances that we live, thus placing all our power in "the outside," without taking responsibility for ourselves and our well-being. Every time we feel and express internally or externally: "Thank you," we are creating new neural networks that are maintained over time, weakening those related to victimhood, discouragement, and complaint [25].

Have you stopped to observe the small details that life offers you "for free" throughout each day?: The gentle touch of the breeze in the morning, the gratifying smell of a flower, the sunlight, that dinner with your friends, the smile that suddenly someone gives you ... if we pay attention, we can discover in every moment a multitude of details that really make us feel completely alive and awake, details, which we can thank [9].

We have many things and we do not notice how grateful we can be for them. Have you stopped to observe how grateful you can feel for having a roof under which every day shelter you, enough money so that all your basic needs are covered, of the food dishes that you enjoy every day? Do you appreciate that kind greeting from your partner at work, that unexpected hug, the interest of who asks you how you are or who gives you a complicit smile? Do you realize what you can thank for people in your life you can trust? Do you appreciate the mechanism of breathing in your body that moment by moment holds, the oxygen you breathe every moment, the gift of being alive here and now?

Even in times of great stress, if we look closely, every moment of life can be a moment of gratitude. For many problems we have, if we are attentive, it is impossible not to find something to be grateful for. In order to appreciate all the good that is in our lives, we have to be "present" in truth at every moment, and in this way, we will connect with the constant abundance and generosity of the life we live [24].

The first of these is that during today you keep the sustained attention to thank, either internally or externally, for every detail of the day to day that you can receive with appreciation [24]. Probably stressful processes do not allow you to experience it. Pay attention moment to moment to everything that happens that you can really recognize and value. If you are attentive to the infinity of things for which you can thank in more and more moments and more and more people, little by little you will begin to feel worthy of receiving the good and beautiful of life, you will contact the deep feeling that in truth, life is easier and kinder than you have sometimes believed [26]. By feeling appreciation and gratitude more and more frequently, everything you reject and for what you complain will have less strength; it will be transformed by the look that your new and wider "glasses of seeing the world" will offer you.

The second practice in this Zero Stress program that we propose is a powerful exercise that in a short time, entails major neurological and reprogramming changes for your mind.

It is about every night, before going to bed, you go through the "movie of your day" in your mind in detail. Recreate every moment you have lived in your journey since you woke up in the morning, focusing your attention on everything that has happened that you can appreciate. Get a notebook or notebook and every time you find a gesture, a detail, an event, a person for whom you can be grateful. Whisper your emotions with kindness and affection, connecting with the frequency of gratitude.

Experiment to treat you through a kind and loving treatment. In a state of calm and connection with you, you can experience what happens if you call yourself internally, as an internal whisper, by your name with a hard, abrupt, and derogatory tone and you can observe what happens. See what happens in your body if you call yourself sharply and disparagingly. As if you were addressing yourself.

Now experience hearing your name in a gentle, loving way. It is a way of saying internally through a subtle and delicate whisper. You can experience what happens in your body. When we whisper our name to ourselves, we can see how our frequency and our state of vibration changes. Highly recommended to perform it in stress processes.

8.1 Practice: whisper meditation

Find your position of attentive presence to meditate. Ensure a good rooting sitting in the chair. Notice the vertical elevation of your column. Pick up the chin slightly, allowing the cervical area to stretch gently. Become aware of your body posture, firmness, grace, and subtlety. And now become aware of the breath. Feel how you inhale and exhale, softly and deeply. You watch the air in and out freely. Anchor your attention in your breathing.

Now you are going to shift the focus of your attention to your body. Connect with the emotional frequency you are living in this moment. Feel that emotion in your body.

Now you are going to start calling yourself and listen to your name (through an almost imperceptible whisper) with an abrupt and hard tone of voice. You can call yourself whatever you want with your name and in a very derogatory way even. Watch what happens in your body and your being. Now you will start calling yourself and hear your name (through an almost imperceptible whisper) with a very soft and loving tone of voice. You can call yourself whatever you want with your name and in a very compassionate way [9]. At the end, let the image dissolve through your breath and thank yourself for this experience in which you dissolve your stress through the whisper meditation.

9. Large conscious zenith chamber

Mindfulness could be defined as the process of developing the observer, that is, of developing metacognition [13]. A large overhead camera, in a large format of silence that visualizes the entire narrative from a healthy perspective. It is the technique of splitting the mind so that a part of it, the observer, becomes aware of the objects of the mind, without identifying with them. In the initial phases, the observer and the zenith chamber are very weak and the objects very powerful, so they tend easily and identify with them, especially in times of anxiety [24]. Over the months the observer becomes stronger and the mental objects are diluted.

With the strengthening of the great zenith chamber, or the witness observer, three phenomena of the mind will occur that allow us to connect with a high transformative understanding:

- There are less and less stressful thoughts. By not identifying with them, they lack gasoline, and they lose strength. When a thought appears (for example: "I will not be able to face this challenge that I have been assigned"), a cluster of concatenated thoughts is not generated thoughts is not generated (for example: "surely my boss will realize that I am not the right person to face this challenge," or "I am not able to face all that has been assigned to me," "I will disappoint people who have trusted me").

- There are more and more gaps between thoughts of anxiety. With fewer thoughts, it is easier to see that there are gaps between thoughts, something impossible to make aware before practicing meditation. In contemplative traditions, the practitioner insists on finding the gaps between thoughts, because of the true nature of the mind. Space between stressful phenomena.

- Every time we believe less the thoughts of alteration. We are aware that they are only mental phenomena that they are not reality that we have not voluntarily generated them and that, if we do not pay attention to them, they will disappear from the mind in a few seconds.

9.1 Practice: meditation in 8K

Update the sensations of your body and verify the conscious presence of your thoughts and emotions. Ensure a good rooting sitting in the chair. Notice the vertical elevation of your column. Pick up the chin slightly, allowing the cervical area to stretch gently. Become aware of your body posture, firmness, grace, and subtlety. And now become aware of the breath. Feel how you inhale and exhale, softly and deeply. You watch the air in and out freely. Anchor your attention in your breathing.

Expand now your awareness in 8K toward all the internal experience that you are living in this moment. Ask yourself for a few moments: what is my experience right now? What thoughts go through my head now? What feelings or emotions are occurring right now? What impulses appear?

Breathe in 8K very consciously. Be aware from your perception of your zenith camera of your experience at this time in a global way, observe all the sensations and emotions that appear, whether pleasant or unpleasant, but without getting involved in them, only taking note of whether they are present and if they change over time. Perception in 8K without involvement or attachment to the content.
At the end, let the image dissolve through your breath and thank yourself for this experience in which you perceive in 8K without attachments [9].

10. The endless story of our mind

You already know that a fundamental aspect of the nature of stress is that thoughts, which you think are absolutely true, suddenly assault you and recreate in your mind continuously. If your thoughts suggest that everything is going well, and that you have control, your stress levels are kept at bay [9]. On the other hand, if your thoughts become obsessed with the negative and make you feel that you have lost control, your stress levels increase, and the internal dialog becomes almost endless on the screen of your mind. In general, thoughts take the form of small stories and desires in your head: the speech of the mind: cognitive storytelling. Since man is man, stories go from generation to generation and connect with the human soul. Literature is full of stories, from Aesop's fables to Shakespeare's works. Historians conjure up images of ancient cultures telling stories about a bonfire, in an environment to share and nurture.

Imagine that the brain is a machine to tell stories. We call it cognitive storytelling. It is a kind of story factory that has no end. From the moment you wake up in the morning, you start explaining the story of your life. In the second one immediately after waking up you are present and nothing else, without your story. Have you ever noticed? [27]. But then suddenly, your personal history invades your consciousness, usually without you noticing. Your brain reminds you who you are, where you live, and what you have to do. It is an automatic process. It is an unfinished production of stories every moment.

Become aware of the nature of the discursive thoughts of the mind. Attention to discern the rumination of the film of the mind against the stable presence of your screen. You tell stories continuously about all kinds of people, situations, and difficulties. If you become aware that you are telling a story about a particular stressful situation, you can weigh if the story you tell is really true. Your identity is constructed in two ways: with stories built over time, or through your experiences with direct experience [28]. If I asked you who you are, would you tell me your name. If I asked you again, would you tell me your story: where were you born, what do you work for, what do you do in your spare time, etc. But you can also feel who you are without your story. And for that you have to connect with your senses. It is a way to connect with your essence.

The narrator brain is a network that is activated by default, which includes its activity in the part of the brain responsible for memory. When you queue at a mall, your mind disperses, fantasizes, and worries. However, that network is also easily activated when you go for a walk in the park. Instead of seeing the beauty around you, you get stuck in your little world of worries and inner stories. It is the endless story that you tell yourself about your own life, the lives of the people you know, and our interactions.

There is nothing wrong with the part of your brain based on the narrative. But nobody wants to limit his life to his personal narrative, since it is very easy to get lost in negative thoughts and emotions, if we do not pay attention to the present moment. In stressful situations, if we get lost in the internal argument of the endless story of each narration of our mind, the possibilities to increase anxiety levels increase considerably [29].

There is more and more scientific evidence that the more time we spend lost with the stories that our minds tell, the more prone we are to stress and anxiety. The way to deactivate the identification with the narration of the endless history of our mind is through the activation of our attention to direct experience and our senses [28]. A way to discern the endless narrative of the present moment.

That activation of direct experience is a state of mindfulness. You live in the present moment. It is the "way of being" of operation. When you walk through the park, you perceive the aroma of the trees, the color of the flowers, and the sensations of your body. Especially in times of stress, we propose that you activate the direct experience on the activation of the brain narrator of the endless story of your mind.

10.1 Practice: dissolve stress from the mountain

Observe your posture and accept the feelings of this moment. Ensure a good rooting sitting in the chair. Notice the vertical elevation of your column. Pick up the chin slightly, allowing the cervical area to stretch gently. Become aware of your body posture, firmness, grace, and subtlety. And now become aware of the breath. Feel how you inhale and exhale, softly and deeply. You watch the air in and out freely. Anchor your attention in your breathing.

Now we invite you to imagine that we are sitting on the top of a mountain, in a kind of chair carved into the rock. From there we can see the sky extraordinarily clean and clear, without clouds that represents the mind. Over time clouds begin to appear, representing stressful thoughts and emotions, which progressively cover the entire sky.

Now begin to breathe consciously from the top of the mountain and experience how with each breath the clouds gradually dissolve. Focus spatially on your exhalation for the dissolution of the clouds.

At the end let the image dissolve through your breath and thank yourself for this experience in which you dissolve stress, through your conscious breathing from the mountain, and without the attachment of your cognitive storytelling [9].

11. Lego of emotions. Build the emotions in your body

Feelings are the conscious experience of the state of the body. Not only do they correspond to facts, they can also originate in brain representations (thoughts and images), that is, feelings that are different from those that would normally correspond to what is happening and that is why we can decide which feelings to choose [30].

Emotions are point reactions, reactive, rooted to the body, short-lived, automatic, and manifest with different intensities. Unlike the mood that they fed back with the internal dialog of our mind. All emotions are tremendously useful [30]. It is the magic of the simplicity of emotions. In fact, there are no positive or negative emotions. Emotions with expansive and contractive but all contain a deep household about our being that it is important that we listen with full attention to discover and decipher its content. From this perspective, the relationship with our emotions must be of an opening and celebration because the arrival of each one of them, including the stressors, has a demonstrated and transcendent function and a self-discovery [30]. All emotions are deeply useful and appear to be understood at a high level of consciousness.

The canvas of emotions is not in the mind, it is in the body. All emotions always manifest in the body and that is its way of existing. Stressful emotions arise through our thoughts but ultimately reach their compositional fullness through production and settlement in the body. It is the habitat of emotions. When we are watching a scary movie and feel a scary emotion, that emotion always goes to the body. That emotion goes to an area of the body where you feel comfortable and strong. Our body is like a hostel and emotions freely find a room and a place to settle. And of course a way.

The healthy way to manage the stressful emotions that settle in our body is not to fight with them. I cannot deny the presence of an emotion of anxiety because my mind decides, or as an order. In fact, the more we fight for an emotion to leave the center of our being, the bigger and stronger the emotion becomes in our hostel. It is like fighting with a wave, I cannot fight her I have to look her in the eye, and trying to surf her is fluent. Looking into the eyes of emotion is the first step to set off the dissolution of stressful emotions that settle in our body.

Stressful emotions like pieces of a Lego have form, texture, weight, temperature, depth, morphology, and color. Experiment with them as the first step of deep acceptance. Like the pieces of a layman, the formalization and manifestation of emotions allows an experiential experimentation of the feelings in our body [30]. When we become aware of the shape of the pieces of an emotion, we are loving its presence, and it is a way of bowing to it allowing its deep identity and its morphology in our body.

The main objective of the narrative recreation of the form of emotions is to increase awareness about the emotion to work, through bodily sensations. If we materialize the emotions and focus our attention on the bodily sensations that they generate in our body, there is an irremediable decrease in the internal dialog, which is the main cause of stress [28]. There is a greater awareness of bodily processes, such as breathing, posture, movement or listening to sounds. The sounds appear geolocated.

What we see and experience appears with a three-dimensionality and a special brightness. An example of this is to perceive an emotion like fear with a gray color, in the form of a very heavy anchor, with a cold temperature and with a very approximate temperature [30].

11.1 Practice: construction and deconstruction of emotional pieces

Examine your body posture and prepare your presence to begin the meditation. Ensure a good rooting sitting in the chair. Notice the vertical elevation of your column. Pick up the chin slightly, allowing the cervical area to stretch gently. Become aware of your body posture, firmness, grace, and subtlety. And now become aware of the breath. Feel how you inhale and exhale, softly and deeply. You watch the air in and out freely. Anchor your attention in your breathing [31].

Connect now with your stressful emotions at this time. Start observing how they manifest in your body. What part of your body do you feel? What shape does that anxiety have in your body? [32]. Does it have for example the shape of a ball in your abdomen? What temperature is it? Does it have a very cold temperature? What color does that anxiety emotion have? Does it have a very dark and penetrating color? What texture does that emotion of stress have? Do you have a very rough texture? How important is that emotion? It is a very heavy emotion that hinders the flow of air in your body? [9].

Explicitly shape your emotion in the body so that you can look into the eyes at the emotion manifested in your body. Then start consciously breathing with that part of your body so that the shape of that emotion anchored in your body dissolves. At the end, let the image dissolve through your breath and thank yourself for this experience in which you build and deconstruct through your breath your current emotion.

12. Conclusion

Congratulations for having reached the end of this transforming journey of self-discovery, growth, and inner look. But as much as this seems like an end, it is not, in fact, more than another wise step of self-consciousness forward, in the direction of a commitment and new lifestyle. The practice will allow you, as you progress, to cultivate ever-deeper levels of self-understanding and compassion, and manage your health and well-being with life intelligence, and in a more active, and effective way [33]. The more clearly you can identify and discern, stressful situations and be attentive to them, the sooner you can untangle yourself, and detach yourself, from automatic reactions and mind traps, which will open the doors to new possibilities and more appropriate responses. Inspiring.

One of the greatest difficulties in the practice of our Stress 0.0 program is to incorporate the practice into the day to day and maintain it throughout life. This problem of the live maintenance of this process over the years does not occur only in our program, but in many other areas, such as healthy living habits (regular physical exercise, healthy diet), artistic activity (practice with some instrument musical, theater, dance) and, practically, in any human activity. In the first months, the practice is usually intense and frequent, but, over time, it is increasingly spaced and shortening its frequency and duration [33]. We always find reasons that justify abandoning the practice. This process is understandable, because in life we can choose between multiple activities that can be satisfactory, so it is difficult to choose between them, since the life time is limited.

Relapses of our stress levels are considered another phase of the healing and healing process. Everything that happens to us appears to be understood, and we must maintain a frequency of transpersonal wisdom that allows us to understand that much of the experiences will become transforming seeds that will flourish when they have to. In the same way, the abandonment of the practice of our program should be considered as another phase of the learning process and should be prepared for when it arrives, using preventive measures from the first moment.

Preventive measures to maintain the practice of the Stress 0.0 program [34].

- Related to motivation: for the program to remain in time, it must have a mature and relevant position within our values and our sense of life. Experience teaches us that the people who maintain the practice of the program for years are those who have a clear sense of life linked to the practice [34].

- Related to the expansion: an excellent and healthy way to maintain the practice consists in its propagation and expansion, in order to improve the global well-being and the quality of life in our environment [34].

When you cannot follow the practices of the program for different reasons, remember with a clear mind and deep acceptance, maintain a curious and kind attitude to return to the path of presence, instead of taking it as a stressful factor [34].

Thank you for making this transpersonal Stress trip with us 0.0. We are deeply honored that you have shared this vital process with us from within. Remember that, no matter how bad your past is or how daunting your future looks, you are not alone, and you can find relief in the present moment. In the face of anxiety and acute stress, take life moment by moment, conscious breathing to conscious breathing. Heart coherence, joy, peace, and transformative understanding are really within your reach. We wish you all the happiness in the world.

Author details

José Jesús Vargas Delgado
Universidad Europea de Madrid, Madrid, España

*Address all correspondence to: jjesus.vargas@universidadeuropea.es

References

[1] Stahl B, Golstein E. Mindfulness To Reduce Stress: A Practical Guide. Barcelona: Editorial Kairós; 2010. pp. 27-56

[2] García Campayo J, Demarzo M. What Do We Know About Mindfulness? 1st ed. Barcelona: Editorial Kairós; 2018. pp. 172-175

[3] Williams P, Tribe A, Wynne A. Buddhist Thought: A Complete Introduction to the Indian Tradition. Barcelona: Editorial Herder; 2012

[4] Roth R. Transcendental Meditation of Maharishi Mahesh Yogi. Madrid: Oberon Publisher; 2003

[5] Bhajan Y. The Chakras. Santa Cruz, NM: Editorial Kundalini Research Institute; 2012

[6] Shamash A. Beat Stress with Mindfulness. 1st ed. Barcelona: Editorial Espasa Books; 2015. pp. 13-36

[7] García Campayo J, Demarzo M. Mindfulness and Compassion. The New Revolution. 1st ed. Barcelona: Editorial Siglantana; 2015. pp. 19-29

[8] Wallace A. The Attention Revolution, 1st Wisdom ed. Boston, MA, USA: Wisdom Publications; 2006. 26 p

[9] Vargas J. Storytelling mindfulness: Storytelling program for meditations [Internet]. 2019. Available from: https://www.intechopen.com/online-first/storytelling-mindfulness-storytelling-program-for-meditations [Accessed: 24 December 2019] 10.5772/intechopen.86778

[10] García Campayo J. The Practice of Compassion. 1st ed. Barcelona: Siglantana Publishing House; 2019. pp. 63-81

[11] García Campayo J, Demarzo M. Mindfulness. Curiosity and Acceptance. 1st ed. Barcelona: Editorial Siglantana; 2015. pp. 185-200

[12] Germer C. Teaching Mindfulness in Terapy. 1st ed. New York: Guilford Press; 2005. pp. 13-36

[13] García Campayo J, Demarzo M. Mindfulness New Practical Manual. 1st ed. Barcelona: Editorial Siglantana; 2019. pp. 138-144

[14] Vargas J. Creativity mindfulness new conceptual stimulation methodology [Internet]. 2014. Available from: https://dialnet.unirioja.es/servlet/libro?codigo=558019 [Accessed: 24 December 2019] ISBN: 9788470746215

[15] Vargas J. Metacine Mindfulness. Book The Invention of Hugo. Cinema in the Cinema. 1st ed. Madrid: ACCI Editions (Ibero-American Cultural and Scientific Association) ISBN: 978-84-17519-97-1; 2019. pp. 293-303

[16] Kabat-Zinn J. Living the crisis fully: How to use the wisdom of the body and mind to cope with stress, pain and disease, 2007. In: Full Catastrophe Living: Using the Wisdom of Your Body and Mind to Face Stress, Pain, and Illness, Delta, 1991. Barcelona: Editorial Kairós; 2018. pp. 205-219

[17] Vargas J. Mindfulness composition digital new teaching methodology of conscious digital aesthetics, in applied visual persuasive communication [Internet]. 2015. Available from: http://webs.ucm.es/info/especulo/Narrar_en_la_era_digital_Especulo_54_UCM_2015.pdf [Accessed: 24 December 2019]

[18] Vargas J. Creative meditation. 10 steps 1 mindfulness methodological temple to increase creativity [Internet]. 2016. Available from: http://www.redalyc.org/articulo.oa?id=31048901050 [Accessed: 24 December 2018]

[19] Vargas J. Mindfulness paths for conscious leadership transformative and influential perspective of conscious leadership in persuasive communication

[Internet]2016. Available from: https://dialnet.unirioja.es/servlet/libro?codigo=686663 [Accessed: 24 December 2019], ISBN: 978-84-15705-12-3. pp. 531-554

[20] Santorelli SF. MBCP program to the perceptive consciousness, and the comprehensive depth of the art inspired by Cervantes. In: International Congress The reception of Cervantes in the XX and XXI Centuries; Ciudad Alcalá de Henares. Myths and Legends; October 5-7, 2016

[21] Vargas J. Mindfulness Branding: Analysis of the 32 Most Successful Advertising Communication Strategies (1986-2016), in 20 Countries, and Their Communicative Application to Mindfulness. Editorial McGraw-Hill Interamericana de España, S.L. McGraw-Hill Education collection with © 2016. 2016. p. 595-603. ISBN: 978-84-48612-59-7

[22] Vargas J. Communication and mindfulness: Effective communication techniques with mindfulness. In: paper presented at II Congress of Mindfulness in Education; April 25-27, 2019; Zaragoza; 2019. Scientific Poster

[23] Vargas J. Mindfulness based on the perceptive consciousness as pedagogical link between technology and education [Internet]. 2016. Available from: https://www.intechopen.com/books/the-evolution-of-media-communication/mindfulness-based-on-the-perceptive-consciousness-as-pedagogical-link-between-technology-and-educati [Accessed: 24 December 2019]. DOI: 10.5772/68085

[24] Kabat-Zinn J. The Practice of Mindfulness. 1st ed. Barcelona: Editorial Kairós; 2007. pp. 121-150

[25] Vargas J. Communication and mindfulness on whatsapp. 8 essential pillars of persuasive communication through emojis. Tecnos University Editions. within the work entitled emerging themes in university innovation, from the collection of the series 'University Editions'. 2018

[26] Escuela transpersonal [Internet]. 2019. Available from: https://escuelatranspersonal.com/ [Accessed: 24 December 2019]

[27] Doria J. Wisdom of the Simple Life. Madrid: Editorial: The Sphere of Books; 2017. pp. 101-103

[28] Kabat-Zinn J. Mindfulness in everyday life: How to discover the keys to mindfulness/wherever you go, there you are. In: Wherever You Go, There You Are: Mindfulness Meditation in Everyday Life, Hyperion, 1994. Barcelona: Editions Paidós Ibérica; 2009. pp. 49-51

[29] Vargas J. Mindfulness reading. Techniques to develop conscious, present and efficient reading through mindfulness. In: IV Virtual International Congress of Reading Education. Murcia: University of Murcia; 2018

[30] Anchondo H, Ramos N, Recondo O. Full Emotional Intelligence: Mindfulness and Effective Emotion Management. Barcelona: Editorial Kairós; 2012. pp. 13-23

[31] Doria J. The 40 Doors. A Path to Transpersonal Intelligence and Mindfulness. Madrid: Editorial The Sphere of Books; 2016. pp. 184-190

[32] Kabat-Zinn J. The Healing Power of Mindfulness: A New Way of Being. Barcelona: Editorial Kairós; 2019. pp. 261-273

[33] Onelife Clinic [Internet]. 2016. Available from: https://onelife.es/ [Accessed: 24 December 2019]

[34] Vargas J. Formal Meditations Adapted by Dr. José Jesús Vargas for Individual Consulting Mindfulness and for University and Master's Teaching. Madrid: Onelife Publications; 2010-2019